D1738785

(Low)life

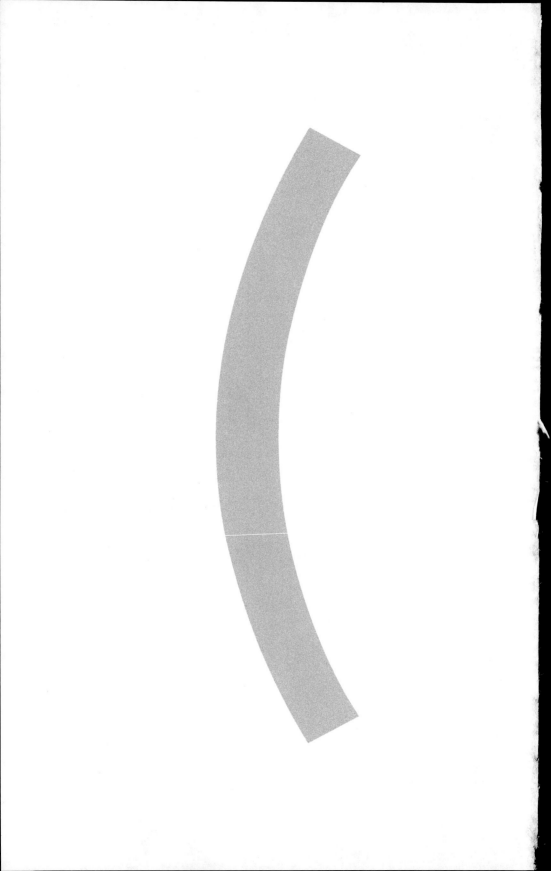

(Low)life

A MEMOIR OF JAZZ, FIGHT-FIXING, AND THE MOB

Charles Farrell

HAMILCAR
PUBLICATIONS
BOSTON

ISBN: 978-1-949590-19-7
Publisher's Cataloging-in-Publication Data
Names: Farrell, Charles, 1951–, author.
Title: (Low)life : a memoir of jazz , fight-fixing , and the mob / Charles Farrell.
Description: Boston, MA: Hamilcar Publications, 2021.
Identifiers: LCCN: 2021934584 | ISBN: 9781949590197
Subjects: Farrell, Charles, 1951–. | Musicians—United States—Biography. | Pianists—United States—Biography. | Mafia—United States. | Organized crime—United States—History. | Sports—Corrupt practices. | BISAC BIOGRAPHY & AUTOBIOGRAPHY / Personal Memoirs | BIOGRAPHY & AUTOBIOGRAPHY / Music
Classification: LCC ML417.F255 F25 2021 | DDC 786.2/092—dc23

Hamilcar Publications
An imprint of Hannibal Boxing Media
Ten Post Office Square, 8th Floor South
Boston, MA 02109
www.hamilcarpubs.com

On the cover: Polaroid of Charles Farrell with Floyd Patterson in Pensacola, Florida, 1994.

This book is for Ruby and Betty, even though neither of them would have been able to read it.

CONTENTS

A Word Before Starting

Most of what you'll read about in this book can be fact-checked.

Some of it can't.

I'll make sure some of it won't be able to be.

In the book, bad things happen to some people. Some of those bad things were done by—and sometimes to—bad people. There are reasons I don't say everything I could about those bad things and bad people.

Bad things don't only happen to bad people. There are a lot of people in this book who didn't deserve what was done to them. I'm sorry for that. Sometimes you're just in the wrong place at the wrong time.

There are also instances where people did good things for me that, strictly speaking, they probably shouldn't have done. I would hardly be repaying them by mentioning their names, which is why I won't.

I'll add that I too have done a lot of bad things that I'm not going to forgive myself for. I won't talk about all of them here. You can't undo damage that's been done and it's theatrical to write about what a bad person you've been. But I'm aware of having been a bad person at times.

For the record, none of the things I'm sorry for have anything to do with fight-fixing—a subject that shows up frequently. I'm happy to have fixed fights. I wish I'd done more of it.

The book recounts a lot of illegal activity. In cases where the Statute of Limitations has run out, or where the people involved are no longer living, you'll get the whole story, names and all.

Fuck the Beginning

I've talked with a lot of people who have collectively read thousands of memoirs and autobiographies. Except when the early years are the story—or without which the story can't move forward—early-life chapters bore everybody.

I'm not going to waste your time. With a few exceptions that help shed light on who I am and what I've done, there's nothing about my family. I'll confine the early years to explaining how things got to the point where they might start to be of interest to you.

1950s

Prerational

Light and dark, moving from one to the other; feeling myself being bumped as my carriage was wheeled over the cracks in the sidewalk. In the light, it was warm. When the carriage was wheeled out of the light, it got cool. I liked the warm better than the cool, the bright better than the dark. But I held people's earlobes because I liked the feel of their coolness. I'd hold onto them until they'd warmed up under my fingers, then let go.

I grew cranky when someone wore earrings. Earrings got in the way.

All this was from the time I lived on Mass Ave. between Central and Harvard Squares. My first three months of life.

A Little Later: Ruby and Betty

From my first point of conscious thought, I paid attention to just two people. They were the only ones who seemed worth listening to. Functionally illiterate and given to primitivism, Ruby and Betty lived lives governed by signs and portents. They were underclass survivors who made relative good—one through limitless talent; the other from hard work paired with unquenchable courage. Making relative good was plenty for them. Neither was ambitious. Getting some fun out of life was the main thing.

Ruby and Betty, my maternal grandparents, were entirely dissimilar from each other in appearance, temperament, and behavior. They were an improbable couple who lived together more companionably than any two people I've known.

When they met, Betty was twenty-four—short, stout, blue-eyed, peach-complexioned, preternaturally strong, and as foul-mouthed as the most underpaid immigrant dock worker. She had been seven years divorced, with three children and years of alcoholism forever part of her mysterious past.

Ruby was a teenager who was already a ladies' man. In all other respects he was fastidious almost to the point of fussiness, conservative in appearance, language, and personal comportment. Newly signed to an exclusive recording contract with RCA Victor in New York, he was approaching his early prime as a pianist, orchestra leader, and composer and arranger of musical theater.

After their nightly performances at the Strand Theatre in Dorchester, Ruby and his cronies would adjourn to the Boston coffee shop where Betty was waitressing. As sure-handed as a card sharp, she managed to dump hot soup in Ruby's lap to get his attention.

The ploy worked. Within a year they were married. Or so everyone who knew them believed. From 1923 onward, various city censuses stated it. It turned out not to have been the case. After my grandparents died, my mother found their marriage certificate while going through their belongings. Ruby and Betty hadn't officially tied the knot until they were in their sixties, two years before their deaths. They'd kept the news to themselves.

The young family left Boston toward the end of the Jazz Age to give the showbiz bonanza of Chicago a shot, closing out the '20s by setting up housekeeping in a well-established hotel uptown. From its lobby my mother, three or four at the time, witnessed with fascination—but no apparent alarm—the gangland bombing of a dry cleaners across the street.

In later years, Ruby would entertain with his tale of going to the Musicians' Union Hall run by the notorious Jimmy Petrillo and being ushered into an office by an official who placed a pistol on the table in front of him and explained that "we just want to get a look at your kisser."

In Chicago, my mother watched Betty and her friend deftly shoplifting cheap trinkets from the Five and Dime. She thought that the two women might also have been turning tricks together. It wasn't that Betty was hard up for money; Ruby was earning buckets of it, and would routinely hand her all she could dream of. She stole and hooked because those were things she'd always done, and she still thought they were fun.

My mother also retained an indelible childhood image of Betty clutching her hand and marching past the hotel elevators to barrel up the stairs and force her way into the room of a woman Ruby had been fucking. She grabbed the floozy by her hair, dragged her into the bathroom, and repeatedly flushed her head in the toilet.

"That'll learn ya not to two-time another gal's husband."

Back in Boston's Mattapan section and living in a triple-decker on Blue Hill Avenue, Betty took in distraught neighbors who were on the street watching their house burn down. Betty had never met Winnie McCauley before, but didn't think twice before giving her family a rent-free home until they got back on their feet. Betty and Winnie stayed lifelong best friends. Whenever Betty went to visit the McCauleys, it would take the two women an hour to stop crying.

Betty always gave away or shared whatever she had. Sharing came easily to her. Orphaned at four and separated from her two brothers and sister, she spent the next ten years being abused in various Irish orphanages and foster homes. She was forced to put in long days of adult work and got married at fourteen to escape a life of servitude. She wouldn't talk much about her past, but she came away from it with a small butterfly tattoo on her left thigh and a scar where the woman who ran one of the foster homes had thrust a scissors through her left hand.

Those years also left her with a drinking problem like the ones that had caused the deaths by misadventure of her parents before they'd reached thirty. Her mother had been killed stumbling under a horse-drawn trolley. Her father had tottered into a field and fallen. Unable to get up, he'd frozen to death. Both were drunk at the times of their deaths.

Betty's marriage to an older man named Evans ended when she was seventeen, but not before she'd had three sons. Her marriage wasn't the only thing that ended then: from the day she left Evans, she never took another drink.

It's a lucky thing that she didn't. Through both blood and marriage, drunkenness continued for generations to run rampant through her family.

My own childhood was studded with incidents where Betty's relatives fell asleep while smoking, burning down their houses and taking themselves out in the process; others passed out behind the wheel as they veered crazily down the highway, slamming into an embankment or another car, empties piled up in the back seat briefly unsettled on impact. At family get-togethers, it would be only a matter of time before Uncle Coogie and Uncle Lenny squared off over some perceived insult. Betty had to explain to me what "Shanty Irish" meant.

I've never tasted alcohol. That's surely because of Betty. I've never taken any kind of drug and I don't take medicine. This comes from a clear understanding that indulging to excess is in my blood. Everything I do—including abstaining—I do to excess. If I'd ever started on liquor or drugs, I never would have stopped.

Betty was also responsible for my lifelong refusal to do menial work. "Don't *never* clean up nobody else's shit, Charles," she'd tell me. "That's what *I* had to do. It's not for you."

Betty couldn't read or write, but she could speak enough Irish to tell people to "póg mo thóin."

Ruby was an even bigger influence than Betty. Having piano in common sealed our relationship. Through Ruby, I was born able to play the piano. This wasn't simply a matter of inherited musical talent; a lot of people have musical talent. Ruby also passed birthright along to me. Birthright was the ironclad inborn knowledge that, finding yourself anyplace on earth, you could walk into a hotel or nightclub and walk out with money in your pocket and a place to stay that night. Birthright was something that would always bail you out of trouble. It would keep you free. There's no way to overstate this: birthright was what set you apart. It's what Betty meant about menial work when she said, "It's not for you."

Ruby was compact, dapper, and handsome—a serious-looking man of effortless grace. Despite having lived a reckless life in his younger days, and having the entertainer's ability to assume the role of bon vivant and raconteur, he was by nature reserved. And he took the business of playing music seriously. My heedlessness toward the piano bothered him. He couldn't understand why I didn't practice and refused to learn to read music.

"You have to learn the language, my boy."

"Why? I can play whatever I hear, and I can hear everything."

"You'll still need to be able to read someday. Things will come up where your ear won't be enough. And you shouldn't neglect your left hand."

"I play *chords* with my left hand. Besides, all that stuff you do with *your* left hand is what *bass players* are for."

"There isn't always going to be a bass player. You have to be able to play the whole piano. Not just the upper half."

"You're too old-fashioned, Ruby. Pianists stopped using their left hands the way you do thirty years ago."

Even though I'll probably never play in public again, I still practice piano diligently six days a week. I've become a world-class sight reader. And anything I can play with my right hand I can play with my left.

That comes from listening to Ruby, because he was right and I was wrong. I'm sorry that he didn't live long enough to hear how I eventually wised up.

Ruby and Betty, born to, but escaped from, lowlife, were inextricably drawn back to it in the revised roles of innocent bystanders. Nothing would stop them from going to housefires so they could sit in their car and gawk. After going out to eat, a favorite pastime was to drive home slowly, counting the number of bars they passed along the way. It was an added bonus if they saw a drunk staggering out of one of them; better yet if someone was being thrown out; best of all if the unfortunate was a woman. They had a commiserating sound—a kind of "tih, tih, tih" with their tongues against their teeth—that they used on these occasions. They were viewing the fates that they had escaped, and their appetite for reveling in their emergence from those fates was never-ending.

They also pointed out weirdos, the afflicted, the deformed, and—my grandmother's favorite—fairies. What they felt toward these people was hard to pin down. They were sympathetic, but thought themselves superior. They felt pity and even a kind of affection.

But mostly they felt safe and lucky. The house next door had burned down. Theirs hadn't.

My life trajectory was established early. I can even point to the things that showed me which direction to take, because there were surprisingly few of them.

The first was spending most of my time with Ruby and Betty. They believed that the sole purpose of life was to have fun. They didn't stretch, they didn't grow; they were like dogs, they were like the lilies of the field, perfect in their existing forms.

Their pursuit of pleasures coincided with mine, even though we came to those pleasures from different angles. By the time I was born, Ruby and Betty were at the stage in their lives where they were endlessly repeating the things that brought them happiness. I was discovering those things for the first time. Life when in the company of my grandparents was an ongoing series of strange and beautiful lowlife surprises and entertainments. They never failed me. Throughout my childhood, one or the other would wake me up and ask, "Are you ready to go to Wonderland?"

Shortly after I turned three, I simultaneously discovered boxing and reading. I found I was able to play anything I heard on the piano.

These commingled to bring me choices in life—choices that acted to define who I was and would become—and to then, through their mutual incongruity, narrow those choices down to a near foreclosure. Encouraged to understand that "breaks" emerged through talent, where they were met by signs coming through portents and voodoo and then further combined with birthright and a gambler's luck, forever removed for me the option of seeking advice or education from outside sources.

Who could possibly teach or show me anything? Surely nothing could be learned from any institution. Why bother? Wisdom was immanent. I had *birthright*. I'd been handed the key to the highway. I didn't need anybody. I was too big for my britches at three, and have stayed that way ever since.

Rockaway Inn

In July of 1955, Betty brought me on vacation to Rockaway Inn, a seaside guest house in Marblehead, Massachusetts. I would be turning four in late August, gathering information and experience more rapidly than I ever would again. It wound up being an educational summer.

Rockaway Inn was an old-fashioned and spacious estate with blue and white awnings over the windows and bunting over the archways. Pennants would catch the breeze off the ocean. Everything felt salubriously slow and lazy and restful. The lobby was vast and open, with a high ceiling where an enormous wooden fan slowly circulated tangy ocean air. There was an abundance of mahogany, and the dark wood made the interior vaguely umbral—a refuge from the heat of the day. In the evenings when the lights came on the entire place glowed, and the dining hall was warm and welcoming.

Rockaway Inn was one block from the beach, where Betty brought me in the late mornings, first sending me running for the ice cream truck so we could have creamsicles. "Oh, ice cream man," Betty's voice could be heard blocks away. "Wait for us, ice cream man." She'd thrust coins or even a bill into my hand. "Catch him, Charles. Let him keep the change."

Each day we'd be joined at the ocean by Betty's two most recent best friends, Eva and Magda Gábor. At three, I wouldn't have understood the concept of celebrity, but could see that there was something glamorous about the women, especially Eva. Glamour was like an added dimension—a glow that made you different. Eva was so beautiful that I assumed Magda was her mother. It wasn't until years later that I found out they were sisters. I sat on a beach towel and read—reading was my newly acquired obsession—while keeping one ear open to the women's gossip, finding it funny when the Gábor's snipingly referred to their sister Zsa Zsa as "the whore."

Eva Gábor was the first grown woman I ever saw naked. It wasn't by accident, and it didn't happen just once. After coming in from the beach, I would take my afternoon nap with Eva in her bedroom. She always undressed before joining me under the covers. She did this without hesitation or inhibition. There didn't seem to be anything out of the ordinary about it. Fascinated by her body and determined to commit its details to memory, I intuitively knew not to appear overly interested, lest I kill off this vacation lagniappe. Eva and I would doze for an hour, and she would then take my hand and walk me downstairs to dinner.

You would assume that Eva Gábor was the only nude female I saw that summer, but she wasn't.

The owners of the Rockaway Inn had a teenage niece who did housekeeping, laundry, and kitchen chores. Although I understand that there is no culturally acceptable provision for a child experiencing pedophilia as a positive event, that's how I remember it. Removed from any philosophical discussion about appropriateness, and reduced to my honest impressions, everything about these encounters was miraculous.

I've tried to dig into my memories of the events to find out whether there's something I'm missing or whether I'm kidding myself in some way—if any hidden trauma, any hint of victimization, anything beyond a series of happy but vague recollections of highly charged secret meetings shows up. Nothing does.

We didn't do much. An outdoor shower had been set up for guests who wanted to wash off the sand and salt water after coming in from the beach. The girl—I don't even remember her name—would take off her clothes, get under the shower, and guide my hand to different parts of her body.

I couldn't wait for her to knock on our door to ask Betty if she wanted me taken for a walk. I understood that what took place in the shower was in no way similar to my daily nap with Eva. The girl didn't have to tell me to keep my mouth shut.

My experiences with the girl in the shower didn't turn me into a predator later in life and didn't make me a victim at the time. More than anything else, it taught me from an early age to be comfortable around naked female bodies. My positive feelings about what took place are personal; I'm not making light of the real damage similar experiences have caused children.

The other important thing that took place was that by the end of summer I could read fairly well. I don't remember exactly how I learned, but know that it started by being read to. My mother read to me. So did Ruby's sister Sophie and her son Sonny.

Eva read to me too. It turned out that she advanced my education in a couple of life-changing areas.

Old Orchard and Two Early Wins

Gambling was magic. It was being paid to do something you got through some inkling, something you could feel in your blood. I was encouraged to think about gambling in this vibrational way, since Ruby's and Betty's betting was guided solely by hunches, signs, sounds, and numerological tip-offs—all of the things that represent the worst possible ways to gamble. Your neighbor's dog Molly barked at you as you left for the track, so Molly's Luck would win in the 8th at Suffolk at 35-1. Skill and study never factored into Ruby's or Betty's choices. I was in my teens before I figured out that they'd better start factoring into mine.

Like nearly all gamblers, my addiction was triggered by early luck—the instantaneous gratification and reward for guessing right. You put your small money down and it came back to you a minute or two later as big money. If you win early, there's a good chance that it won't matter to you that you lose forever after. You will spend your life chasing the feeling your first scores brought.

The yearly carnival held in the parking lot of the Sacred Heart Church was exciting in the way that all carnivals—no matter how modest—with lights, music, rides, games of chance, and concession stands are exciting to children. You'd run into friends from your elementary school, and you'd meet kids from the other schools.

I'd fallen in love with a girl from out of town, one grade ahead of me, with whom I'd rendezvous each year at the carnival. We would walk around the crowded midway together, secretly holding hands. Just before her group of kids was rounded up to go home, we'd slip behind a booth and she would kiss me once, then dart away as quickly as a gazelle.

It was into this destiny-charged atmosphere that Ruby and Betty brought me one summer night. I looked everywhere for my perennial soulmate. At Ruby's urging, I tried my hand at a game of chance. I got a premonition that if I bet number seven, my girlfriend would appear. It hadn't entered my mind that I might win until Ruby started yelling, "A whole box! A whole box, my boy!"

That first score for me was candy—twenty-four Baby Ruth bars for a nickel. That's a 24-1 payoff. Any gambler would be blasted away by those odds. Except that, other than on the rarest of occasions prompted by inside information, no competent gambler would *take* a bet at those odds.

As a child, however, the message I received along with the candy bars was that gambling was easy, fun, and paid off. My win not only brought me cavities, it brought me the lucky number seven. You could imbue this number, through force of will, with efficacy, with potency. Number seven would make your horses run faster, would cause roulette wheels to do your bidding. You just had to project "seven" onto the operation. You could will "seven" into being. Even if a six or an eight hit, it could be seen as not quite a loss; you were only one off. The cosmos was *trying* to work for you. A little more mental energy would have pushed you over the line into the winners' circle.

It's instructive that I had at least momentarily forgotten about my yearly assignation. The girl didn't show up that year or the next, after which I'd outgrown the Sacred Heart carnival.

Old Orchard, where I spent my summers as a small boy in the mid-1950s, was safe because it wasn't safe. The fun houses, roller coasters, and live animal rides, the pizza and fried dough stands, the rigged games of chance, the peep shows and freak shows all taught me things I'd need to know later in life. To be comfortable in what looked to be unpredictable surroundings. To recognize that, embedded in the whirling lights and movement, the noise, the scents, in the dark, in the floors that moved under your feet, in the walls that weren't where you expected them to be, embedded in the uncertainty of the racetrack daily double, in the midst of people's drunken and irrational behavior, there was a reliable bedrock that you could find the center of, where you could thrive and go forward.

To an unformed mind, this was all just like gambling. It represented one small part of what could prepare you to be a gambler. No kid who gambles can understand how there can ever be a potential downside to it. The money you're given to gamble with isn't coming from anyone's rent or mortgage money; no one is risking not having food on the table. A child losing a bet is *cute* to adults—"Oh, you lost. Too bad! Here, try again." So, even though losing is not as good as winning, it's still fun. The bet is just one stop along a lengthy concatenation of pleasurable sensory overloads that start before you even leave home for the afternoon or—better still—for the evening.

Gambling was really a series of planned activities that began with choosing how to present yourself at the track. Your luck might depend on your choices. For the men, these could include what hair tonic and cologne to put on, what rings or watch to wear. Ruby, although as conscientious about his appearance as the next fellow, was much too tasteful to slather himself in lotions, to drape on gaudy clothing, or to festoon himself with gewgaws of any sort. His wedding ring, a good non-decorative timepiece, a clean, one-color or white shirt of natural fabric, expensive slacks held in place properly by a slim belt minus ornate buckle, and—weather requiring—a simple sports jacket told the world plenty.

Betty's coiffing and fashion choices were more eye-catching than Ruby's. She favored large pieces of jewelry with brightly colored stones in their centers. Lipstick was to be applied liberally, with only unadulterated red being acceptable. Whether this was to compliment her freshly blued hair, set off by her light-skinned complexion to complete a patriotic facial triptych, nobody knew. Betty's dresses were undramatic and modest, generally of neutral colors chosen not to draw away from the admiring or invidious attention paid her mink or ermine stoles, those darkly glossy mélanges of heads, paws, and tails.

The excitement of the midway—shared with Ruby and Betty—was twinned with the thrill of betting on the sulkies at Scarborough Downs. At the Old Orchard Pier, we would fill up on French fries drenched with malt vinegar and salt in the preferred style of vacationing Montréalais, then hit the track, Ruby and Betty with their Pall Malls and me with my Muriel cigar, all smoking contentedly, windows rolled down on the short drive over.

I had been reading about the Orinoco River in South America the day before. Orinoco, the number-seven horse in the fourth race, was listed at 14-1 on the board. I calculated how a five-dollar bet would pay seventy dollars when she won—a fortune for a seven-year-old.

My grandparents were as sure as I was that I'd picked the winner. The signs pointed directly to it. Ruby walked me to the betting window. "Here's a fin, my boy. Place it on the nose." There's a joy at that age in no longer needing to ask what the voodoo of inside language means.

At the gun, Orinoco jumped to the lead and held it wire to wire, the winner by two lengths. Betty screamed her head off the whole route. At the ticket window, I was handed seventy-four dollars and change, an exchange that sealed my fate.

"Are you ready to go to Wonderland?"

Uncle Joe Martini and Family Mob Connections

My uncle Joe Martini, who was married to Ruby's sister Sophie, was the first real gangster I ever met. Joe brought Sophie and their son Sonny to visit Ruby and Betty every year. Joe was a large, bald, emotionally expansive man who wore dark, expensive suits with open-collared shirts. He preordered a new red-interiored Cadillac Fleetwood every year. His munificence and the pleasure he took from life immediately sold me on becoming a gangster. Like Ruby and Betty, but on a larger scale, Uncle Joe and Aunt Sophie spent their time solely in pursuit of fun. Joe kept his wallet stocked with hundred-dollar bills.

Joe Martini was also the first man I ever met who called other men "Honey." It's a New Jersey–Pennsylvania working-class thing; Joe Biden does it.

Uncle Joe would ask me about my grades whenever he saw me, often multiple times in a day. When I'd tell him—I was a good student in elementary school—he'd slide a five-dollar bill into my shirt pocket with a slick gesture that I learned to imitate. He'd ask me a math question, and slip me a ten when I got it right. I didn't know it, but Joe had a far greater aptitude for numbers than I could ever dream of having.

Despite being a tough character, Uncle Joe didn't do any kind of muscle work for the Mafia. He collected the drop and did their books. Then he skimmed from the till. It's still hard for me to believe anyone doing something that stupid would be allowed to remain alive. But Uncle Joe was so universally liked and so generous that he was "retired" by the Mob. He was given a million dollars, a diner in Keansburg, New Jersey, and a free pass to live the rest of his life in peace. Everybody loved Uncle Joe Martini.

Piano and Boxing

The ability to play piano was no mystery. On my mother's side, we were professional musicians for the four generations that I knew about, and likely further back than that. Ruby's father had been a vocalist; my mother was an extraordinary vocalist; Ruby was a great pianist, a first-rate bandleader, composer, arranger, and a highly trained all-around musician. It would have been a shock if I *hadn't* been able to play the piano. When I accompanied my mother, she might ask that I "bring that up a third" or "lower it from C to A-flat." She didn't think there was anything out of the ordinary about an eight-year-old kid transposing standards into any key, and I never wondered about how I could do it.

Boxing aptitude was harder to trace. It seemed to come from nowhere, yet I felt the same certainty about it that I did about piano. Mine was never a child's take on the sport. I could recognize subtlety and nuance. I loved feints, head movement, setting an opponent up. I knew which combinations would work. I thought strategically.

I recognized that Ray Robinson was untouchable; that would have been obvious to anyone. But I couldn't get enough of Harold Johnson, Joe Brown, and Joey Giardello—fighters whose work came more through the craft of adumbration than any overt display.

1960s

Turning Professional

I think of myself as leaving home and quitting school when I was twelve, but that's not quite what happened. Neither occurred overnight. At twelve, I stopped spending much time at home and began sleeping elsewhere, occasionally on the street. And although eighth was the last grade I'd officially pass, I continued to go to some classes for a little longer than that.

Much about leaving home and quitting school early tied into an unusually strong antiauthoritarian streak. I could never stand being told what to do. This renunciation of authority started with my parents, then my teachers—I wouldn't pray or pledge allegiance to the flag in class; both required in public schools during the 1950s—but soon expanded to include any institutional figures, including bosses, officials of any kind, military personnel, judges, and cops. *Especially* cops.

My insistence on doing things without instruction or advice relegated me to the scattershot information-gathering of the autodidact. This guaranteed that there would be enormous gaps in my education; I'd be stuck for a lifetime making wild guesses at things I knew nothing about, even if I did sound authoritative in those guesses.

I was also very impatient to start my life, having dreamed up a vivid picture of what that life would be. It didn't occur to me that enjoying a childhood *was* living a life.

Twelve: The Magic Number

There's our real life. Then there's the dream life that we imagine for ourselves. And we are always two—the person going through their day and the person projecting what their dream life might be.

What if your real-life aptitudes and a willingness to incur risk coincide with the dream life you imagine for yourself? Does your real life become your dream life? Or does your dream life get constantly reconfigured in order to remain a dream?

Before turning twelve—the age I had picked to become an adult—I imagined ways my life might go. Real things had drawn me toward those ways, but those real things had arrived through the prism of magic—pure voodoo. Spellbound by the magical qualities only, I was not yet alert to the practical requirements needed to turn them concrete.

JFK Slept Here; I Did a Little More

Beale Street in Brookline, Massachusetts, will always have great historic significance for me. It was the childhood home of President John Fitzgerald Kennedy.

That's beside the point. The important thing is that it's where I lost my virginity.

I intended to start my adult life at twelve, and reasoned that if you were a virgin you weren't really an adult. Summer of 1963 had begun; there were only a couple of months to get it together if I was going to make it under the wire by late August.

I hit the street, with intuition sending me by subway—paying the kids' fare of ten cents and transferring once in Cleveland Circle—to Coolidge Corner in Brookline. The same intuition propelled me directly down Harvard Street to a mom-and-pop candy store called Irving's. Brookline—a wealthy town just west of Boston—was the furthest place imaginable from a red-light district and candy stores weren't teeming with sexual opportunities. I wasn't thinking at all. Fifty-seven years later, I am still certain that some prerational cognition was in play. I knew exactly where I was supposed to go.

I was so sure that the girl would be there when I got to Irving's that I was completely unsettled when she wasn't. How could I have possibly been wrong about something so essential?

Then Veronica walked in.

Seeing her forced me to come to terms with the enormity of her *realness*. This shut my insides down entirely, as if everything had flash frozen. Time slowed. Details of Veronica's appearance and the surroundings were vastly intensified in definition and color. For a moment, there were *literally* colors I'd never seen before. There was a steady D-flat hum in the air.

I had wished for the girl to be beautiful. Veronica *was* beautiful. She was obviously older than me—which I knew she would be. I couldn't tell how much older.

Although often mistaken for an adult by my mid-teens, I still looked like a child at eleven. I already wore size twelve shoes—I'd wind up at thirteen and a half—but was only 4′10″ and weighed under seventy pounds.

Veronica couldn't have mistaken me for someone her own age, but somehow understood that I hadn't wandered into Irving's to get a soda. We were in this improbable place for the same reason.

She said, "Buy me a coke? I like the syrup they use."

We talked about nothing. We were trying to figure out how to get to where we needed to be.

After a few minutes, Veronica asked, "Would you like to come to my house? It's right around the corner."

"Will we be alone?"

"Yes. My mother works. She doesn't get home until five. We'll have three hours before she comes home."

We walked around the corner to a tree-lined street of brick and stone duplexes. The girl told me her name. She was fourteen. I thought I'd never seen anyone so beautiful. I knew enough to put my arm around her.

When we got to her house, we began kissing. It was the only time in my life that I was scared before fucking, and was involuntarily shivering. I was pretty sure that I knew what to do, but there'd be no way to tell until I'd actually done it.

I said, "I haven't done this before."

"It's easy. You'll see. It feels really good."

"You've done it?"

"A few times."

Veronica was evolved in ways I didn't understand, smarter than I'd ever be. She was already an adult.

And she was right about fucking. It turned out to be very easy and it felt really good.

Chubby and the Turnpikes

Chubby and the Turnpikes were five Cape Verdean brothers from New Bedford, Massachusetts, by way of Providence, who fronted a good R&B band centered around their spellbinding harmonies. The vocalist Ralph Graham hooked me up with them when I was about fourteen.

The Tavares brothers were wild kids. They liked to drink, and I guess some of them were involved in minor criminal activity. But they were friendly and funny, and it was a blast rehearsing with them. It may have been the first time I thought I might be in a band that would become famous.

Then Chubby went to prison for stealing cars. At least that was what I was told. Just like that, I was out of a gig.

A decade later the brothers did wind up becoming famous. As Tavares, they were one of the most successful bands of the disco era. Tavares sounded exactly the same as when they were Chubby and the Turnpikes. Years later, it would gall me a little bit to have to cover "Heaven Must Be Missing an Angel" for Ric Ricardo. Ric, who was Portuguese, would tell the audience, "You all know this great hit by my Portuguese irmãos."

"They're Cape Verdean, asshole."

Charlie Mariano

Although by the time I was sixteen I'd been playing jazz for a few years, gigging with Charlie Mariano was a big jump forward. I knew Mariano's lead alto work from Charles Mingus's *The Black Saint and the Sinner Lady* album—possibly the bassist's finest. Mariano's playing gave voice to all of Mingus's feelings of love and pain, loneliness and longing.

Charlie's drummer Louie Peterson got me on a New Year's Eve gig with the two of them. No bass player. It paid $165 apiece—really big money for the time.

I could already play piano, but didn't have a wide repertoire. New Year's Eve gigs are entirely about playing standards. I had good ears and picked up tunes fast, but some standards had entirely unpredictable transitions. If you didn't already know "All the Things You Are" or "Body and Soul," you weren't going to guess the right chords.

I know this for a fact because Charlie played both during the first set. He didn't think being sixteen was an acceptable excuse for not knowing the material. I was getting adult money. Realizing I didn't know many standards, Charlie and Louie played it safe from then on, choosing tunes that I could pick up right away. But neither was happy with me.

When we went on our first break, Charlie Mariano took me aside. He wasn't known for his patience to begin with, and I had stretched what little he had as far as it would go.

"Look," the great altoist said, "I've been hearing about you. Louie's told me good things. And, you know, you might be a genius and all that. But you still gotta learn the fuckin' tunes."

Putting the Kids Through School

I was good at taking tests. Like IQ tests, SATs were designed to benefit white males who lived in the northeastern United States. They fed us the exact questions we were most likely to know. I might as well have written them myself.

In the 1960s, there were no safeguards ensuring that the person taking an SAT test was the actual student whose name was on it. You could walk into any testing room on your scheduled day, give the monitors someone else's name, and take their test. No one asked for an ID.

In the town where I grew up 90 percent of the high school graduates were accepted to four-year universities. Parents would do almost anything to get their kids into good schools.

I'd taken the SATs and scored an 800 in what used to be called the "verbal" section and a 790 in math, so I knew I could guarantee minimum scores of 750 in each category to anyone who'd pay me $500 to take their test. Over a two-year period, I took about ten SAT tests in four different high schools—twice for girls—and never turned in less than a combined 1540 score. I was probably responsible for bringing in some tuition money for Harvard and Yale. Or maybe the young polymaths wound up receiving scholarships based on my scores.

Christmas in Des Moines 1966

Des Moines in winter was barren and without color; the snow reached the streets already dirty. You could smell the slaughterhouses just beyond downtown. We hung around the bus station, trying to figure out where to go and what to do next. There wasn't a lot of money, and I worried that we were going to run out. Nobody in Iowa looked anything like us. Instead of being invisible, as I'd hoped, we were objects of close scrutiny.

The people we were spending our time with were objects of close scrutiny too, although we didn't realize it yet. We knew our new friends were thieves and that they fenced stolen goods. We knew that Alvin Hummel, who brought us to the Walnut Hotel where we wound up living down the hall from him, was a failed bank robber who had been emasculated during the ensuing shootout.

The Des Moines underworld was a close-knit community of cultural rejects, many of whom were related by blood, marriage, and quasi-marriage. Although they all engaged in illegal activities, they were more like outsiders than lowlifes. They maintained certain ethical codes, behaving reliably within their guidelines.

When he started talking to us at the bus station, one of the first things Alvin told us was, "I'm a queer and a bank robber. But you don't have to worry about me."

I asked him, "What makes you think we're worried about you?"

"I'm not saying you are. I'm just saying that there's no need for you to be."

I thought about it. I had someone in my care in Des Moines; different principles applied to what chances I could take. During the few weeks I'd been there, I hadn't been able to properly see to things.

I'd managed to rent a small apartment above a used-car lot where pennants snapped sharply in the wind day and night. The owner of the property was a gaunt, taciturn man to whom I introduced myself as Allen Turner—the name I'd been living under since arriving in Des Moines.

"You're taking the place for yourself?"

"No, my wife will be living with me."

"It'll cost you an extra twenty-five dollars a month, seein' there's two of you and I pay the heat and electric."

"That's okay."

"And you can't keep no pets."

We had brought our cat Alban with us.

"We don't have any pets."

"When was you plannin' of movin' in?"

"If it's ready, we can move in today."

"I got to have the cleanin' lady go through the place. Last people here didn't keep it up. You can move in tomorrow, but I'll need a deposit. It's seventy dollars a month, plus the twenty-five. Give me twenty-five now and drop off the rest at the lot tomorrow. You can pick up the keys then."

We were lounging around the apartment two days later when a key rattled the door and the owner walked in.

"I'm giving you back your money. You got to leave. This girl can't be more than fourteen or fifteen. She's not your wife."

"She's my wife. And she's eighteen."

"I'll give you an hour, then I'm coming back with the police. Pick up your money on your way out."

We were desperate to find a place, which was why we let Alvin Hummel walk us over to the Walnut Hotel and then talk Rose into reducing her rates and renting us a two-room suite with kitchenette for twenty-five dollars a week. Alvin managed to arrange it so that the rent was due at the end of the week.

But it wasn't as if the Walnut Hotel didn't have plenty of vacancies. It might have been a decent place in its day, but its day was a half-century past, and it was now a seedy rattrap that supported a community of damaged, deficient, and demented rejects who spent their days with their doors wide open, eating frozen dinners and cookies in bed while watching TV, mumbling to themselves or laughing hysterically. Some stood in their doorways waiting to reach out and grip our arms as we walked by. There were urgent things they needed to tell us.

The Walnut also supported a parallel-universe community of vermin just behind its peeling wallpaper. Mostly you would hear them scurrying throughout the night, but occasionally one would break through, and you'd find it crouched in your living room or perched on the kitchen counter or even suddenly and frantically scrambling onto your bed from a hole in the plaster, unhinged and searching for which way to jump.

The Walnut Hotel was a place where people who had lost went to finish out their days. We hadn't lost, and we weren't finished.

"Allen, you ever been to Greenwich Village," Alvin Hummel asked. "What's it like?" He pronounced it "green-witch."

"Crowded. Dirty. Cheap. Fun. I like it, but I've never thought of living there before. Maybe it'd be a good idea. We need to get out of here."

Alvin was in his late thirties or early forties and had never left Des Moines. To uproot to the heart of New York City took a lot of courage.

"It's probably a lot better for queers there."

"I'd guess so. Des Moines seems like it's not a good place for anyone except Iowans."

We agreed to bring Alvin with us. It felt like bringing someone to Oz to find out if the Wizard would give him some balls. And some new friends. We'd wait until the end of the week, pay Rose, then get on the bus.

It didn't happen. That night at around 3:00 a.m. there was a powerful banging on the door, followed by a loud voice. "Police Officers. Open the door."

When I let the two cops in, the first thing one of them said was, "You're under arrest. We're taking you with us."

They looked at the girl. "You'll have to come too, Miss."

I couldn't think of what to say. I was very afraid, but it was important not to let on.

"What are we being arrested for?"

"She's not being arrested. You are."

"For what?"

"For Statutory Rape. She's underage. Let's go."

"She's my wife. She's not underage. We just got here."

"Got here from where?"

"New York."

"Then you've also violated the Mann Act."

"We've got a cat."

"Leave it with Rose."

Rose, having let the cops in, was standing in the hallway.

"It's okay, honey," she told me. "You can leave your kitty with me. I'll take good care of her until you get this straightened out."

The girl was braver, tougher, and smarter than I was, but she was frightened and silent. We were brought to a paddy wagon—not a police cruiser, but an actual vehicle used to round up miscreants—and put inside. The cops were aloof and officious, not trying to be menacing. I asked them questions, more out of fear than anything else, but also in an effort to appear in control.

"How did you even notice us?"

"The Walnut Hotel is the residence of known felons. We keep an eye on the place. We saw you two coming in and out with Alvin Hummel."

"That doesn't make us criminals."

"This girl is underage. That makes you a criminal."

We reached the precinct house, where the girl and I were separated, presumably to each be questioned. I was taken to a small interrogation room, where a lone detective talked with me. He was tired and bored, going through the motions.

"Statutory Rape will put you in prison for a long time. Where did you pick her up? Is she a local girl? Have you been pimping her out?"

It would have been pointless to keep up the fiction that she was my wife and eighteen.

"Look, Detective, I can't be guilty of Statutory Rape. I'm fifteen years old. She's my girlfriend. We live together."

"Bull*shit*. You're not fifteen years old."

"Yes, I am."

"You got a way to prove that?"

"Not on me."

"You're going to need a way to prove it. Meanwhile, you're staying with us in the back."

I spent the next five days alone in a jail cell. It was always cold and it was incredibly boring. There was literally nothing to do. No books, no television, and only one window that was too high to see out of. The only activity was listening to trains passing below the jail. The bed was a crosshatched metal cot. No pillow, one threadbare blanket. Because I was a vegetarian, I couldn't eat any of the food provided, sticking solely to black coffee.

After a point, I figured out that I wasn't in any real trouble. It was embarrassing to have to call my parents to verify my age; worse still that, because I was underage, I could only be released into their custody. This required a totally unnecessary trip by my father and the girl's mother to the precinct house so we could be released from jail.

Rose had, as promised, taken good care of Alban—who she still referred to as "she"—and we picked him up on our way to the airport in Omaha, Nebraska, 135 miles unpleasant miles away. We never saw Alvin Hummel again.

Beacon Hill: Summer 1966

I had a friend named Paul Shavitz, a precocious kid who got involved in dealing heroin for the Mob and tried to keep their money. He wound up dying of a hotshot when he was fourteen—payback for not turning over his earnings.

Paul was one of the first hippies on the East Coast. He'd already taken a ton of LSD, but it was surprising that he got mixed up with the decidedly non-hippie drug heroin. He grew up in Revere, though—a real Mafia stronghold—which might explain how it happened. Everyone in Boston rock circles knew Paul. He could walk into any club for free, hang out in the band's dressing room. Before any psychedelic music had made its way to Boston, Paul had advance copies of all the albums by the bands from Haight-Ashbury. He played Country Joe and the Fish's "Electric Music for the Mind and Body" for me—considered to be *the* seminal psychedelic album—opening a door to something brand new from the other Coast.

Paul was friends with a local classical music conductor named Steve Myers, who had an apartment on Phillips Street on Beacon Hill. Steve was staying in Italy for the season, and so—just like that—I was given a third story walk-up for the summer by someone I'd never met, courtesy of Shavitz.

The place was small and spare, clean and utilitarian. There was a fire escape off the bedroom window. Stepping onto it placed me just underneath the streetcar tracks to the Red Line, where trains passed within a few feet, on their way from Park Street to Charles, heading toward the Harvard Square terminal. I had always been fascinated by the Edward Hopperesque experience of passing apartment windows from a train, swiftly catching glimpses of people cooking in their kitchens, watching TV in their living rooms, sometimes changing clothes in their bedrooms.

These were single-reel silent movies, never to be seen again, but vivid during their moment of occurrence. On the nights I stayed on the Hill, I would occasionally feel as if I were passing myself from the train and wondering what the life of the kid idly lying out on the fire escape drinking a cup of coffee might be like.

I anticipated spending most of the summer in that apartment, but I didn't. I loved the place too much. It was the same as when I wound up leaving an apartment over a small mom-and-pop grocery store on Cremazie Boulevard in Montreal the summer before.

Both were too perfect and too cinematic. They connected to vibrant neighborhoods that were real and, as a consequence of their realness, focused me on romantic notions of what day-to-day living could be. Living an adult life that's well integrated with the goings-on around you may be the bedrock for authenticity *if you're an adult*, but it's a French New Wave film if you're still a kid.

I couldn't have been happier in my Phillips Street apartment. Waking up to make a strong cup of espresso in a good coffeemaker, the sun gleaming on clean dishes in the dish rack, being able to throw on a pair of pants and a T-shirt to walk barefoot through the morning heat to the deeply shaded Pinkney Street Market around the corner to pick up a few groceries were activities of a real life. And activities of real life on Beacon Hill would lead to adventures.

> *Why leave a place that seems perfect? It took me a while to understand that the adventures I kept having only happened because any fifteen-year-old living alone on Beacon Hill would have adventures. An adult living under identical conditions would not.*
>
> *Disregard what having an apartment in a vibrant city at the start of the hippie era would mean to a fifteen-year-old. What would it say about the same person, now in middle age, to live in a third-floor walk-up studio apartment?*

Coltrane

I got the first major answer I needed about work from John Coltrane. Trane was the only musician I ever saw in person who really scared me. Sitting a few feet from him at the Jazz Workshop instantly undid everything I'd always believed about my not having to work to be a great musician. My involuntary first reaction was, "Oh, no."

I was so frightened, jealous, and angry that it briefly blocked out everything I'd always loved about his music. It was as if Coltrane was telling me, "You must learn how to work." My free ride was over.

There's some irony to this because, although John Coltrane showed me the practical steps to becoming a real musician, his more important lesson was about meaning.

Coltrane is the most influential tenor saxophonist jazz has produced. Like all innovators, his legacy includes an astounding amount of terrible music played by terrible musicians. More than a half-century after his death, he is still the primary jazz source for horrible playing.

Musicians—particularly jazz musicians—seldom understand that, putting aside nonmusical issues of intention, all that can be gained from innovators is whatever new language they've added to the vocabulary. That new language can now be incorporated by anyone able to use it.

But the better you can imitate the musician who has influenced you, the more uninteresting and valueless your playing will be.

I knew right away that being influenced by Coltrane had nothing to do with playing like him. That door was now closed; nobody was ever going to come close to out-Coltrane-ing Coltrane. Years later, I got a firsthand understanding of the same principle when playing with Ornette Coleman. Ornette had the Ornette territory covered.

Coltrane not only taught me to devote myself to practice; he also gave me the freedom to use my own voice.

"When I grew up, I put away childish things."

In music, mimicry is a childish thing.

Coltrane taught me that I needed to practice, just as Ruby had advised. I began to concentrate on the conventional disciplines associated with classic piano technique—scales and arpeggios, sight-reading progressively difficult literature; developing a more comprehensive background in harmonic theory, and rigorously building my left hand to equal my right. It took me a few years of trial and error to have a focused method as to how to do these things, but once I did, they stayed with me. I still practice exactly as I did almost fifty years ago—an approach that will allow me to improve at a measured pace for the rest of my life. My goal is to play my best on the day I die.

The End

Coltrane had been dead for a couple of years on the cold January night I went to hear the Elvin Jones Trio at the Jazz Workshop. I didn't know how I was going to make it back to my parents' house after the subways stopped running in order to see Betty, who was staying with my mother while Ruby was in the hospital.

Elvin had kept Jimmy Garrison from Trane's quartet as his bassist, and brought in multi-reed player Joe Farrell to complete the trio. It was a high-powered group, pushed hard by the leader. Farrell, with enormous shoes to fill, found an effective strategy for holding up his end of the bargain. He had mastered Coltrane's harmonic language, but could move backward from it and he wasn't averse to sometimes phrasing boppishly. He also played soprano sax much differently than Trane, and added flute, alto flute, and piccolo to his arsenal. He was not stuck playing in Coltrane's shadow.

Elvin came to my table after each set. I don't know why, since we didn't know each other. His wife Keiko joined us a couple of times, but let Elvin do the talking. He was a great talker—sharp, funny, irreverent—a street guy with a brain. Between sets, Elvin smoked and drank without letup. The breaks were long ones, and the conversation got easier and easier. We talked about playing in Europe. He'd just come back, having run into the exiled Phil Woods in France. I mentioned that I was considering trying my luck there.

"You're not going make a lot of money. But you'll get more pussy than you've ever had in your life."

Keiko smiled indulgently. Elvin threw his arm affectionately over her shoulder. He was a little bit drunk. He was drenched in sweat and grinning like a wolf. I liked him immensely, and felt as if I'd known him my whole life. I'd told him that I'd gigged with Charlie Mariano.

Elvin said, "Man, I've been sitting with you so long I feel like you owe me, since you're not buying the drinks. At least come up and play a set with us."

I froze. I couldn't do it. I'd never been afraid to play with anyone before. And I wasn't afraid to play with Elvin, Joe, or Jimmy. I was still afraid of Coltrane. Elvin was a lifeline to Coltrane, and I wasn't ready to play with Trane. Trane and Bird were too much for me at seventeen. Anyone else would have been fine. A year later, they would have been fine.

But that night at the Jazz Workshop, Coltrane loomed too large and was still too close at hand.

I was embarrassed to back out—I saw it more as backing *down*—of playing with Elvin Jones. He tried to convince me to come up, but was cool about it when I didn't. After the trio's last set, he, Keiko, and I hung around for a while. Elvin reminded me of some of the fighters I knew; he had the same kind of natural warmth and emotional generosity. Elvin Jones might even have made a good fighter if he could have knocked off the cigarettes, booze, and drugs.

I had to hitchhike back to my parents' place, and it was very late by the time I got there. I was still bothered by not having had the courage to sit in with Elvin Jones's trio.

The moment I entered the house I knew that Ruby had died. Betty was sitting with my sister Paula in the kitchen. Paula has always been good at taking care of people, and she was trying to take care of Betty, but it couldn't be done. Losing Ruby had ended Betty's life, as losing Betty would have ended Ruby's. Neither would have known how to live without the other.

There was nothing to be done for any of this. Betty cried through most of the night, periodically reminiscing with us about Ruby. She managed to take a cup of coffee. She managed to laugh a little bit.

We loved Betty too much to disrespect her with the platitudes people use. We waited the night out. We endured it the way animals endure trauma.

At dawn, Betty went upstairs to get some sleep. She was exhausted. Now she had to figure out how to die.

As it turned out, there was nothing to figure out. Betty had liver and brain cancer and was suffering from renal failure. She'd never told anyone. Her doctor said that she should have been dead a decade earlier. He couldn't understand how she could possibly still be alive.

There's one existing photo of Betty as a little girl, taken soon after she was orphaned a year or two into the twentieth century. Her face is innocent and serious; she looks at the camera straightforwardly without the trace of a smile. She has the most determined expression I've ever seen on a human being. Betty would have stayed alive as long as she needed to—as long as Ruby was still around.

After Ruby died, Betty said goodbye to my mother, my siblings, her kids from her first marriage, her two remaining siblings, and me. That took a few months. Then she let herself go.

Ruby and Betty dying ended the first phase of my life. As a kid, I learned everything from them. I was who I was—and who I am now—because of them. I can play piano because of Ruby. I can happily give away anything I own because of Betty. They brought me to the beautiful part of lowlife. The bad part I brought on myself.

At the end of their lives, I wasn't spending nearly as much time with them as I should have been. I'd visit once or twice a week and I'd stay at their place sometimes, but I was preoccupied with my own expanding life and I was selfish about it. In some meaningless ways, I'd passed them.

When people you love deeply go, you go too. They don't ever come back, and the part of you that was with them doesn't ever come back. What remains of you is reincarnated on the spot. That's where you find a place for them: the reincarnated you is where *they* are reincarnated.

The Summer of Love

During the Summer of Love, Janis Joplin tried to pick me up at a concert. She looked sweaty, old, and not very clean. She had bad skin.

I had already fucked a few minor celebrities, but was quickly outgrowing any remaining starstruck phase. After tallying up the benefits of again fucking someone famous against Janis's general unattractiveness, I passed.

I'm now embarrassed by that kind of thinking.

But that's not the point here.

That you could be a teenager sitting on a darkened club's concrete floor as the concert's headliner, traipsing through the crowd on her way to get a drink or smoke a joint, stopped to pick you up said a lot about The Summer of Love.

Joseph E. Levine

In the early spring of 1968, I was approached on the street by a girl. It was one of those first warm days of the year—the kind that causes you to think about what might happen next. It was easy to feel optimistic. It was the weather.

She asked if I remembered her.

"Were we in English class together?"

"Yes, Miss Nicholas's class. You stopped coming."

"Yeah, I wound up doing different things."

"It's so strange that I ran into you. My folks and I were having dinner at the Café Vendome a few weeks ago and you were playing piano. I told them we'd gone to school together. I would have said hello, but didn't think you'd remember me."

"You should have. You would have broken up the monotony."

She laughed. "My parents were going to ask you to play at a birthday party they're having. I told them I didn't think you'd want to."

"No, I want to. Tell me about it."

Do you know who Joseph Levine is?

"It doesn't ring a bell. Did we go to school with him too?"

"Joey Levine? Oh, no. He's a Hollywood movie producer. Joseph E. Levine. But he's from Boston. His birthday's coming up and my parents are giving him a small party. Could you play, like, movie theme songs for a couple of hours?"

"Sure. Do you have a piano?"

"Yes, and we'll get it tuned. I don't know what to offer you. A hundred dollars? Does that sound okay? We'll feed you too."

Grown men in factories were making half that for a week's work.

"That would be great."

"And you can play 'Happy Birthday'? I know that's pretty hokey."

"I can play 'Happy Birthday'."

"Joe's wife Rosalie might want to do a few numbers, if that's okay. She used to sing in the movies."

"Whatever she wants."

"That would be great. Rosalie's nice. Give me your number and I'll call with the details. My folks will be so happy."

The party took place a couple of weeks later in a surprisingly modest house in an upscale section of Newton. That afternoon, I got an early lesson in celebrity.

The conversations I overheard were all centered on Joseph E. Levine, who was upstairs taking a nap. Joseph E. Levine was sleeping. Joseph E. Levine was tired. Joseph E. Levine had a new picture coming out. Had everyone seen Joseph E. Levine's *The Graduate*? Wasn't it incredible that Joseph E. Levine himself was right upstairs? Joseph E. Levine would be coming down soon.

In the meantime, Joseph E. Levine's wife Rosalie introduced herself. She was a fun-loving woman whose life as the wife of a Hollywood producer hadn't gone to her head.

"You're too young to know this, but I'm going to ask anyway. Do you know "Lulu's Back in Town?"

"Everybody knows "Lulu's Back in Town." What key?"

"Good God, *what key?* Where have you been all my life? E-flat."

Rosalie was good. I wasn't so callow as to not recognize that she was someone special. I wondered what this Joseph E. Levine guy was going to be like.

Then Joseph E. Levine made his grand—albeit sleepy—entrance. He slowly descended the stairway, yawning as he did. He seemed ancient.

When I looked Levine up while writing this, I was shocked to find out that he was then seven years younger than I am now.

More shocking still was that Levine lived another twenty years. At his party, he looked as if he wouldn't live another twenty minutes. It wasn't that he looked unwell. It was more that he looked *done*—like a man who'd seen everything he was ever going to see and for whom life no longer held any surprises.

Levine was allowed to walk down the stairs alone, but then he was surrounded. He was a shortish stout man, and he withstood the eddying like the small private island he undoubtedly was. Everyone wanted their special moment, needing something from him. He didn't resist their overtures, but neither did he absorb them. Levine stood there and waited for it to be over.

He was led to the piano and introduced, giving me the cold-fish handshake of the success story who fears that every introduction will cost him money—that everything comes with a pitch attached.

I didn't feel sorry for him exactly; I was too young and poor to feel sorry for anyone that wealthy and successful. But I *got* it. Levine couldn't be part of anything, not even his own birthday party.

I paid attention to him while I played, thinking about my future. I could be famous if I wanted to be. Never Joseph E. Levine–level famous, but all the signs were already pointing to my making it in music.

Observing Joseph E. Levine gave me a sinking feeling that celebrity might require burning through experiences, leaving yourself Levine-like before your time. I'd *already had* a lifetime of experiences, and hadn't even started becoming famous yet.

Watching a tired Joseph E. Levine slumped down in an easy chair, unreadable except in projecting the clear wish to not be there, made me think about my own agency. Because I was young and talented, I was headed places if I wanted to go.

I was looking directly at someone who had made it to the top of Hollywood's corridors of power. He was not only miserable, he was finished. If what this weary and emotionally bankrupt man had was fame and success and wealth, wouldn't it be smarter to stay a happy nobody?

How You Look Is How You Play

I came up during the first wave of musicians whose looks didn't necessarily correspond to the kind of music they played. Fashion that was specific to idiom had always been the norm until the later 1960s. There was virtually no overlap: the way you dressed was a near-certain tip-off to what you played. There was some militancy about this: concert musicians were buttoned-up, jazz musicians were urbanely stylish, rock musicians were outer-limit-seeking, folk musicians tended toward the rusticated, and blues players were either citified or countrified according to whether they were Chicago or Delta affiliated.

The shift away from sound/sight consistency may have started when white rock musicians fell in thrall to the blues and soon became proficient enough to join working bands with black musicians. The old pros didn't alter their appearances, but the white kids made minor symbolic adjustments, modifying their combing patterns or even cutting their hair, and adding ironically retro sports jackets over work shirts and jeans.

Then the first wave of kids who'd grown up with the British Invasion and the San Francisco psychedelic bands found their way into jazz. At first, the veteran jazzers maintained their allegiance to cool, but Miles Davis—that touchstone for where things were heading—began closely observing his teenage drummer Tony Williams's cultural metamorphosis, and decided that neither his appearance nor his music could be allowed to stagnate. It didn't matter if what the transition produced was better or worse; things needed to keep moving.

My 1951 birth date placed me at the epicenter of '60s hippie culture, but my sensibilities hewed closer to the formalism of the generation that preceded me. I wound up embodied in a kind of cultural bifurcation. There's a photo of me at sixteen wearing a white shirt, black sports jacket, and necktie. I have a carefully trimmed beard—in what I've discovered was called the "royale" style—and black shades. All of these fashion choices come straight out of the 1950s. My hair, combed back severely, would be consistent with those fashion choices if it didn't fall to my elbows, a length that would have been seen as radical even at the time the picture was taken. The earring wouldn't have fit in either. When you're that young, you often pick up your style from things you've seen elsewhere, and those things aren't automatically culturally congruent. What you don't realize is that, by combining elements of disparate styles, the hybrid you come up with might add up to something brand new.

Drafted

On turning eighteen, I got stuck in the first draft lottery, drawing the unlucky number ten. Within days a notice summoned me to my local draft board for a pre-induction physical.

Having dropped out of school and with no usable training, I was prime shipped-off-to-die material for Vietnam. There were ways I could have gotten a deferment, but I didn't want a 1-Y classification. Only 4-F would keep me out of the service no matter how fucked up the US draft policy became.

I wound up sending a letter to my local draft board. I knew this was taking a risky approach in banking on my local draft board being against the war. In the South, the board would have me on the next plane to the Mekong Delta.

I wrote that, because I was a strict vegetarian, I wouldn't eat the meals provided by the army. I wouldn't wear the leather belt and boots that would be part of the uniform. Forced to pick up a gun, I'd choose for myself who the enemy was. I warned the Board that I'd be a misfit inductee winding up with a dishonorable discharge or in a military prison, possibly killing someone, while costing US taxpayers a lot of money.

A certified letter arrived four days later. I was no longer required to report for my pre-induction physical. I'd been reclassified 4-F.

Plato's Plum: Boston, Massachusetts

I started working in Mob clubs in the summer of 1966, just before I turned fifteen. I was still young and inexperienced enough to be excited about playing piano in an upscale nightclub—young and inexperienced enough to not immediately figure out what kind of place I'd wandered into.

Today the '60s are often thought of as a whole: the period when the United States went from black-and-white to color. But up until the middle of the decade—and, in most places, later than that—it was really a continuation of the '50s, still more parts Ike than JFK.

There was also a kind of alternative cultural overlap that incorporated elements of both eras while acknowledging some shifts in fashion and music happening in other parts of the world.

These changes had only recently shown up in Boston at the time I began playing at Plato's Plum. The mentholated air, the breezy bossa nova music through the club's state-of-the-art sound system, the small round tables with white linen tablecloths and cut-glass ashtrays, the dress code requirement of sports jackets for men, the recessed lighting, and the tiny bandstand that barely fit a baby grand piano; these were all quintessential early-to-mid-1960s signposts, transitional period artifacts. It was too light and loose-limbed to belong to the era that preceded it, but bore no connection to the massive cultural overhaul just around the corner.

It was cool in a way that things would never be cool again. There was a formalism to this kind of cool, a sense of care and good taste. This was somehow even true about the things that were a little bit tacky.

Plato's Plum on Boylston Street in the heart of downtown Boston was the only Mob club I ever enjoyed playing. At the top of a short winding stairway from the street, the lounge had a panoramic view of bustling Copley Square. It felt special to be there; you felt onto something. The underworld presence in the place was undetectable by anyone not trained to spot it. Customers were treated cordially, even on the rare occasions when someone had had too much to drink.

During my stay at Plato's, my daily routine was like a movie version of a jazz musician's life. I'd lounge around my house into the afternoon. In the early evening, I'd put on the gray lightweight sports jacket recently purchased at Louie's, belt expensive darker gray slacks, add a slender tie that complemented the jacket, then make a final check in the mirror. Looking back at me was someone I'd convinced myself looked the way a jazz musician should look. I belonged. Playing the piano professionally allowed me to be a boy with a man's confidence and sense of entitlement.

If playing piano was adult work, it was fun adult work. Because I was not yet sixteen, I assumed it would always be fun. My arrangement was to play five nights a week at thirty-five dollars per night, payable at the end of the two-week run. I'd be making more money than I could spend.

I drifted into an affair with Bobbi Kelly, the club's vocalist. Bobbi—a recent Playboy Bunny—was the glamorous antifeminist, men's magazine personification of the ideal woman. She was in her mid-twenties and already divorced.

If I hadn't been caught up in a romanticized notion of what it meant to be a working jazz pianist, Bobbi wasn't a woman I'd have become involved with. Because I was young, having her on my arm seemed incredibly prestigious—a confirmation of my status as an adult. The Playboy Bunny imprimatur still carried weight with some people, and I was too dumb not to be a show-off.

If Bobbi's singing had been even passable, her looks would have allowed her to finesse her way through. Her vocal deficiencies couldn't be masked through the judicious choice of chord voicings or strategic obbligatos. Her voice was so bad that it drew attention away from her beauty. Once on the bandstand, she briefly balanced on a teeter-totter—her voice on one seat, her looks on the other. Back and forth the seesaw went before it finally clunked down hard, landing her first on her ass, and then out the door.

After Bobbi was fired, things went on as before. There were enough people in the crowd who wanted to sing to satisfy anyone who enjoyed hearing someone at the mic. They all sang better than Bobbi.

The gig went fine until it was time to collect my money. The owner wasn't a tough guy kind of gangster. With his stylish suits and expensive jewelry, his small well-trimmed mustache, he was too urbane to convey menace. I should have been tipped off that something wasn't right about the guy by his excessive use of aftershave.

We'd barely exchanged a word during my two-weeks there. Now he told me, "The club didn't do good business during your run. You didn't bring in the people."

The owner had nicked himself shaving that morning. He was carefully examining the nick in the mirror, pulling the skin on his neck taut. It wasn't worth his effort to look at me.

"Yes, we did," I said. "Even if we hadn't, you'd still owe us the money."

"Sorry. Payroll doesn't have it."

He continued looking at himself in the mirror, now fixing his hair and straightening his tie.

"We won't play tonight."

"We already let you go. You weren't drawing. Another band is coming in tonight."

I couldn't think of anything to say or do, so I left. I came back two hours later with a lawyer—an acquaintance whose age might add gravitas. I couldn't bring myself to just walk away even though I didn't think we'd get the money. I was wrong. My friend's lawyerly monologue worked. The owner wasn't intimidated by it. He just wasn't in the mood to argue. The pile of bills extracted from his jacket pocket barely made a dent in the wad.

Although I didn't know it at the time, beginning my Mob club career at Plato's Plum had started me near the top of the heap. A number of years passed, during which I learned my craft, playing a wide variety of music in a wide variety of places, steadily building a reputation. I had more interesting legitimate work than I could handle, so assumed that my lone Mob club experience would be my last.

My Introduction to the Mob

My uncle Joe Martini always tried to help people he liked. He got Ruby's brother, also named Joe, the sauna and massage concession at the Ritz-Carlton in Boston. This is indirectly where I came into the Mob picture.

As a teenager, through my connections at the Ritz-Carlton, I became friendly with some Boston-based fighters. The one I was closest to was a remarkably slick operator named Tommy Tibbs. Tibbs wasn't just slick in the ring; until the day he was shot to death outside a bar in Roxbury, he was good at wheeling and dealing with gangsters. He introduced me to some of his Mob friends, telling them that I was the best boxing handicapper he'd ever seen.

This brought me to the attention of some mobsters running a record store called Minuteman in Cambridge. Minuteman was a money-laundering and fencing operation. No one there talked directly about what they were doing, and they weren't like any other Mob guys I've known. What I know about Minuteman's operation is through deduction.

For one thing, although the owner appeared to be the visionary rock 'n' roll pioneer and general lowlife Morris Levy, the minions who ran the store were buttoned-up Midwesterners who acted more like FBI agents than Mobsters. If anything, they were like the Mormons who handled Howard Hughes's day-to-day business.

Minuteman seemed to specialize in merchandise that either had fallen off a truck or been listed as missing, damaged, or stolen, but then found its way to the second floor of the store, where it was resold for about twenty cents on the dollar.

The Mobsters provided an out-of-the-way desk where I could write down my betting recommendations, adding in my own bets as partial payment. My choices generally paid off, and I would get a percentage along with my winnings. I was also invited to take as many records as I wanted.

I never met or even saw Morris Levy, as far as I know. From what I understand, he was a dangerous motherfucker, if an extremely gifted one. In addition to being a notorious loan shark, he opened the jazz club Birdland in New York City, discovered Frankie Lymon, and was the owner of Roulette Records, an odd label that's primary function seemed to be to lock its artists into slavish contracts. Levy was a legend in the music business—*The Sopranos*' character "Hesh" was based on him— about whom rumors circulated for many years after his death; one story persisted that he hadn't actually died, but had disappeared with millions of dollars in cash to an unreachable island. Which island it was varied with the telling.

I got in trouble with the henchmen at Minuteman when I grew too cocky. I was only about sixteen at the time, so might be forgiven my indiscretion. One of the cashiers at the store saw me taking an enormous quantity of records home. I invited him to do the same, saying, "It's okay. They're on me."

This didn't go over well with the Mobsters. It couldn't have been about the money. The amount I was encouraging the employee to lift wasn't a fraction of what I was bringing in through my betting advice. But you don't steal from the Mob. Unless you're my Uncle Joe Martini, apparently.

The Kings and Queens: East Providence, Rhode Island

I told myself that the early-career fiasco at Plato's Plum put an end to my gigging in Mafia-owned establishments. That resolution ended a few years later when I ran up against some poker losses I couldn't afford.

I was worriedly weighing my options when a call came from a pianist who asked if I could find musicians for a trio gig that he was unable to make. It entailed some travel, but paid twice my asking price—more money than I could turn down.

The Kings and Queens was a nondescript bar just over the Massachusetts border off Route 95, visible from the highway. I immediately wondered why the gig paid so much. The club appeared to be closed, but the door was unlocked so we went in. There were no customers, most of the lights were out—along with the outdoor entrance sign—and there was no staff to speak of. A couple of serious-looking guys sat at the bar drinking.

"You guys can set up over there," one of them told me.

"There's nobody here—do you want us to start playing?"

"That's up to you."

"You don't care?"

"Don't make no difference to me."

We waited to see if anyone would arrive. No one did.

I started to feel a little guilty and brought my guys up to play a short set to an empty room. While we were on our break, a neatly dressed couple came in and sat at a table near the band. Nobody served them, so they soon got up and left. This scenario repeated several times during the evening. Clearly, customers were not encouraged to drink at the Kings and Queens.

Again, I asked the serious-looking guy, "You really don't care if we play or not?"

"I don't care what you do."

"Do we have to stay here?"

He looked at his friend, raising his eyebrows with a "you believe this guy?" expression.

"Yeah. You stay the whole time if you want to get paid."

So, we stayed. Each night, we dutifully arrived at the Kings and Queens fifteen minutes before starting time. Our first set, which we didn't play, began at 9 p.m. We then didn't play three more forty-minute sets per night and left promptly at 1 a.m. We didn't play from 9 p.m. until 1 a.m. three nights a week for two weeks. We were paid in cash at the end of each week.

You'd think that I'd have been sorry to lose such an easy free-cash gig, but I was strangely relieved when the serious men let us go after the two weeks were up.

1970s

Oh, Jesus

How did I wind up back in Mob clubs? The same way I wound up doing anything I didn't enjoy: I was broke and in trouble. There were plenty of other gigs, but Mob clubs paid twice as much.

Most of the time I accompanied a Portuguese-American vocalist named Ric Ricardo, a gifted entertainer who loosely based his act around Tom Jones's Vegas Revue. He was an alternately unctuous, obsequious, tyrannical, and moody runt, who frequently headlined or emceed Mob joints to pay off his gambling debts.

Ric was so cut off from mainstream American culture that he didn't know why his name made people laugh and start speaking in high-pitched Spanish accents.

When he first introduced himself, I shook his hand and said, "I'm Fred Mertz."

"Nice to meet ya, Fred."

The wiseguys loved Ric's singing and impressions, but looked down on and made fun of him relentlessly. Their scorn caused him to fear his largely Mobbed-up lowlife audience, making it impossible for him to develop a smooth stage patter, relying instead on a hokey word-for-word repetition for every set.

Some of it made no real sense. Occasionally he'd refer to himself and me as "Ric Ricardo and the Riviera Show Band." He wasn't trying to be funny.

He was a great vocal mimic but dampened the impressions with horrible intros. "Can you picture Tom Jones on *The Dean Martin Show*? Can you picture Walter Brennan on *The Dean Martin Show*?"

Because Dean Martin's show had long before been canceled for poor ratings, nobody in Ric's audience knew what the fuck he was talking about. And why would Walter Brennan, who couldn't sing or dance, have even *been* on a variety show?

When thrown off his game in any way—which happened often—Ric had the unfortunate habit of blurting out, "Oh, Jesus."

If a request was made for a tune he didn't know, Ric, forcing a pained, wheedling smile, would blame the band. "I don't think my guys know it."

"We know it, Ric."

"Oh, Jesus."

Both bully and victim, Ric worried constantly about saying the wrong thing to gangsters, bosses, and audience members. Mistakes were inevitable: Ric once assumed that a high-ranking Mobster's mistress was his daughter and sang "Daddy's Little Girl" in her honor as the Don's horrified underlings frantically attempted to signal him to shut up.

He insulted the musicians constantly but excluded me from any outbursts. I was always on the verge of quitting, looking for a reason, so any ill-timed comment would send me out the door. Ric would have been fucked without me, and he knew it.

I turned out to be a prize commodity in the New England Mob clubs. I could instantly figure out tunes I'd never heard and intuitively transpose them into whatever key made the vocalist sound best. I could handle any kind of music the audience wanted. Mobsters appreciated that, so I was treated better than most musicians. Still, I charged a lot and word got around that "the guy's a little bit difficult." And while gangsters' patience for artistic idiosyncrasy wasn't unheard of, it had its limits. I had to be careful to never step over the line.

As I made my way from club to club, my sense that circumstances weren't quite right began to coalesce. Each gig seemed worse—and more bizarre—than the previous. They weren't always intolerable, but they were almost inevitably surreal.

Many of these gigs required backing up vocalists, comedians, exotic dancers, and an assortment of novelty performers that included X-rated hypnotists, vocal impressionists, and even a woman in short shorts and halter top whose entire act was to roller skate around the stage.

The Grey Finch: Nantasket Beach, Massachusetts

Ric Ricardo and I did our first gig together at an open-air honky-tonk called the Grey Finch on Nantasket Beach, a tawdry, dying carnival town on the Atlantic Ocean.

It took over an hour to get there from Boston. You had to pass clam shacks, fried-food take-out places, soft-serve ice cream carts, pre-computerized arcade games, and a decrepit amusement park that had once been wildly popular but was seeing its last days. By the time you finally drove down Nantasket Boulevard to reach the Grey Finch you had made your way to the end of the United States, where life seemed to drain into the ocean. The impassive, freezing Atlantic was right in front of you, and that was all that was left.

And now you had to go to work.

Ric Ricardo was a glutton for doing lengthy afternoon rehearsals in the club—in effect providing entertainment the musicians didn't get paid for. He called it "moving the room"—playing breakless sets to keep restless customers from heading to another nearby honky-tonk.

The Grey Finch was where I first figured out that I was exempt from the rules that other musicians, easily replaced, had to live with. I could demand double pay and get it. I discovered that the Mob guys didn't object to my holding them up for more money—they figured that if you had the balls to go for it, more power to you. Later, I'd learn what could happen when a less respected musician tried this.

Nights at the Grey Finch never seemed to end. We played terrible music for terrible people. The set list included losers like "Tie a Yellow Ribbon Round the Old Oak Tree," "After the Loving," "What Would You Say," and the morbid "Green, Green Grass of Home." I would pray for older wiseguys to come in so that we'd at least be able to throw in a little Jimmy Roselli.

The monotony was shattered on occasion. One guy who dropped by often was always treated with nervous deference. Even the muscle seemed uneasy in his presence.

It was hard to figure out why everyone was so skittish around him. He was a compact, good-looking man in his late thirties, convivial, stylishly dressed, and always in the company of attractive women.

He would invite me to sit at his table. When I'd hesitate—I didn't like mingling with the customers—he'd ask, "What's the matter? You're not prejudiced against Italians, are you?" Everyone would laugh like it was the funniest thing they'd ever heard, but the whole table tensed up.

One night I asked Ric about him.

"Be very nice to that guy," Ric said, looking grave. "That's Franny the Killer. He's a hit man."

"We're talking about the same guy? That pleasant, well-dressed guy?"

"Just be nice to him, Sir Charles. I'm not kidding."

I already knew enough to be nice to nearly everyone at the Grey Finch. You never knew who was who. Or, as the wiseguys say, who was *with* somebody.

One night, leaving the club very late at night, our car wouldn't start. Nobody could get it to turn it over, so we went back inside to use the phone. Franny the Killer, having a late drink with his friends, called me over.

"Here," he said, handing me a set of keys. "Take my car."

"No, thanks, Franny. I can't take your car. I'm not even the one who does the driving."

"But you're the leader, Sir Charles. And you're the guy I want to have the car. You're responsible."

"That's why I don't want to borrow the car. I don't *want* to be responsible."

"Charles, take the fuckin' car. What do you think? If something happens to it, I'm gonna kill you?"

Everyone laughed.

"Let's not put that to the test. Really, we're all the way out in Newton. It's too big an imposition."

"How ya gonna get home? Just take the car. Bring it back tomorrow night."

I took the car. We drove it back to Newton at about 35 miles per hour.

Franny was a hitman with non-Mob ambitions. He owned a good Italian restaurant in Boston's North End, and later opened another in Bourne on the beach in Cape Cod. I played at both places and he spent time showing me around. He was always very cordial and generous. Nothing in his demeanor hinted at how he earned his money. The Mobsters' treatment of him showed how deeply feared he was.

I only knew Franny to do an uncharacteristic thing once. While showing me the kitchen of the Bourne restaurant, he threw his arm over my shoulder and said, "It's funny how a guy will do things he doesn't want to do just to be able to do the one thing he does."

It seemed like he was talking for both of us.

I played countless gigs with Ric Ricardo during my Mob club years. Largely against my will, I got to know him well. He was a degenerate gambler—and a terrible one. Once he had a few drinks in him, he would giddily throw his money away on anything. He'd bet outlandish sums that he didn't have, which was exactly what the club owners wanted. They'd slap him on the back with his wins, and laugh along with him at his losses. His credit was always good; his glass always kept full. We'd play poker for a dollar, then five, then twenty, and finally a hundred-dollar ante. The stakes escalated every few minutes, and Ric's playing style got steadily more frantic as it did. He would stay in on virtually every hand. All of the players knew to simply let him raise.

Poor gambling had gotten him into trouble before. He had once disappeared for months, and the rumor was he'd been badly beaten. But Ric was beyond rehabilitation; he wouldn't let a few broken bones get in the way of his having fun.

Ric Ricardo had a pal named Joe Finnegan, a 400-pound Mob enforcer who was a regular at the Grey Finch. Ric would sing a modified version of the 1908 George M. Cohan tune "Harrigan," changing the lyrics to fit Joe's name in his honor. "F-I-double-N-E-G-A-N spells Finnegan."

Joe Finnegan was not someone who looked for trouble. But when the collectors had been put off long enough and Ric's debts got too big for him to pay even by working for free, Joe was given the contract to break his legs with a baseball bat. Breaking deadbeats' legs with a baseball bat was Joe's specialty. He was well known all over the East Coast for it. "Here comes Teddy Ballgame."

When Joe Finnegan came into the club and sat at the bar without greeting Ric Ricardo, everyone in the band knew something was going to happen. Ric thought if he somehow delayed the end of the gig indefinitely, Joe would give up and go home. What resulted may have been the greatest performance of Ric Ricardo's career. He took the "Hardest Working Man in Show Business" crown from James Brown that night.

He kept putting us through two-hour sets, giving us five-minute breaks, then calling us back to the bandstand, never leaving the stage himself.

I talked to Joe during one of the breaks, just past midnight. "He's never going to stop the show," I said. "He'll sing forever. He'll sing until you fall asleep at the bar, then sneak out of the club."

Joe sipped his Coke. "I've got all the time in the world," he said. "He has to stop sooner or later, and I'll still be here when he does."

We wound up playing all night, slogging through every tune we knew, and then every request anyone made until we could barely raise our heads from our instruments. Finally, at three in the morning, I decided enough was enough.

I knew a secret about Ric Ricardo. If he tried to sing higher than G-natural, his voice stopped cold. It wouldn't break or the notes come out as a croak; he'd just hit a wall past which was dead silence. I'd always made sure I put his tunes into keys that wouldn't take him out of his range. But this time I made sure that "What Now My Love" would end his night.

Although he was a very good vocalist, Ric wasn't a trained musician. He couldn't tell that I was transposing the tune up in half steps chorus by chorus. He handled things well until we got to the bridge the second time. By this point, I had subtly shifted the key from F-natural up a major third to A-natural, which required him to hit a G-sharp.

He went for the note. His arms were theatrically spread, his eyes closed, and his mouth wide open, but no sound emerged.

"Oh, Jesus."

Our night was over. So was our time at the Grey Finch. And Joe Finnegan took Ric Ricardo someplace private and broke his legs with a baseball bat.

> *While that violence troubled me, it struck me at the time as condign; everyone knows that failure to pay one's gambling debts will result in bodily injury or worse. To me, that Ric had finally been cornered in a Mob joint like the Grey Finch didn't make the Grey Finch worse than any other lousy place to perform. If he'd been beaten at his house, it wouldn't make his house a bad place.*

But, as time passed, it became increasingly clear to me that Mob clubs, even in all their variety, consistently invited peculiar and, ultimately, destructive behavior. Things always moved downhill.

Your treatment by the Mob—it doesn't matter if it's the Mafia, the Russians, the Irish, or the Jamaicans—is not based on meritocracy. You can do everything right and make them a lot of money, but you really are only as good as your last score on their behalf. Their overall mindset is punitive; Mob guys stay poised for you to fuck up so that they can retaliate. This was a lesson I eventually learned the hard way.

My nights of ennui at the Kings and Queens began to seem less surreal than metaphorical. The bulk of a Mobster's life is spent waiting, endlessly waiting. The term "soldier" they bestow on themselves is more apt than most of them ever realize. Low-level Mobsters, like low-level military personnel, spend numbingly long periods of tedium, very occasionally broken up by spasmodic episodes of activity, some of them violent. With the military and the Mob, the foot soldiers seldom know why they're being told to do what they're doing.

So, they wait for their orders and then wait to carry them out. They wait for rewards that will always be less than what they expect. But mostly they wait for nothing.

After the leg-breaking incident, I didn't hear from Ric for a year or so. I assumed he'd left Boston or at least figured out that it was unhealthy for him to work the kinds of rooms that had been his bread and butter for so many years.

I should have known better. What else was he going to do?

"Charles, can you take a ride up Route 1 Saturday night?"

Ric sounded like we'd spoken fifteen minutes earlier, and as if nothing untoward had taken place.

"I'm working a killer room—Paula's Lounge."

"I don't think so," I said, taking my usual opening position before shifting to my usual opening question. "What does it pay?"

"Well, I'm still trying to build the room."

"How long have you been there?"

"About two months. But I don't have my *guys*. I need my *guys*. I told Paula I had a dynamite piano player. I really built you up big. You know I love ya, babe. Paula wants you to come in with your guys."

"What happened to the band that was in there?"

"Oh, Jesus."

"That doesn't sound good."

"No, it was a terrible tragedy. The piano player was moving his equipment and fell down a whole flight of stairs and broke his neck. So sad."

"How is he?"

"He's dead."

"Where did this happen?"

"At the club."

"I think I'll pass."

"I can get you double pay."

"How much does that come to?"

"Uh, I'll have to ask."

Nothing ever changed with Ric or the Mob clubs. But the offer came at one of the many times I needed money, so maybe nothing ever changed with me either. The double pay would most likely come to more than what I'd ordinarily charge. I could hold them up for more once I'd made myself indispensable.

Paula's Lounge: Peabody, Massachusetts

Paula's Lounge turned out to be a strange gig even by Mob club standards. The place was an enormous, no-frills, 300-seater in Peabody—a long, unpleasant ride from Boston, one of an unending series of pathetic clubs and restaurants dotting Route 1.

Paula's gimmick was a floor show featuring has-beens with recognizable names headlining, a comedian or novelty performer, Ric Ricardo, and a jaw-dropping assortment of local nobodies who'd do any fucking thing asked of them for free simply for the opportunity to perform.

Then there was Paula herself, an abrasively brassy "old broad" from London who'd married an ancient, high-ranking absentee Mobster; she worked as MC for the floor show, told risqué jokes, cajoled the audience, and treated almost everyone who worked for her like shit.

Paula's MO was to bring in one-time stars who were in serious gambling trouble with the Mob. In this hangar-like hellhole in the middle of nowhere, they could work down their debts. Frankie Fontaine, formerly of Jackie Gleason fame but now down on his luck, regularly headlined.

There was a hefty cover charge, but Paula packed the place tighter than a cattle car. As soon as the early show would wrap up, everyone would be shoved out the door and the "late show" crowd would be hustled in to replace them. Nobody working for Paula got close to a square count, but the place was a gold mine for her.

I've seldom worked with weirder performers than I did at Paula's. Possibly the weirdest was a Miami Beach regular named Tubby Boots. Tubby was a 400-pound comedian who did a drag show. He sang "specialty" numbers, performed a striptease with tassels on his tits, and told the dirtiest jokes imaginable. Paula and Ric were both incredulous that I'd never heard of Tubby Boots. A lot of other people had, though: he did turn-away business for his entire two-week stay. And he worked his fucking fat ass off for every show.

Tubby Boots and I got off to a bad start. He had brought the orchestral score for his show, arranged for an eight-piece band. At Paula's, I fronted a trio, playing a piano that was a half-tone flat. It's impossible to sight-read a score for an entire band, spot-reduce it to a piano part, and transpose the whole thing at the same time.

Like most old-school show-business veterans, Tubby Boots didn't know what could or couldn't be done musically. He just knew that he had a successful show in Miami Beach and that his eight-piece band could play that show—end of story. He paced the club during rehearsal, complaining to anyone who'd listen, especially Paula, about my inability to accommodate him.

Tubby Boots was the headliner, and he was bringing in a lot of cash; Paula was a Mob wife who'd had the previous piano player thrown down a long flight of stairs to his death. I didn't want to anger them. But what they were demanding of me couldn't be done. I had to explain why in a way they'd both understand.

Luckily, neither was stupid. I called them over to the piano.

"Do you see that?" I asked. "Where it says 'trumpet'?"

"Yes," answered Paula. The two huddled over the piano, their talcum powder cutting off most of the available air.

"And that?"

"'Tenor saxophone.'"

"And there?"

Tubby Boots spoke up. "It says 'trombone.' I get it. So, what are you saying? That you can't play my music?"

"I can play your music. But I can't make the piano into a trumpet or a saxophone. I can't make my trio into an eight-piece band. Now I've got two suggestions."

"Go ahead."

"Paula, I can do a written reduction of the charts. That's time-consuming, difficult, and it'll be expensive. Or I can listen to Tubby's records and learn the shows from listening to them."

"How much will that cost me?"

"Give me a couple of hours. You can pay me an extra hundred bucks."

"Sure. Fine."

Paula hated to part with money, but doing so got Tubby Boots his music played right. And at some level, he understood what had been done for him. We got along from then on.

There were some serious distractions at Paula's Lounge.

Paula had a silly Ginger Rogers parody number—Ginger Dodgers—that she insisted on doing as part of the night's show. She may have been a hard-edged gun moll, but she still had dreams of being in showbiz. She led a "dance troupe" consisting of three conspicuously attractive young women, two of whom were local trailer-park hookers, the other a lesbian who taught legitimate dance.

For no discernible reason, their dressing room had a window allowing anyone onstage to see into it simply by looking to the left. Everyone performing onstage kept their heads turned directly to their left, at a ninety-degree angle from the audience.

Members of the crowd noticed this and, offended by not getting our undivided attention, asked Paula what we were looking at. They wanted to know why the musicians weren't paying attention to the show—which we could all do in our sleep—and why we refused to interact with the audience.

"Sir Charles, please tell the boys that when they're onstage they have to stop staring at the nude women," Paula said.

"Is it that obvious?" I asked.

"If they turn their heads any more sharply, they'll get whiplash. Haven't they ever seen a naked woman before?"

"Well, you know, probably fewer than you'd imagine."

"I'm going to have that goddamned window sealed up. That will solve the problem."

"It *would* solve the problem. And it would create a new problem. The band needs some form of diversion to get through the night."

"Other than the show itself?"

"Definitely other than the show itself."

"Will you tell the boys to at least make an occasional show of paying attention to the performers and the audience? We'll leave you your window, Sir Charles."

Paula's Lounge was also where I got my first glimpse of an odd subset of show business: the X-rated hypnotist.

This particular mesmerist was a vain goofball with an unfortunate name for anybody facing a Mobbed-up audience. Jerry Valli, by necessity, began his act by having to explain to disgruntled patrons that he wasn't Jerry Vale, the crooner wiseguys held in such reverence. And he wasn't Frankie Valli of Four Seasons fame, there to sing his hits.

Because of his name, Valli started every new show with two big strikes against him. He may have been good at his craft, but not good enough to hypnotize the crowd into not hating his guts for deceiving them.

If you work bullshit gigs like Paula's Lounge, you learn surprising things. I had always assumed that hypnotism acts were fakes, conducted with confederates and audience plants. Although all hypnotists have a ringer or two planted in the audience—characters who know how to play "hypnotized" in order to get laughs from the crowd—most of the participants are actually picked legitimately and become authentically hypnotized.

For half an hour, these dupes would reveal embarrassing things about their sex lives, bray like donkeys, and take off as much of their clothing as the market would allow—always to be awakened at the point of maximum exposure and embarrassment.

The biggest laughs invariably came from getting men to "act like a bunch of queers." Every hypnotist using this surefire bit understood that it came with serious risks. Mob club audiences were homophobic and uniformly thin-skinned; they could quickly turn on the performer. They often adopted an us-against-them mindset against hypnotists.

"That fuckin' jerk-off in his white tuxedo is gonna make half-faggots out of all my friends. He might even make an asshole out of me if I get drunk enough to go up there."

Hypnotists had to be careful not to take things so far that there'd be retaliation. And they had to be cautious getting to their cars after the show.

As much as working at Paula's Lounge was tiring, nothing untoward happened there. I finally left because I no longer needed the money. Paula was miffed, but I stuck around for a couple of weeks until Ric found a replacement. There was no steep flight of stairs waiting for me in the end.

Mob Club Royalty

I've sometimes wondered about the admiration and identification that Mob club owners, managers, and even patrons felt toward British royalty.

At least three of the places I worked had "Kings" or "Kings and Queens" in their names. Four club owners or managers called me "Sir Charles" independently of each other. The title was always enthusiastically taken up by their customers with a grateful sense of relief. An acceptable way to categorize me had at last been found.

Still, I believe what drove these conceits was not the same: the reason for calling a club "The Kings and Queens" wasn't the same as the one for calling me "Sir Charles."

The first had to do with destiny, saga, and privilege, no matter the circumstantial evidence pointing to lives of mediocrity or worse.

The people who were part of these crowds felt they weren't just some assholes off the street despite the fact that in most of these clubs some asshole off the street could walk right in. Nonetheless, the thrust of the insiders' royal decree was, "This is our place. You keep the fuck out."

Still, why was I knighted at every Mob place I played? Why would people to whom I gave no more than aloof professional courtesy make it a point to elevate me? These were people who were usually unduly touchy about being slighted and quick to respond violently to perceived insults. "What, you prejudiced against Italians?" was an oft-repeated question, partly as an inside joke, but with enough underlying threat attached to guarantee the desired answer.

The way the wiseguys could accommodate my lack of sanguinity toward them was to designate me a figurehead, a minor piece of sovereign real estate—one they might claim for their own palace. By giving me their blessing to be detached—which could translate as the bearing of royal superiority—they removed the need to straighten me out for not paying any attention to them.

Rechristening me "Sir Charles" also gave Mobsters license to voice heartfelt artistic opinions and float profound philosophical theories. A feared enforcer could request Della Reese's "Don't You Know," a popular oldie stolen from Puccini's "Musetta's Waltz," with no embarrassment, then cry his eyes out as I overloaded the number with vulgar arpeggios. Women would love him for it, and even his cronies would be impressed.

"Honest to God, I can't help it," he'd sob. "It's so . . . fuckin' beautiful."

At a certain point in the night, the music would make a sentimental pilgrimage, starting with Tom Jones, moving on to Frank Sinatra, and veering slightly upward toward the operatic leanings of Jerry Vale and Jimmy Roselli, which would then open the door for Mario Lanza and Ezio Pinza, before hitting its pinnacle with Enrico Caruso and "Pagliacci," and gradually rolling back down the hill to settle with Engelbert Humperdinck's "After the Lovin'" and "Release Me." Of course, all these songs were being sung by Ric Ricardo, which limited the depth of interpretation for some of them.

When the cycle had been completed, there'd be a palpable atmosphere of depression in the room as it hit home that we were back near where we started, or maybe someplace even slightly worse.

The Stupidest Man Alive

In the early 1970s I became good friends with Margaret Chaloff, a major figure in piano pedagogy. Her ex-husband was the celebrated concert pianist Julius Chaloff, noted for his work with composer Ignaz Friedman. More significantly for the thousands of jazz musicians living in Boston, she was the mother of baritone saxophonist Serge Chaloff, a talented player whose early death had been hastened—as were those of many of his contemporaries—by being in thrall to the various romantic excesses of bebop mythology made flesh in Charlie Parker. Margaret's iconization was further elevated when, in her late sixties and despite not being a jazz musician, she joined a leaderless quartet with Sam Rivers, Tony Williams, and John Neves.

Margaret Chaloff had taught Keith Jarrett, Herbie Hancock, Chick Corea, Kenny Werner, Bob Degan, and Steve Kuhn, among others, championing an elusive Russian technique that focused on breathing, weightlessness of fingers and limbs, with power and control emanating from the base of the spine and shoulders. Her students shared an unusually limpid, singing quality in their tone. They also had precise articulation from hand to hand and finger to finger.

I called her Margaret, but she was referred to as Madam Chaloff by most who knew her and as Ma by her assistant, Avram David. She was in her eighties when I met her—a tiny, unflappably enthusiastic bundle of energy with beautiful naturally red hair and a chirpy voice—birdlike in almost every way—who was the biggest deal in any room she entered, no matter the company.

A devout Catholic, Margaret was also a mystic. She exuded a profound spirituality that went beyond talent and conviction.

The first time I visited, Margaret yelled at me from her top-floor apartment, "Get up here. Hurry. We have so much to discuss."

I made a show of running up the stairs.

"That's good! Now sit down and play something for me."

I sat at her Steinway, then noticed that it had only eighty-four keys instead of the standard eighty-eight.

"I can't play this piano. The center is in a different place than I'm used to. I won't know where the notes are in relation to each other. Everything will be off."

"Oh, get with it, Grandpa. Let me hear something."

I played for a minute or so, then stopped.

"Oh no, you play with too much power. That's all *sex energy*. You're a lot of trouble. What will I ever do with you?"

As I started to tell her that she didn't need to do anything with me, she bounded out of the room, then bounded back in clutching a small figurine.

"Take this. Keep Him near you. You're going to need Him."

She handed me a statuette of Jesus.

"Thank you. But I'm not religious."

"You'll need a Protector. You have important work to do and I can't be with you all the time."

"If you say so. Will you play something for me now?"

"I will play one note for you. Maybe you'll learn something."

I was about twenty then, making more money than anyone playing in Boston, working constantly, on my way to gaining a reputation, and deeply invested in being a self-made force of nature on piano. Nobody was going to show me anything.

Margaret—all ninety pounds of her—sat at the piano, placed her ten fingers on the keys, breathed in easily, and, as she exhaled, made an abrupt movement with her wrists, using no weight, her hands never leaving the keys, and traveling no distance at all.

The room exploded. It was the loudest sound I'd ever heard—loud enough to make me jump. I almost yelled, "What the fuck was *that*?"

Margaret moved aside on the bench and beckoned for me to sit back down.

"Now play something for me again."

"I can't play when anyone is within the range of the keyboard. It ruins my sense of balance."

"Art Tatum used to play this piano with me sitting next to him. Charles Ives has played this piano. Charlie Parker has played this piano. Grow up." She poked me in the ribs.

I didn't want to play; it was being put on the spot too much. I did it anyway.

Margaret Chaloff punched me in the head. Not hard, but not gently either.

"*No*," she said. "You don't press *down* on the keys. You draw the sound up *from* the keys. You have to breathe the notes."

I was the leading jazz pianist in Boston. Everyone knew that. I started to play again.

Margaret Chaloff slapped my hands off the keys.

"No weight. There shouldn't be any weight."

"I didn't come here for lessons, you know. I don't need piano lessons."

"And I'm not giving you lessons. You're too stupid to teach. You're even *stupider* than Keith. And I didn't think such a thing was possible."

The first session was the only time Margaret Chaloff ever told me how to play. It's the only time anyone has ever told me how to play. And yet it had a greater effect on my piano playing than anything else has. When I went home that day, I couldn't stop thinking about what had happened. There was something elemental that I'd been missing—something I had to learn in order to be able to play the way I needed to.

For weeks afterward I'd play one note, knowing I wasn't getting it. My playing now felt leaden; the notes trapped inside the body of the piano. The piano was a mechanical device. How would it be possible to connect with it? There had to be a point where I not only was breathing in conjunction with the production of sound, but where somehow the piano would be breathing back. I had to learn to recognize the vitality within the piano.

It seemed impossible right up until the moment it fell into place and became self-evident. The best thing about attaining this skill was that once you had it it would never leave you. Finding life inside the piano—the life *of* the piano and your connection to that life, a vibrant exchange through interaction—came through shedding fear and inhibition.

Until just shortly before her death, I would visit Margaret a couple of times a week. She believed in the discredited pseudo-science of phrenology, so my shaved head was of particular fascination to her. She would impulsively explore it the moment we sat on her piano bench, the place where nearly every one of our conversations took place. Phrenology may have been bullshit, but I was a big believer in the conveyance of energy through the hands—maybe my bullshit theory replacing hers—so I was grateful to have a genius doing whatever she felt like doing to my head.

Margaret came to one of my last concerts, part of a series at the Emmanuel Church on Newbury Street. Her acolyte Avram David approached the piano a few minutes before I was about to play.

"Royalty has just entered the building," he said.

I looked up, and there she was—floating across the floor, beaming and weightless, her corona of red hair piled on top of her head. She didn't come to the piano. She sat in the front row of pews.

Playing concerts was difficult for me physically. They required one straight hour of playing at full speed and volume, not stopping or slowing down for any reason. My fingers would rip open within a few minutes, and I dreaded that part of it; looking down and seeing blood on the keys was unsettling. I'd try to block all distractions out, but the pain was hard to ignore. I don't think of improvised music as having a beginning or an end per se, so the one-hour preset was arbitrary. The house lights would blink on to start, then blink off to signal that I could stop. When the pain was at its worst, I'd remind myself that the lights would eventually blink off.

A lot goes on while you're improvising for an hour without interruption. Although it is not entirely without mystery, playing music—even music that seems entirely spontaneous—has very little mystery to it.

Jazz was no longer serious music for me by the time I was twenty, so none of my concerts included any. I didn't play music written by other people and I didn't compose my own. Jazz musicians operate from a framework that provides preexisting information that can be called up as needed. What I did when playing concerts was similar. I had a repository of information ready to be called into service. Once I started to play, I could use whatever best reflected how I felt. These ideas were entirely fluid, subject to adjustments triggered by a wide variety of stimuli and many aleatory factors. The information consisted of—but wasn't limited to—harmonic progressions that gave me ammunition for chordal improvising, simple thematic material that could be expanded easily, physical patterns that would allow me to make difficult leaps over the range of the keyboard with great velocity, and even emotional trigger points that would elicit certain types of creative responses.

I wouldn't have played a concert without having practiced for months beforehand without missing even one day; even an hour off my schedule would have caused a postponement. The unbroken months of practice got me into shape. It made it possible to have ready the technique and ideas that were default mechanisms to get myself started, to push myself past rough or inspirationally fallow spots, and to guarantee that there'd be no mechanical failings. That was all pure pro-forma stuff—protection against meltdown. A lot of any given concert is spent in attendance to this aspect of the playing. There is nothing transcendent about it.

Part of the time during any concert was spent watching the people who were watching me, noticing who was in the audience, making note of my surroundings—all a sort of real-time reconnoitering. There is nothing transcendent about this either. It was no different than how I would have spent part of the set when playing in a club. This kind of taking in the terrain neither helps nor hurts your playing. Depending on the proximity of the piano to the audience, it's almost unavoidable.

Once or twice, sometimes three times, the right conditions would show up unexpectedly, and I could become invisible in the music, finally *finding my way deeply enough inside so that I was—as I always tried to become—lost, unconscious. When I finally got to this place—and I never stayed in it long, unfortunately—nothing existed.*

Many segments of the playing were pure architecture. I would be working on structure, thinking theoretically. This mostly meant building patterns that made a kind of linear sense, with chords or individual lines moving in relation to one another. This aspect of the playing was what was most like jazz improvisation and classical composition. It was workmanlike—the product of what I'd been practicing prior to the performance.

Now and then there was actual inspiration stemming directly from technical or theoretical rigor. This happened only rarely, almost always as an offshoot of the times when I was thinking architecturally, my hands suddenly executing without effort. Things had reached a point where all was going well, and I could allow myself to shift over to autopilot. From that vantage point my vision was clear, leaving me free to make leaps that I knew were impossible. I'd make them anyway, and they'd work.

During the concert I spotted Margaret with a faint smile on her face. She brought her fingers to her lips and then lightly waved them toward me.

To this day Madam Margaret Chaloff will occasionally visit me in dreams. She comes to ask why I didn't follow the path she told me was my birthright and my responsibility. It's a good question; one that still I ask myself. Stupider than Keith, no doubt.

The Craziest Dream

Margaret Chaloff was responsible for my playing with Sonny Rollins. She had a Finnish piano student named Heikki Sarmanto who was playing and composing for Sonny. Heikki heard some of my playing and recommended me to Sonny.

I was going to play at my house with saxophonist Jimmy Lyons and bassist Sirone—who were at the Jazz Workshop with Cecil Taylor that week—on the day that Sonny called. I assumed it was Sirone, whose call I was expecting, on the line.

"Hey, man. We still on to play today?"

"I thought we'd play tomorrow. Are you in the City?"

"Boston? No, I'm a couple of towns over. I figured we'd play here."

"I think it'd be easier if you came to New York than to have the whole band come to Boston."

"You're not still in Boston?"

"No, I'm in New York."

Then it hit me.

"Wait. This is Sonny, right?"

"Yes."

I explained my mistake.

"Oh, good. I thought one of us was crazy."

I hadn't made the best first impression, but it turned out to be a lot better than my second.

I got to New York City early and promptly turned the address and street numbers around, going to a wrong location halfway across the city from where the rehearsal was taking place. To make matters worse, I wound up at a jazz record store that had small recording studio in the back, so it took me a while to figure out I wasn't in the right place.

By the time I got to the correct address, Sonny's band was a couple of hours into their rehearsal.

I was shocked by how bad they sounded. Sonny aside, none of them could play at all. I was set to replace Walter Davis Jr., who I'd always thought of as kind of a journeyman—decent feel, nice time, mediocre technique. Compared to the three guys who made up Sonny's rhythm section, Davis was Bud Powell.

I listened to a tune, thinking about the ordinariness of the music, and wondered why I wasn't excited being about to play with Sonny Rollins. I was twenty-one and already bored. And, for some reason, mildly annoyed.

Masao, Rollins's guitarist, played like a robot. Bassist Chin Suzuki, neither bad nor good, dutifully plugged away at the changes. David Lee, the drummer, was noisy and kept clunky time, made worse by drums tuned to sound like soggy cardboard.

I was invited to join in on "Three Little Words." Sonny Rollins wasn't exactly a responsive player because he didn't have to be. He was Sonny Rollins. If you were a jazz musician, you were supposed to know how to play with him. You'd been playing with him in your head your whole life. Playing with him for real was exactly as you imagined it.

Behind Sonny the zombies trudged grimly onward—one gadget mechanically replicating the same basic chords chorus after chorus, one tin woodsman addressing his daily civil service job unsmilingly, and one obsolete gizmo clanking and sputtering in the pursuit of nothing—a trio of joyless jazzmen inching their way around the never-ending circular track. Trying to work with them was like trying to push a humorless boulder up a steep hill.

Sonny would have known they were three little stiffs: he chose them. But why? New York was filled with good players; he could have had his pick of any of them. There had to be a reason why he worked with such weak musicians.

Not surprisingly, he was ignoring them, so I did too. Essentially, I was playing duets with Sonny Rollins. At one level I recognized that the man standing next to the piano reeling out an unending stream of entirely singular improvisation was one of the greatest improvisers the world had ever heard. His tone was enormous, yet controlled in every register, authoritative even as it remained conversational. He was capable of holding fifteen, twenty, and more minutes of unimpeachable creative logic in his head, seemingly without effort. I *did* understand all that about him. Yet, on another level, because his voice was so completely familiar, playing with him was as easy as playing along to a Sonny Rollins record, and so a strangely emotionless experience.

I was certain that he liked my playing, although he may not have liked me. The group played for an hour or so, and then Sonny called "I Had the Craziest Dream." I had never heard of it.

"I'll teach it to you," Sonny said.

He pulled a folding chair up to the piano stool, sat, and turned to face me.

Then Sonny Rollins started to sing.

"I had the craziest dream," he began, "yes I did. He had a slight speech impediment; it came out "the cwaziest dweam."

His right foot, a couple of inches from my foot, started to swing lazily in time to the music. I wear a size thirteen and a half shoe, and Sonny's feet were about the same size, so our two enormous feet looked like we were both wearing clown shoes.

Sonny gazed at me directly the whole time he sang, giving the lyrics a thorough reading, paying attention to the precise melody as written, adding no embellishments, no jazz inflection. He was teaching me the tune, trusting that I would somehow figure out the chords from the melody alone.

"I never dreamed it could be.

Yet there you were, in love with me."

He sang with no sense of embarrassment. He sang the tune at the slow tempo he intended the band to play it.

"I found your lips next to mine, so I kissed them

And you didn't mind it at all."

I thought, "This is going to make a great story someday."

"When I'm awake, such a break never happens

How long can a guy go on dreaming?"

"Okay," I told myself, "it goes to the F-sharp minor 7 flat 5 at the start of the turnaround."

"If there's a chance that you care

Then please say that you do

Say it and make my cwaziest dweam come true."

Sonny was right: he had taught me the tune.

I didn't take the gig. This shows how little understanding I had of the music business. It never crossed my mind that it might be a good career move to play with Sonny Rollins for a year or so, then see what my options were.

The band had a two-week engagement scheduled in Philadelphia that Monday. I asked about the money.

"It's $265 a week."

"I can't possibly play for that. I make more money than that walking around the corner."

"That's what I pay all the fellows."

I suddenly understood why he had such awful players in his band.

"That's okay. Just pay me more."

"I can't do that. How would that make them feel?"

"Don't tell them."

"Oh, no. That wouldn't be right. They've been with me for a long time."

"Sure, I understand. But I can't work for $265 a week. I'm sorry."

I wasn't unhappy about not taking the gig. It would have been an honor to have played with Sonny Rollins for an extended period of time, but having to fight that rhythm section night after night would have been brutal. I'm not sure there was any kind of money that would have made it worth it.

Columbia, the Gem of the Ocean, and a Sailor Adrift

A feature article had come out about me in *The Boston Phoenix*. It was meant to be favorable and generous, but presented me as an exotic.

The piece *did* have one unexpected consequence. It reached the desk of Columbia Records A&R executive Tom Werman, who called to ask if he could fly in from New York to talk about signing me to the label.

I knew Columbia wouldn't be interested in my serious work and I wasn't interested in recording anything else. But Werman was from Boston and could make the trip into a family visit if it turned out we had nothing to discuss. Either way, he wanted to hear me play.

Tom wound up at The Backyard, where I was gigging every night, playing mainstream jazz to earn a paycheck. Werman expressed an interest in recording what he heard. That wasn't the music I wanted to record, but the conversation was enjoyable, so after the gig we continued it at my place.

Tom asked to hear my real playing. I played for about thirty minutes, and it gave him an idea.

"If you'd be willing to tone it down, maybe incorporate some of what you were playing at the club, I think we could do something with this."

"I wouldn't want to do that, Tom."

"Don't change it too much. Just throw in something where people won't feel they're being conned. There could be a market for this. Columbia's jazz roster is pretty thin. We're really leaning on Miles, and we're looking to expand."

I was making $30,000 a year at The Backyard—in the early '70s more money than I knew what to do with. I owned a home and kept a seven-room apartment on the block between it and the club. I told that to Werman.

"I understand. But just think about it. The option is always there if you change your mind."

A couple of years passed. Through a series of bad decisions, I found myself in big trouble.

The Backyard, too ambitious in its attempt to run a restaurant, lounge, and disco simultaneously on three separate floors, was sold. I could see the writing on the wall and left with the owners. I fell into a long losing streak at poker. After a few good years, I was broke again.

My friend Nick Gray called Tom Werman in New York to let him know that I'd changed my mind about recording with Columbia. Making the call myself seemed like a signal of weakness. Tom asked if I was ready to record. Backed into a corner, Nick told him that I was. Two days of sessions were booked for a week later.

Once again, I was caught bluffing without a playable hand. There was no group; there was no material. There was literally nothing to bring, and I had no clear idea of what kind of music might land a record contract. This caused me to take the worst of approaches: I decided to compromise and go with something for everyone.

For the next six days, musicians lived at my house, spending the entire time rehearsing music that was being written on the spot. I stationed myself at the kitchen table with manuscript paper and endless pots of coffee, trying out first one type of music, then another. The beleaguered musicians were run ragged, often being forced to negotiate styles of music they'd had no previous experience playing. Tunes would appear and get a cursory run-through, only to be abandoned. Members of the band would like one piece and dislike another, opposed by other members who had opposite opinions.

Everyone was a pro and tempers never wore thin, but by the time we made it to New York City, we were all burnt out, with still no clear consensus about what would work and what wouldn't. Worse, there was an uneasy feeling within the band that none of it would be what Columbia was looking for.

It wasn't bad music, but it had neither vision nor conviction. It *sounded* calculated. The woman I'd chosen to sing the music was a powerhouse Gospel vocalist of vast resource, poised to become a star in her own idiom, and her talents were undeniable. But I was asking her to work against her strengths, requiring her to memorize material that was quirky and technically demanding. A week's constant singing had driven her voice to its breaking point.

Some added last-minute pressure was brought to bear. On the morning of our first session, the band was shown the studio at West 54th Street. We were to be given the "Big Room," with Miles Davis being bounced down the hall.

"He's just got the five guys and doesn't need any extra equipment."

I seriously thought about sending the band home. I'd brazen it out by myself, carry the whole thing on my shoulders, not get the deal, but at least blow everyone out of water with my playing and leave holding my head up.

It wouldn't have been right. The band members had worked nonstop without pay for an entire week. They weren't making money for the recording session. They'd earned their chances.

After visiting the studio, my sister Paula, drummer Jim Schapperoew, and I went for breakfast next door. The woman waiting our table was disconcertingly good-looking. She was a small black woman with high cheekbones and a dancer's graceful movements.

My sister said, "She likes you."

"Don't be crazy. Look at her."

When the woman brought coffee, she told me, "This is your lucky day."

"It is? How do you know that?"

"You met me, didn't you?"

I thought she was kidding around.

"You're going to bring me good luck? I need it today. I'm recording next door."

"At Columbia? You'll do fine. Let me bring you your check."

The check had no charges, but there was a message. "Good luck today. Call me and let me know how it goes. Angela." She'd written down her phone number inside a heart.

After meeting Angela, I suddenly didn't give a fuck about the recording session anymore—I knew I wasn't going to get the contract anyway—and was totally loose about whatever was going to happen. I was relaxed enough to ditch the piano for the marimba on one piece, even though I'd never played marimba before. I even used four mallets on the tune, nailing it in one take.

The band completed four tunes in two days of recording, although we really only needed the first session. We didn't improve on anything when we went back.

The tunes bore no resemblance to one another: one was a Gospel piece with topical lyrics, another was a sophisticated ballad that I'd written with Dionne Warwick in mind, the third was a threnody for the wrestler Gorgeous George, and the final piece might have shown up in a sentimental *New York City at Night* romance movie. In other words, it was unsellable. Worse, it showed real weakness of character on my part. The music itself wasn't weak, per se—it was vaguely original and adequately played—but it advertised desperation in its unattractive eagerness to please. Arrogance—sticking to my guns—would have suited me better. I only took two brief solos on the whole project.

Columbia had told me beforehand that they were interested in Charles Farrell. What I gave them had nothing to do with Charles Farrell except that it showed him to be a studio flunky willing to kowtow when there was money on the line.

All I got from Columbia was silence. Experience taught that silence always meant no. Silence meant "we're now done with you."

I gave in and called Tom Werman after a few weeks. It was my final weak move.

"I don't have any idea what to do with this, Charles. It's not what we were expecting."

If I hadn't asked, he wouldn't have told me. He didn't owe me an explanation. I still have the original reel-to-reel tape around somewhere, one of my few possessions that somehow hasn't gotten lost. I haven't bothered to listen to it in over forty years.

The Squire: Revere, Massachusetts

I had been gambling heavily. Not Ric Ricardo–level gambling, and not incompetently. But all gambling has ebbs, flows, and reversals of luck. I'd hit a recent cold streak that brought me limping back to the steady employment and good paydays of Mob clubs. Unfortunately, now these places grew steadily darker and more dangerous. People where I was gigging started dying.

In December 1976, about a year after the gig at Paula's Lounge, I was hired to accompany a small-time gangster and aspiring vocalist named Freddie Guarino at the Squire, a recognized Mafia stronghold owned by a taciturn Mob boss named Richard Castucci, who had close ties with the powerful Providence-based Raymond Patriarca family.

Freddie Guarino hustled up a living by staging accidents—many of them his own. These mishaps ran the gamut from minor car crashes that could combine vehicle damage with whiplash claims to falling on icy sidewalks in front of downtown office buildings. He would break into people's homes, ransack their places, and have insurance adjusters lined up to pay off the fraudulent claims. He knew doctors, chiropractors, physical therapists, and even psychiatrists who were all in on the scams.

Freddy was a good-looking, fast-talking con man whom everyone liked. He was self-deprecating—full of funny stories about scores gone comically wrong. He sang passably well, sticking close to the Vic Damone model so dear to the hearts of all Mobsters.

In order to get out of working at the Squire without appearing to be impolite, I imposed conditions that were sure to be rejected. I demanded twice what other clubs paid. A grand piano had to be brought in. There would be three sets a night instead of the customary four.

Freddie waived his own fee so I could get my asking price. Somebody heisted a grand piano from a warehouse and had it shipped to the club. Three sets a night was okayed.

I was stuck with a gig I didn't want. Castucci made me uncomfortable. He was a small, silent man who wore a soft fedora. He had a reputation as a dangerous killer with several hits on his resume. With most people, these sorts of rumors were just talk. With Castucci, they were not.

The Squire felt instantly wrong in every way. There were too many bad people in too many large rooms cooking up too many dangerous deals, with too many hangers-on listening in. There were Mobsters, drug-dealers, gunrunners, FBI agents, and snitches. There were undercover cops who worked for the gangsters and gangsters who worked as undercover cops, plus all manner of small-time boosters. There were alliances and double-crosses. Everybody had something going. The atmosphere simmered with violence, betrayal, and seething anger, itching for combustion. The sum of this dissonance was unnerving to the ear.

The large club was a bunker on the outside, but its interior was garish and bathed in overbright golden light. Function rooms were scattered throughout, cubicles on the second floor where massages were given, three separate bars, and a kitchen. So much dangerous shit was being done it was hard to believe that a contract hit didn't take place every hour.

I'd been playing Mob clubs for years, for killers, gangsters, and even Mafia bosses; I was accustomed to being in questionable places with questionable people. This was different. The Squire's sole reason for existing was to promote nefarious business. Despite the lights and the noise and the music, the atmosphere was still more menacing and oppressive than anything I'd experienced. Nobody had fun at the Squire.

In most Mob clubs, a vocalist—especially a fellow wiseguy—whose repertoire consisted of Jimmy Roselli, Jerry Vale, Vic Damone, Frank Sinatra, and Tony Bennett with some Louis Prima thrown in would find an enthusiastic crowd. Not at this place. Freddie had some friends show up to hear him, but we were mostly left alone. The Squire wasn't a music club; it was just a club that had music.

After the first set, I knew I had to get out.

"Freddie, this place makes me really nervous," I said. "I don't think I want to work here."

Guarino looked concerned. "What's wrong, Charles?" he asked. "Is there anything I can do? Anything else you need?"

"No, everything's okay. I just don't think they want music here. And the place seems dangerous."

"It's a nice place. Nothing ever happens here. Richard's got people for that."

"Yeah, that's the problem. I'm getting tired of working in places where you need to have people."

"Well, okay. If you don't want to do it, you don't want to do it. Nobody's gonna make you."

"You're sure?"

"Yeah. I mean, sure. If you're not into it, you shouldn't do it. Let's go tell Richard."

I was afraid to tell Castucci. If I were lucky, I wouldn't get paid and I'd have to pay for moving the piano. If not, I'd get roughed up professionally for being an asshole.

Freddie Guarino and I walked into an office off the kitchen. Richard Castucci was sitting behind a desk, doing nothing. He looked up at us from under the brim of his fedora.

"Richard, Charles doesn't think his kind of music is right for the club. He doesn't think it's gonna work out. We figured it was better to let you know before things got started."

"Yeah. Okay."

Castucci gave me a blank stare. I didn't ask to be paid, and he didn't offer. Neither of us mentioned the piano.

A week later, James "Whitey" Bulger's partner Stephen "The Rifleman" Flemmi gunned down Richard Castucci. His body was found in Revere, stuffed into the trunk of his new Cadillac Sedan de Ville, at the time a very popular car with wiseguys.

Castucci's murder hammered home that no one was safe at Mob clubs; not the patrons, not the owners, and not even the piano players. But I kept going back to them because I needed the money, and Mob clubs paid better than jazz clubs.

Why So Many Bad Musicians Worked Mob Clubs

Unless I brought my own players with me, the musicians working Mob club gigs were always terrible. With all of the good musicians to choose from in the Boston area, it seemed odd that nobody doing the hiring ever picked a winner. I finally figured out that there were loads and loads of electricians, plumbers, and handymen who were part-time musicians. Little more than nightclub groupies, they were all thrilled to have the opportunity to play for free in front of real audiences. The problem was that the audience liked these clowns. The amateurs were the crowd's own people, and they radiated a love of what they were doing. Additionally, because they were almost always skilled tradesmen, they would spend hours and hours of their spare time working for free on the lights, the sound, the stage, and anywhere else in the club that needed work. That was the real reason they were allowed to be on stage.

For any good musician, having to work with stiffs is an ordeal. I explained to club owners many times that good musicians made better music than bad ones—a simple and obvious observation. Once in a while I'd be allowed to import good players to back up the acts, but it didn't solve the problem because the bosses never let the lousy musicians go. They would keep the larger group, and the amateur hacks would good-naturedly join in with the pros, delighted to be in such great company. It didn't matter what inappropriate instrument the talentless part-timer played—more was better. Charlie, an elderly Italian paisano who brought his fucking mandolin up to the stage nearly every night, was a terrific pastry chef who'd work in the kitchen before each gig, cheerfully preparing occhi di bue, canestrelli, biscotti, or whatever anyone asked for. He'd then take the bandstand and play for free all night. Charlie was a welcome sight to everyone—except the professionals onstage. He seemed happy to travel anywhere to play. We were stuck with him at both the Grey Finch and Paula's Lounge, more than forty miles apart.

The Lithuania Club: South Boston, Massachusetts

Of all the Mob clubs I played, The Lithuania Club may be the only one that still exists. It bears no resemblance to the place where I gigged over forty years ago, yet seems to have kept the same address.

It's hard to believe it was ever a Mob club, but in its day this small room was, in its mean and miserly way, almost as pernicious as the Squire. While still operating under the Lithuanian rubric, it was run by IRA members, and nearly all its clientele were Irish. Guns for the war in Northern Ireland were cached in the basement.

During the late 1970s, there were nightclubs all over the Boston area—both Italian and Irish Mob controlled—with weapons stashed in their basements. Dealing in weapons was one area where the Italians and Irish did business together. There were IRA guns stashed in Italian Mob clubs in Kenmore Square, as well as in some of the gay and drag show clubs in the Theater District.

Low-level crime ran rampant at the Lithuania Club. Before you made it through the door, someone tried to sell you a fake Rolex. Guys pushed cartons of cigarettes out of the trunks of their cars. Small appliances were a hot item. There was nothing low-level about the gunrunning, though. The Irish Mob and IRA were more hard-core than the Italian wiseguys. The Italian Mobsters were dangerous, and a lot of them were tough, but most didn't seem fearless the way the Irish did. The Boston Irish had direct ties to Belfast, and went back and forth all the time; many of them were in a war that they were personally committed to the death to.

Buddy Ray was the usual headliner at the Lithuania Club. Buddy was a tall, pretzel-shaped sad sack who resembled the legendary poker hustler Amarillo Slim. Without a rigid bone in his body, he melted over the mic, poured himself into a chair when he sat with customers, and collapsed in a heap on a back-room couch during the band's breaks. His default impulse was to try to achieve the next level of recline, whatever it might be.

Buddy Ray seemed like an unlikely performer for a Mob club. Neither Italian nor Irish and not a good vocalist, he was more like a jack-of-all-trades who would vary his material between country and western, oldies rock, pop ballads, standards, and even some big-band swing. His strong suit was understanding the emotional needs of the audience. He wasn't handsome, but the women in the crowd loved him and the men didn't resent that they did.

Despite his adeptness at communicating with his audience, there was something about him that suggested he really wasn't meant for the kind of life he'd wound up in. Maybe that's what his audience was truly responding to. Without knowing quite why, you felt sorry for Buddy Ray. He just seemed out of place—someone who had drifted into the lower depths and couldn't work his way out.

Buddy would say things you wouldn't expect. As I walked to the bandstand one night, he asked if I'd ever read Flannery O'Connor.

"She would've been a good woman if there had been somebody there to shoot her every minute of her life," I slightly misquoted.

"I figured she'd be your type of gal."

He had private routines. Whenever he sang Ray Price's "For the Good Times," Buddy Ray would step out onto the floor and pick a nice-looking woman from the audience as his dance partner, all the while crooning honky-tonk heartbreak into a handheld mic, a lonely and faraway look on his face.

One good thing that happened for me at the Lithuania Club was a chance to make extra money performing a carny trick. The drummer had phoned in sick, having left his drums on the bandstand the previous night. Buddy Ray's music was rudimentary enough that it was child's play to handle piano and drums at the same time, so I offered to fill in for the drummer.

By playing piano with my right hand, I could use my left on the ride cymbal and snare drum simultaneously, strategically placing the stick so it struck both, my feet free to keep time on the bass drum and hi-hat. On rock numbers, I'd switch over to just the drums.

Playing two instruments at once let me get paid as two musicians. Playing two required no more effort than it would have taken to play one—and it was a lot more fun.

The Lithuania Club's audience was not composed of keen observers. At end of every set, Buddy Ray had to make the same pointed announcement: "You've just been listening to Charles Farrell playing piano and drums *at the same time*."

People would *ooh* and *aah* with each announcement, as if they'd forgotten about it every set and needed to be reminded.

"Hon, *look* at that guy. He's playing the drums and the piano at the same time!"

"Yeah, how's he doin' that? I ain't never seen nothing like that before."

Except that he'd seen it an hour earlier.

The Fire Barn: Chelsea, Massachusetts

The Fire Barn was a more or less legitimate restaurant featuring live entertainment. Civilians brought their families there. The Mob presence was very quiet: the back room was a gambling site and a storehouse for stolen goods, but what went on in the back stayed in the back. The manager was a 250-pound bruiser named Big John McManus—an Irishman who worked for the Italians—humorless and wound a little too tight. He was a professional who would never do anything stupid, but he was capable of badly hurting people if things wound up going there. Big John McManus wasn't my kind of guy, and I wasn't his. There was no reason why anything should come of our mutual dislike. And nothing ever did.

The Fire Barn began as just another Mob club gig. It was steady, it paid well, and the nights passed without drama—entirely boring, entirely livable, and acceptably depressing. My trio backed Ric Ricardo and whichever other entertainers were brought in.

One of the sorriest of these was Guy Anthony. If Jerry Valli was the King of the local X-rated hypnotists, Anthony was the cut-rate Court Jester. He was a goateed little softie who got work when Valli was unavailable or the club wouldn't shell out his asking price.

Guy Anthony was a tyrannical bully who ran headfirst into resistance every time he tried to assert any authority. Nobody was intimidated by him. He commanded no fear, respect, or loyalty. He was just a pint-sized clown who never learned, despite his frequent dressing-downs.

"Didn't I tell you to bring me a Seven & Seven?"

"The fuck you just say to me?"

"I meant, I thought I ordered a drink."

"You watch the way you talk to me. I don't work for you."

"No . . . I know. I didn't mean anything. I was just asking if my drink was ready."

"Don't get fresh. You'll get it when I have time."

"Fine. That will be fine, thanks."

"Asshole."

After exchanges like this, Guy would stew in his humiliation, growing increasingly resentful and bitter. It didn't make for having good stage presence.

Unfortunately for him, Guy was booked at the Fire Barn on the exact weekend I discovered that there was gambling in the back room and wound up in a poker game with John McManus, Ric Ricardo, and three or four others. Within minutes, the stakes had risen to the point where we had a moderately big game going.

The band got a twenty-minute break between sets, but the poker game had kept me in the back for an hour. I was up around a thousand dollars, so I gave no thought to returning to the bandstand. John McManus was winning too, so it wasn't bothering him that I wasn't playing piano. The crowd was getting restless, but who cared? Nobody was going anywhere.

Guy Anthony's voice came to us from the PA system onstage.

"I'd like the band to return to the stage please. All band members to the stage."

John and I split a pot. We were in the middle of the next hand when Guy's voice again reached the back room.

"All band members come up onstage now. Musicians to the stage."

I left the table and stepped to the back of the club. I made my voice heard across the room.

"I'll be there in a little while."

"Will John McManus please come to the stage? John McManus to the stage please."

I went back to the game. Guy Anthony's voice droned on, becoming a harangue. It was starting to get annoying.

"I'd like John McManus to come to the stage immediately. Band to the stage immediately."

John got up from the table. For a man of his bulk, he moved very quickly, covering half the length of the restaurant in a few steps.

"Guy, put down the goddamn microphone, get off the stage, and have a drink. We'll send for you when it's time to go back on."

Eventually I took a break from the game to go back to work. Guy was upset, and it threw off his stage act. Because the audience had seen him being embarrassed by John McManus, they felt entitled to take shots at him too. They got their chance.

There's a test that hypnotists use to help them choose onstage subjects. Guy started the test by repeating, "You're becoming stiff as a board. Stiff as a board. Stiff as a board."

From behind his drums, Tony Cerra could be heard saying, "I'm bored stiff. I'm bored stiff. I'm bored stiff."

People started snickering.

A couple of minutes later, Guy had a few audience members hypnotized. He announced that his subjects were going to imitate celebrities. He made the mistake of introducing them as "famous impressionists."

Tony Cerra said, "Monet. Renoir. Cezanne."

The crowd might not have known who the fuck Tony was talking about, but they realized that he was making fun of Guy Anthony, so the line got big laughs.

Things degenerated into chaos. One woman was slow in snapping out of her hypnotic state. That occasionally happened to subjects. It wasn't cause for alarm, but to people who'd never seen it before, it was horrifying. They thought she might never come around, fated to live out her life in some voodoo netherworld.

"Jesus, she's in a trance."

"I know. Like a zombie. Somebody should call an ambulance."

"Could she maybe lapse into a coma?"

"I think so."

"She's gonna be a vegetable for the rest of her life."

"She could die."

"I know. Oh God, this is just tragic"

The woman regained consciousness a few moments later, but the mishap killed any chance Guy had to win over the audience that night. Somehow, it seemed better that way. He was a guy people were happier with when he fucked up.

I went back to my poker game. I thought I had hit the jackpot at the Fire Barn. Within fifteen minutes, I'd raked in more money than I would have playing piano all week. There was some lagniappe, too: The poker players ranged from poor to abysmal, and not one was even adequate. At first, it seemed like free money. The problem was that, for a non–tough guy like me with no official underworld affiliations, the raised stakes moved the game from cash to credit. Once I couldn't pick my winnings up directly off the table, all I could actually do was lose, irrespective of how much I collected in IOUs. The wiseguys decided that if I lost, I lost. But if I won, *they* won, since they weren't going to pay me. I was up nearly ten thousand dollars before I figured out this simple dictum, at which point I stopped playing poker with Mob guys.

The English Social Room: Lawrence, Massachusetts

Though I was afraid of wiseguys and disliked their clubs, I became relatively anesthetized to the ever-present hostility, the penny-pinching, the long hours in smoke-filled rooms, and the pointless music. I even took vague comfort that when people had died in these joints, they didn't die too near me. Until my final underworld gig.

The last Mob club I played, on the New Hampshire border in a city dubbed "Law Town" by its founding fathers—undoubtedly ironically—was the English Social Room. In fact, irony ran amok here, starting with the club's genteel name.

The English Social Room was a wide-open, anything-goes rattrap where the police were paid off and all the strippers doubled as hookers. This shithole attracted losers who became unhinged by watching the strippers. Many of those losers were dangerous psychos who felt that violence was the only appropriate response to arousal.

The bandstand was a cramped space shoved into a corner of the massive club, as if an afterthought. Searchlight-bright, every tawdry detail of the place was on constant display, including most of whatever people were doing to each other.

The Boston underground legend, tenor saxophonist Lester Parker brought me onto the gig. The pay wasn't bad and Lester promised an easy job: back up the strippers, accompany a couple of vocalists—one of whom was Buster, the club manager—and play one dance set. This last assignment was an odd nicety harkening back to the dime-a-dance era or ahead to the private dances of contemporary strip clubs. While we played polite foxtrots, customers moved to the dance floor with the strippers who'd paw their crotches to coerce them into spending money on quickie sex in the dressing room or in the bathrooms.

Rule-free, violence-prone clubs need someone steady at the helm to direct tough but low-key muscle on how to handle the crowd. Buster was not that guy. He pushed everyone too hard, was disagreeable and argumentative, had a loud and corrosive voice, and enthusiastically jumped the gun when calling for his bouncers.

Like many Mob club bosses, Buster thought of himself as a great entertainer whose talent would be appreciated by the clientele: guys who, until they heard him sing, had been under the mistaken impression that they'd come to the English Social Room looking for pussy.

You had to stay on top of Buster when accompanying him. His terrible voice wasn't the biggest problem—most vocalists have fairly terrible voices. His time was the deal-killer. Bar lines varied from three to seven beats, lasting however long it took Buster to sing them. When lines were easy, he dispensed with them early, before his four beats were up. When the lyrics were a struggle, the bar line could stretch on and on.

Anyone could do almost anything they wanted in the club. The strippers, although falling just short of doing live sex shows onstage, had lots of leeway in their performances. Sheri Champagne—far older than the other strippers—had been a headliner during the Golden Era of Burlesque. Statuesque and was still attractive in her early fifties, she served as ad hoc comic MC. Uneducated but streetwise, uninhibited in both word and deed, she also knew whose toes not to step on. Sheri had spent a lifetime pretending to be a lot dumber than she actually was.

Her gimmick was to get me to stop playing during her act. She'd work it into her routine, being deliberately provocative to lure me from the piano. The audience loved it.

"Oh, I know what'll get you," she'd say. "Wait 'til they bring me up next time, baby. I've got something that will take your hands off the keys."

During her next time up, Sheri pulled out all the stops, pushing my face into her tits, pulling off her pasties, and grabbing first one and then the other of my hands and putting them on her ass and between her legs. None of this stopped me from playing the piano.

"Are you a fuckin' robot, Charles? I swear to God, I'm gonna start suckin' your cock in a minute if this don't work."

"I don't play piano with my cock, Sheri."

So, Sheri Champagne never bothered to suck my cock, either onstage or off.

Unified in their misogyny, the crowd targeted strippers they took a disliking to. They were like sharks smelling blood in the water, homing in on and abusing the inexperienced and insecure, deliriously shouting the most vicious epithets they could think of. Their hostility bordered on the physical, and if the bouncers hadn't been so evidently dangerous, violence might have erupted.

One night, a very young, nondescript newcomer came onstage. She was skinny and small-boned, which only accentuated the voluminous size of her breasts. In the pre-enhancement era, her unusual construction was startling to the crowd.

Unlike most of the strippers at the English Social Room, the girl didn't quickly dispense with her bra and pasties. Her T-shirt remained on as she pushed her enormous tits outward, driving the men in the audience nearly apoplectic. Meanwhile she systematically and mirthlessly removed the remaining pieces of her costume as we played dutifully behind her, trying without luck to discern any rhythmic movement.

When her T-shirt was the last remaining encumbrance—everyone straining toward her for the big payoff—she took a pin hidden near the edge of the stage and popped one and then the other balloon.

It was the wrong punch line for patrons of the English Social Room. Rather than seeing themselves as the butts of a harmless if not overly funny joke, they felt they'd been cheated and made fools of. They were used to this happening in their day-to-day lives, but *here*, where they were paying good money, they were entitled to see tits. And goddamn it, they were going to see tits. Big ones.

"Get off the stage, you fuckin' flat-chested bitch."

"Grow a pair of tits!"

"Fuck you. Fuck you. Fuck *you*!"

As the bouncers escorted her to the dressing room, the poor girl started to cry. Then she began shaking, completely unprepared for and traumatized by the crowd's vicious response.

"It was a *joke*," she said. "It's just a joke. It was supposed to be funny."

"That's okay, honey," said one of the bouncers. "Don't pay no attention. They don't got no senses of humor. They're animals."

Had the girl been a little more experienced, she would have understood that the English Social Room wasn't the right place to play cute pranks.

The men's room at the English Social Room was used by the strippers as a place for sexual transactions. Because of my lousy circulation, I had to warm my hands up under hot water before each set. I'd grown used to seeing strippers bent over some anonymous club patron in the furthest stall, its door as likely as not to remain open during the encounter.

On my last night, as I stepped into the men's room, a bouncer rushed over and blocked the door to prevent anyone else from entering. One of the tile walls had multiple splashes of fresh blood dripping down it. A man was lying on the floor, part of his head shot away, clearly dead. Buster and two bouncers huddled over him as Buster frantically gave instructions.

"I put in the call, but we gotta' do it fast."

"Where's he goin'?" asked one.

"Walk him past the fence. It's just gotta be off the property. Like a step or two. But definitely off the property."

"Like by the tree?" the other asked.

"Yeah. By the tree's good. I'll let them know that's where he's gonna be."

The bouncers hustled the body out a side door, handling it like they would a passed-out drunk.

Buster turned to me. "Charles, get up on the fuckin' stage. You're getting paid to play music here."

I Refuse a Request from the Crab King

"Ay, Ay, Ay, Ay!" "Ay, Ay, Ay, Ay!"

The wail came from deep within the recesses of an upholstered booth to the right of and slightly behind the piano. Settled between two good-looking, no-longer-young women, his arms draped over their shoulders, one hand rhythmically waving a cigar like a conductor's baton, the short, stocky man was grinning loopily, like a baby. He was extravagantly drunk.

"C'mon," he slurred. "Ya know it. I know ya know it. Do "Ay, Ay, Ay, Ay." He began to sing. "Everybody wanna hear "Ay, Ay, Ay, Ay. Do the Ay, Ay, Ay."

Wrapping up the final long set at Franny the Killer's upscale Italian restaurant in Boston's North End, it had been a tougher than usual night in a place that was generally fairly stress-free. A small group of buzzed couples, personal friends of Franny's, got onto a kick where they wanted a "classical" piano recital, which required a half hour of me banging out schmaltzy melodies while flinging my hands around theatrically and throwing in arpeggios that would have made Liberace blush. I'd been a one-man version of the Boston Pops playing the "1812 Overture." Now I was tired. I wanted to go home.

"I'm sorry," I told the tipsy toddler, "but I don't know the tune."

"Yeah, ya do. Ev'body know tune. Goes "Ay, Ay, Ay, Ay!"

My friend David Reich, sitting in on flute that night, told me the guy was singing the chorus to "Cielito Lindo." I knew "Cielito Lindo." I actually liked "Cielito Lindo." But I also knew that one request would lead to another, and then another, and we'd be stuck playing bullshit tunes at Franny's until daybreak.

Ric Ricardo pulled me off to the side. "Charles, do you know who that man *is*? That's the *Crab King*! He supplies all of the restaurants around here with their crabs. He controls the waterfront! Are you *turning down* the Crab King?"

"Yeah, I'm turning down the Crab King."

"Oh, Jesus."

Franny hurried over to confer with us.

"What's goin' on, fellas?"

"Charles turned down the Crab King. He don't wanna honor the Crab King's earnest request."

The Crab King was starting to wave around a wad of bills.

"C'mon, he said, "I got hunned dollars for you guys do "Ay, Ay, Ay, Ay." He was dancing around now, wagging his ass in imitation of Carmen Miranda. His lady friends were laughing, goading him on.

Ric was in a panic. "Charles, that's the *Crab King*! You don't turn down a man like the Crab King. He's gonna pay you guys and everything."

Franny said, "Sir Charles, you got a lot of fuckin' balls—I'll give you that. You sure you don't want to do it? He'll put a C-note in your pocket."

"You think I should do it?"

"Honestly? Nah. If you don't want to do it, don't do it. I'd like to get home sometime tonight. Besides, it makes a good story that Sir Charles turned down the Crab King. I'm gonna be a little worried about my next delivery of crabs, though."

Lulu White's: The South End, Boston, Massachusetts

By the time I stopped playing in public at twenty-seven, I was nearly a decade into not being able to stand doing gigs. Lulu White's was where I stopped playing in front of people—my last regular gig.

If you were a jazz musician and didn't enjoy gigging at Lulu White's, you were in the wrong profession. I was in the wrong profession. Lulu White's had a responsive and untemperamental Yamaha Grand, excellent room acoustics, a well-placed stage, and pleasant and commodious seating. It was a listening room, and audiences were generally attentive and appreciative.

I was not generous toward other players. Because I thought of music solely as a way to make a living, I was predatory, especially when it came to pianists. I would make it a point to show them up. This led to my humiliating Jim McNeely, Stan Getz's pianist, one Sunday afternoon.

It's hard to explain my anger. I'd never met McNeely, and it's not that he was a bad pianist. He was completely okay, but it was *the way* he was completely okay that infuriated me. He was cautiously mediocre.

I said to someone seated near me, "Look at that soft parochial school-boy motherfucker." I had just finished playing a strong set, and McNeely had made his light-footed journey over to the bandstand to get a look at the piano. Then he tentatively sat at the keyboard and politely started to play. It made me furious. He played a couple of tunes, and I was waiting for him when he had finished.

"Did you hear me playing?"

"Yes, you sounded really good."

"Yet you dared to get up there after you've heard me play?"

"I'm sorry. We're playing later tonight, and I just wanted to get a feel for the piano."

"You don't hear the difference between you and me?"

"Yes, I hear the difference."

"But you still get up there and play that weak shit. Get the fuck out of my room."

It was true that I didn't like jazz musicians much. That still doesn't explain the degree of anger I felt. Some of it had to do with jazz culture; I had no patience with the endless "that was a good hang" or "those were some really hip licks" apprenticeship shoptalk. Something in me revolted when introduced to musicians whose loftiest ambition was to work for *someone else*. That tended to be the artistic ceiling that jazz musicians diligently strove to achieve. Jimmy McNeely was *Stan Getz's* piano player. That was the end of the road. I'm sure he felt that he'd made it.

A minute or so after my outburst, Jo Jones came into the club. Papa Jo lived upstairs and I saw him every Sunday afternoon when he'd stop by to listen to me.

"*Mister* Tatum!" He put out his enormous manicured hand and flashed his thousand-kilowatt smile—big white braggart's teeth gleaming. He had the posture of a swordsman. Bald, five foot three, and well into his sixties, Jo Jones was still the handsomest man in any room he entered. He knew it, too.

"You just missed Stan Getz's piano player trying to play where I'd just played."

"Oh, really? That didn't work out well?"

"No. The guy's got no balls."

"You've got to have balls when you play. Everybody knows that."

"Exactly. When are you going to play with us, Jo? That's the only reason I come to this place."

"One of these days, Mr. Tatum. One of these days. I don't enjoy sitting behind another man's drums."

Jo would tell me about being the drummer on Art Tatum's last recording. Billie Holiday's last recording. I'd kid him about being afraid to record with him.

Although Lulu White's almost always booked mainstream jazz acts as their headliners, the Art Ensemble of Chicago made its way there one week.

I was sitting with Joseph Jarman, Malachi Favors, and Don Moye during one of my breaks. They were waiting for Lester Bowie to arrive. Moye said to me, "Your boy over there says that you're The Man in these parts." He indicated the writer Bob Blumenthal.

"If that's what he says."

"You can play over chords and all that kinda shit."

"Sure."

"So, if I was to ask you to play "Cherokee" in some crazy key like B-natural or F-sharp, you could do it."

"Of course I could do it!"

"You could play it fast?"

"Any tempo you want."

"You wanna bet about who can play "Cherokee" faster—you or Jarman over here? I pick the key."

Favors and Jarman had started laughing.

"I'll take the bet."

"For how much?"

"Any amount you've got. Five hundred dollars? A thousand dollars? Whatever Chester is paying you for the week here? I'll cover any bet you want to make. You really think your guy is going to be able to play "Cherokee" faster than me?"

An expression of exaggerated alarm crossed Moye's face. "Shit, man. Who said anything about Jarman? I ain't bettin' on Jarman. I'm bettin' on *you*! Joseph can't play over no changes."

Dorothy Donegan, whose playing I hadn't been familiar with, was a frequent headliner. Her piano playing was a flashy hybrid of Fats Waller, Earl Hines, and Meade Lux Lewis. She could sing. She could tell jokes. Dorothy was one of the last of the really great black cabaret performers, and I got a kick out of her. Ordinarily I made it a point to embarrass other pianists, but Dorothy Donegan managed to get on my good side. She would stand at my left shoulder, watching my hands on the keys, making encouraging sounds when I played something she liked.

"I'm stealing your shit, you know."

"I can see that."

"Can you show me how to do those double octave things with both hands?"

"Just watch. I'll slow them down."

"Yeah, yeah. I get it. I'm gonna use that when I come up. I'm serious, man. I'm takin' your shit."

"If you can play it, it's all yours."

Ahmad Jamal came in for two weeks. He'd had nearly unprecedented success for a jazz musician during the 1950s when his rendition of "Poinciana" made it into the pop charts. His trios had defined what urbane nightclub jazz was supposed to sound like, and his audience, largely made up of the black bourgeoisie, had stayed with him throughout the years.

Over time Jamal's playing changed, using a lot of elision and becoming much more allusive, making abstract reference to the Great American Songbook without touching down directly on it. He had grown artistically from the charming and accessible musician he'd been during the period of his greatest popularity.

I loved what he'd come to play over the years, but the audience at Lulu White's didn't. They wanted "Poinciana." They wanted "Surrey with the Fringe on Top" and "Gal in Calico." The theme from "Mash."

Willard Chandler—known only as Chandler—was the manager at Lulu White's. He'd run an ill-fated Mob-owned club before taking over at Lulu's. Earlier, Chandler had been the head of the Pullman Porters' union. There was still a lot of railroad man in Chandler. He was a powerful, imperious, and charming guy who knew how to run things and make them work efficiently. He did most of the booking for Lulu White's, handled its day-to-day operation, and was used to getting his way.

Chandler was almost unflappable, but the situation with Ahmad Jamal was starting to get to him. He was becoming slightly unhinged by the negative comments he was hearing, by the walk-outs, requests for refunds, and by the lack of communication between the pianist and his audience.

"Charles, I don't know what to do. They want the Ahmad Jamal who they know, and this dude doesn't sound like that Ahmad Jamal."

"He does. But he's much better now. It's all in there, Chandler. This is the best he's ever played."

"You can say that as a fellow musician, but the people who are paying to hear him aren't happy with the music. Let me ask you something. Can you play like Ahmad Jamal? You know, sound like him?"

"You mean the old Ahmad Jamal."

"Yes, the old one. The one who people actually want to pay money to hear."

"Yes, I can play like that Ahmad Jamal."

"Do me a big favor, and play like *that* Ahmad Jamal during the two weeks that *this* Ahmad Jamal is booked at the club?"

"I don't suppose I'm going to make *that* Ahmad Jamal–level money."

"I *did* say it was a big favor."

"No, it's fine. I'll sound just like the old Ahmad Jamal throughout his engagement."

"Nobody who comes to the club as your guest will ever spend a dime here from now on."

For the next two weeks, the patrons at Lulu White's were treated to the music of the classic Ahmad Jamal Trio, just not Ahmad Jamal. Later in the evening, Ahmad Jamal would come on to play his sets to an indifferent clientele, many audience members leaving before he'd finished his first tune.

When I finally quit Lulu White's, it was the last regular jazz job I had until almost twenty years later, when circumstances caused me to take a late-afternoon lounge gig at the downtown Holiday Inn in Tampa.

The maybe-owner, maybe-not of Lulu White's was a rich, preening little motherfucker named Chester English III. We couldn't stand each other.

I walked out just before a Sunday brunch gig, leaving a roomful of customers. The final straw was money, and not very much of it. Chester English III owed my band and me for a gig we'd done a week or so earlier—a special concert event backing up the famed tap dancer Sandman Sims, on tour to promote a documentary film that had just come out. I had gone to the penthouse above Lulu White's where English kept an apartment. He was there with the club's publicist.

"We're done here. You better find a band, because you've got a packed house down there. And you need to pay me for the Sandman Sims concerts."

"Can you just fill in for today? I can't get anybody in on such short notice."

"No. Give me my money so I can get out of here."

"If you're not playing, you're not getting your money."

"Then I'm going to throw you out the window."

"Ha-ha. Very funny. Look, I don't have the money to pay you right now. Come back during the week."

I moved toward him.

"You don't understand. I'm really going to throw you out the window. I don't like you, and I'll enjoy doing it."

English held up a hand.

"Okay. How much is it?"

"It's $600."

"I have to go into the other room to get it."

"Then go into the other room."

English left the room, came back with some bills, and handed them to me. I didn't bother to count them. I knew he wasn't going to stiff me. He knew I would have thrown him out the window. I'd learned a few things since Plato's Plum.

So, my final professional act in music was to threaten to throw a rich boy with the preposterous name Chester English III through the penthouse window of Lulu White's if he didn't pay me what he owed. He paid up, no defenestration took place and—except for few brief swerves back in—I left the music business for good.

1980s

An Alternate Use for Gardening Equipment

An enormously fat man showed up at my house one afternoon looking for an associate of mine. I reminded the enormously fat man that in the business I was in I couldn't have people dropping by my house unannounced. The enormously fat man wasn't happy about any of this, but he left without causing a problem.

He showed up again about a week later, once more in the middle of the afternoon. I had been on my front porch waiting for someone when the enormously fat man walked up. Business was taking place upstairs at the time. I told him to have a seat on the outdoor lounger, which led him to believe I'd be bringing out the man he was looking for, although the guy wasn't actually around.

I rushed through my first-floor apartment down to the basement, found a three-clawed gardening tool left by the previous owner—years later Brian Moore told me the tool was a "cultivator"—and ran back to the porch.

I placed the cultivator just under the enormously fat man's eyes and pulled the skin downward.

"If you move a muscle, I will tear both your eyes out," I said. "I asked you not to just show up here, but you wouldn't listen. Now you will. Where's your wallet?"

"In my back pocket." He barely moved his lips.

"I don't know how you'll do it, but get it without making me think you're going to be stupid."

He managed to lift his fat ass off the couch enough to get his wallet. As he did, I made sure to apply a little more pressure near his eyes.

This was all happening in broad daylight on a busy street. But I couldn't allow anyone to show up at the house when business was taking place upstairs.

I took his wallet from him and found his driver's license. He was Wayne Hubler.

"You're going to need a new driver's license and a new wallet. I'm keeping these. Now get out of here. If you ever come back, I'll kill you."

Wayne Hubler left. It was the last I saw of him. I was worried that someone more capable might be sent in his place, but it didn't happen.

When I finally figured it out a couple of decades later that my vigilance and ability to react instantly and without conscious thought came from fear, it took me more than two years to stop shaking. And my breathing still isn't entirely right.

Las Vegas: Learning to Value the Things Around the Thing

When I was first on my own, I'd step onto the sidewalk of a new town and think, "This is where I am, so this is who I am here."

Circumstances and situations varied depending to a great degree on my financial status. Over the years, I've awakened temporarily homeless on park benches in South Florida, weightless, empty, and free on beaches in La Romana and Rincon, momentarily in the chips in hotels in Paris and London, and even foolishly optimistic in houses that I was briefly lucky enough to own in a couple of different countries.

This practice of waking up brand new somewhere other than my home reached its spiritual apotheosis in Las Vegas in the 1980s.

Las Vegas offered unique possibilities for constant reinvention; gambling could make a day-to-day difference where and with whom you'd be waking up and what you'd be waking up to.

Despite its lights and crowds and larger-than-life bombast, Las Vegas was a loner's town. As soon as you moved off the Strip you were in a small, dusty place in the American West—a loser's habitat of efficiency apartments, weekly rentals, trailer parks, hookers, hustlers, pawnshops, and sob stories.

In that tilted world, it was easy to be a king. Las Vegas was about waking up at 11:00—whether a.m. or p.m. didn't matter. Grabbing a cup of sludgy coffee and heading to the bus-terminal-at-dawn drabness of Caesar's Sports Book. Checking the morning lines for Pimlico, Santa Anita, or Belmont, putting something down on a couple of fight tips. Drifting over to the weary and slowly dying Dunes to pick up walking-around cash from the beatable Tens-or-Better video poker machine.

Going to the fights presented a unique social experience if you were attending a card where those ringside consisted of real boxing people. A specific insider language let everyone leapfrog over the usual introductory niceties. You could form temporary deep friendships.

I started to understand how attending a boxing card could move me beyond the solitary viewing exercise that was a function of my business. Going to the fights could be part of one's cultural identification, extending past seeing what took place in the ring and radiating outward to help define how you inhabited space in the world at large, and even where that space might be.

You could run into someone who knew as much or more about boxing than you did, and your conversation might resume the next day at Johnny Tocco's gym, helping cement the first steps toward not just a lifetime friendship but a mutually beneficial business relationship. This new friendship might then lead to phone calls from half a world away six months, a year, ten, and even twenty years later—calls clueing you in on a valuable scouting tip picked up by someone's trained eye while watching a sparring session.

Said another way, if who you were was determined in part by the company you kept and the nature of the time spent in that company, you'd be free to creatively enter the flow of wherever that company and those experiences could take you.

"I live here now" is a Zen sentence. Each word is essential. "I live here now" can be seen as an individual's gateway to collective experience—where individuation gives way to common cause in space and time (the "here" and "now").

A fight, in this instance, is no longer a fight at all. Or, although it's a fight, the punches-thrown-and-landed part of it might not be as important as what it means as a cultural and economic signpost. And economic implications are always cultural implications.

Boxing energy radiates outward from a very tiny nucleus. I once sat in a cramped office off to the side of an antique shop in Manhattan, talking with two men about an unknown fighter with an impressive but entirely built-up record. We drank coffee, discussed the feasibility of putting the unknown fighter into the biggest fight in boxing history, and then loosely worked out issues of money.

That was the whole deal: three individuals who were friends through the boxing business—one with close connections to its power structure, the other two no more than small-time outsiders—spending a few hours on a sunny afternoon in midtown pitching good ideas back and forth about how to lock into a small piece of Mike Tyson's comeback money.

"Are We Gonna Get Out of Here Alive?"

I owed the Superstar a favor. A big one. And, unfortunately, the Superstar intended to collect.

The Superstar was an intrusive life-of-the-party—a full-time plumber by trade, an occasional part-time home contractor, and a weekend DJ and one-man-band wedding and birthday entertainer who still held out dreams of making it in show business.

The Superstar was incapable of introspection, happy only when he was the center of an audience's attention, which he would go to any lengths to get. He wasn't an unkind or vindictive man, but he was a boor—a loud vulgarian who assumed that his pleasures must be everyone else's.

On his weekend gigs, he'd show up early with a truckload of equipment: a Kurzweil keyboard, an unsubtle drum machine with pre-programmed simulacra of assorted rhythms that included showy snare and tom-tom fills, two mics, a long cord and a stand, cocktail drums, all manner of percussion equipment, a passel of gag items, prop clothes—men's and women's—makeup, and a variety of wigs and funny hats. The Superstar wanted to be sure he'd covered all the bases. He sang, he played, he did impressions, he lip-synched, he told jokes, and he did cheap gimmicky tricks. He'd dance his way into the crowd, gripped mic ready to be thrust into revelers' faces for some good-natured badinage or an impromptu vocal duet. Most of the Superstar's material was upbeat pop garbage and oldies, all delivered at earsplitting volume. The rest consisted of overly sentimental tearjerkers, also delivered at earsplitting volume, but with added reverb.

The Superstar would do anything to get me to play piano on his gigs. He knew it would make him sound much better than when he accompanied himself with his basic keyboard chords—often wrong ones—and botched arpeggios. He didn't care about money; he'd take nothing for himself and throw in additional money if need be. The problem was that I wasn't taking gigs anymore, so we were stuck negotiating for appropriate barter.

Mostly we traded my playing piano for his doing plumbing and carpentry work at my houses, always smallish stuff. Then one day the Superstar hit the mother lode.

I'd decided to have my house rehabbed. I had about $100,000 to spend—this was around 1980—but no idea of how to establish the legitimacy of the contractor, no instincts about what questions to ask or what things were supposed to cost. I couldn't even tell the difference between good and bad work. I also hated everything about dealing with tradespeople. Because I knew nothing about what they were doing and could be easily victimized, I'd find myself growing obsequious around them, asking wide-eyed questions, feigning interest.

I might have used the Superstar for the job from the start, but couldn't bear the thought of having him around the house for months at a time, smoking Marlboros and tiny cigars, barking orders, bringing in take-out food that would be left lying around in soggy napkins, listening to loud music on a boom box, filling the place with his cackling laugh, scattering half-empty coffee containers and cigarette butts everywhere.

I remembered how, during one of the times he had done some repairs, I had asked him if he could not smoke in the house.

"It's not your house. It's a work site. The workmen make the rules."

I hired Jim Johnson because he was the third of three contractors I'd interviewed, and I was sick of doing the auditions. He was also much cheaper than the other two and could start immediately. It turned out that there were reasons for both those things.

Johnson was a taciturn former woodchopper from Moncton, New Brunswick. He looked like the big outdoorsman that he was; he also looked like someone to be wary of.

By a strange coincidence, I owned fifty acres of woodland in Moncton, but had never been there. If I had, I would have known not to use anyone from Moncton to do anything other than chop wood, and I would have stood well away from him when he did.

Johnson showed up with his younger brother—a bigger, jollier, and more psychotic convict version of himself. The brother was also a song-writer. To prove it, he brought his guitar along every day. Each morning he'd ask me if I could tune it for him.

From the start, everything with the restoration went wrong. Even to my untutored eye it was evident that the Johnsons' work was substandard, sometimes comically so. They seemed to be trying to turn my home into a primitive treehouse, a standard tool shed, or a home in Moncton. The Johnson brothers weren't even qualified handymen.

Worse, they grew truculent when I expressed dissatisfaction with the quality of their work or was unhappy with their daily early quitting time.

The Superstar showed up one day and instantly saw to the heart of the situation. He spotted a charlatan and a crook in Johnson, and over the next few days built his case against him, beginning amicably but working his way toward ridicule and finishing up at outright hostility.

He then began quizzing Johnson about the work itself, plying him with technical inquiries he couldn't answer.

"Why would you use two by fours to build a porch railing, buddy? It's a million-dollar house. You're making it look like a chicken coop."

"I'm trying to keep Charles's costs down."

"Did you look into installing high-end precut porch railings? You can buy them at Home Depot. Let's take a look at what those would cost."

"Well, I didn't think to do that."

"I thought you wanted to keep Charles's costs down. It's not just the railings. Let's look at the back porch you put in. I'm gonna show you how you could have saved him money if you'd done this the way anyone who knew their ass from their elbow would have."

The next day, the Superstar started singing verses to a song he was writing, adding lyrics as he went along. "Moncton Man" was a jaunty, heraldic piece of music.

"He's a Moncton Man," the Superstar would begin. "He can't read a slide rule. He can't follow a plan. He's a Moncton Man."

And, "He's a Moncton Man. Can he learn to pull a plow? Not even if you show him how. He's a Moncton Man."

Or, "He's a Moncton Man. Whatever he builds will come out wrong. And so I wrote this little song. He's a Moncton Man."

The next day, Johnson's brother told me, "Jim don't like the stuff that guy Steve is sayin' about him. And he don't like the wiseass songs. You should tell him he better stop that."

I knew it was time to cut Johnson loose, but I was worried about how to do it. He'd been paid a lot of money up front for work that hadn't been done right or hadn't even been started yet. And I was concerned about retaliation.

When I told this to the Superstar, he said, "Come with me. We're gonna take a little ride. If I'm right about what I think the Moncton Man did, you'll get your money back. And he'll leave with no problem."

The Superstar had seen all of the packaging from the kitchen cabinets that Johnson had installed. His instinct told him that Johnson had worked a deal with someone at the factory warehouse, that the items were all stolen, and that I'd been charged full price for them.

We took a longish drive down Route 24 to Avon, the Superstar telling me the entire way, "You'll see. They won't have any invoice for those cabinets."

"But the cabinets arrived on a Star Kitchen Cabinet truck. They pulled right into the driveway."

That made the Superstar burst into his loud cackle. "We *got* 'em! He's in cahoots with someone at the factory."

When we got to the Star Kitchen Cabinet factory warehouse, the Superstar marched straight in and demanded to see the manager. He asked for the invoices for my cabinets. As expected, there were none.

"Do you know a character named Jim Johnson?"

"Sure. I know Jim. He's Mike LeBlanc's brother-in-law. They're from Moncton."

The Superstar turned on his heels. "Let's go," he told me.

When we got back to the house, he thrust himself directly under Johnson's chin.

"We're gonna have a little powwow, Chief."

"*Whaaat?*" He had no idea what the Superstar was talking about.

"Sit down. I've got a few things to say."

Once Johnson was seated, the Superstar began.

"Here's what you did. You and your Moncton brother-in-law, this Frenchy LeBlanc guy, swiped the whole kitchen's worth of cabinets. They're probably scratch-and-dent too. You got Charles to pay full price for them, and you split the money."

"No, no. We used Charles's money to buy the cabinets. We didn't steal nothing. I'm no thief."

"Let me see the invoices."

"I don't have them with me. But I can get 'em."

"You sure about that, Chief? Because the warehouse has no records of them. We just came back from Avon. We can call the manager now if you want."

Johnson said nothing.

"I'll bet you want to punch me in the face right now. Do you want to punch me in the face?"

He pushed his face near Johnson, daring him.

"You'd love to punch me in the face. But you're not going to. You're not going to do a fuckin' thing."

"I'm not going to punch you in the face."

"You're damn right you're not. You're gonna pack up your shit and get outta here. You got twenty minutes. You ain't gettin' another dime from this man. You're paying him back his money. And there better not be any trouble from you. No busted windows, no flat tires. None of that shit. You're outta the contracting business, pal. I'm going to check to see if you're advertising in the area. Take your business back to Moncton."

"I'm no thief. But if Charles isn't happy with the work, we'll go. We don't want no trouble."

"If I wasn't right, you'd punch me right in the face. But you're not going to do a fuckin' thing. I'm watching the clock. Twenty minutes, then I'm calling the cops."

The Johnson brothers were gone in fifteen. They even left some of their tools. That was no great loss. They'd never learned how to use them anyway.

The Superstar was willing to work on the house, but he wanted me to hire another builder to do most of the heavy stuff. He'd oversee the hiring and he'd supervise the work. Now I owed the Superstar whatever he wanted. I would have been happy to pay him his going rate, but knew that that wasn't going to be enough.

He wanted four things. All of them were bad.

"If I do the house, you're gonna have to give me carte blanche. I choose what to put in. I'm gonna try to save you money."

"Blanche" had come out sounding like the woman's name, but I got the message.

"Fine. You're saving my life here. Whatever you want."

"Two. You've gotta give me a week in Vegas. I want to hit the shows. And I want to do Karaoke at all the lounges. I read where at the Dunes you can get a videotape of your performance. I can tell people that I played Vegas."

"Sounds like fun. Done."

"And if there's a piano there, you gotta play for me."

The Dunes was my de facto home away from home in Vegas. It was the casino I liked best, and where I had found a poker game I could quietly beat consistently. It was an out-of-style little place where I could be left alone. It was going to make me sad to have to think about it as the place where the Superstar made Karaoke videos.

I put on my game face. "Keep your fingers crossed about the piano."

"Three. We gotta go to The Golden Palomino. It's supposed to be the classiest strip club in Vegas. I don't want to go to a shithole. This place features fifty hot chicks."

"I played in a lot of strip clubs. I'm not big on them, but we can go. Absolutely."

"And finally. And I want to go to a whorehouse. It's the one state where they're legal."

"Not in Vegas. But it's easy to find beautiful hookers on The Strip."

"I don't want a hooker on the strip. I want you to take me to a real whorehouse."

"Please trust me on this; you're going to hate it. They're the most depressing places in the world."

I knew there'd be no talking him out of it. There'd be no talking him out of any of his wishes. I was going to have to do things I couldn't stand, all the while faking enthusiasm. It would be like taking an overactive child to the carnival, putting him on every ride, then having to listen to him giddily shriek, "Look at me, look at me" all day.

I was able to get a good deal on rooms at the Imperial Palace, one of the lesser hotels on The Strip. It was a charmless place where you could stash your stuff, catch a little sleep, and have easy access to wherever you needed to go.

In Vegas, the Superstar was angered and confused by the conclusions that people jumped to about him, even though many of those conclusions were correct. From his drooping black mustache, baseball cap, and baggy jeans—from which his ass was on conspicuous display each time he bent over to fix any of the multitude of broken things he found on his daily rounds—to the bulky set of utility keys jangling from his back pocket, he looked like the guy who could replace the lightbulb, jigger the air conditioner, and see to any plumbing crisis that might arise. The Superstar could really do all of those things and more. But in Las Vegas his Right-Man-for-the-Job appearance played havoc with his self-image every time he was in a casino or walking through a lobby.

Casino employees would hail the Superstar with respect. "Hola, Señor!" they would beam upon him proudly, standing at attention. Hotel guests would confront him to demand that he come to their rooms to see about their air conditioners or to check the hot water in the showers.

"Why does everyone keep asking if I work here? I'm not Mexican!"

On our first night in Vegas, we visited The Golden Palomino. It was an outsized video-arcade-like place with flashing strobe lights, buzzing and beeping machines, screaming customers, bass-heavy dance music that pulsated at brain-damaging volume, scores of naked women bumping up against boisterous college-aged groups of white guys alongside older loners and losers who seemed to be trying to melt into woodwork where there was no woodwork, and two vast brightly lit stages on which an array of young women practiced an advanced hybrid of cheerleading, yoga, and gymnastics, spreading their legs and—if the money thrust on them was right—assholes for close inspection.

The Golden Palomino operated on a kind of tier system, with women assigned tasks determined by where on the "hotness" scale the management placed them. On the bottom rung of this totem pole were the plain outcasts whose function was to mingle with the crowd, single out weaker members of the herd, wrangle them off to a comparatively quiet corner, and then inveigle them to spend all of their money on a variety of private interactions.

Among this lower caste was Mary, who attempted to solicit me when I sought respite from the churning, calculated cauldron.

She seemed sad. Hers was an uphill battle at The Golden Palomino. Although she was totally nude, she had the appearance of being totally *dressed*, such was her disembodiment from her surroundings. If anyone had actually given a shit, they might have asked her, "What's a nice girl like you doing in a place like this?"

Mary complimented me on my suit, cautiously fingering its lapel, leaving her hand on my arm. Then, as coached, she asked if I'd buy her a preposterously overpriced drink of soda water passed off as vodka.

I explained why I was a poor choice as designated sucker for the night—I didn't drink, didn't like strip clubs, understood the policy behind the hustle to buy her watered-down booze, and was only there out of obligation to a friend. I offered to buy her one drink based on the principle that anyone could fool me once.

She surprised me. She asked, "What would you like to drink?"

"Orange juice, no ice."

"I'll be right back. Don't go anywhere, okay? Don't talk to anybody else."

Mary returned a few minutes later with a glass of orange juice, a glass of something clear and effervescent, and a small brochure.

"An orange juice, no ice for you. A club soda for me. And I brought my book. Will you look at it for me?"

"What is it?"

"It's my jewelry. I design jewelry. I had a guy print out photos of it. It's all original. I get my inspiration from Navajo handicraft."

Did Mary honestly believe I might be a mark for the clunky silver and turquoise trinkets that had come into being through whatever demented visions she had when she looked at other clunky silver and gold trinkets? If not lap dances, was *this* her choice for how to hustle me?

It was here that my own unfortunate hustler's instinct kicked in, alerting me to Mary's various tells—the signals she desperately sent out indicating her need for someone in this devaluating place to *see her*. Any kind word would win her heart and whatever further body parts could be taken along with it.

I briefly warred with my better self and lost.

"This is beautiful work, Mary. You have the soul of a real artist."

"*Really?* Do you think so? Whenever I see Native American crafts, they *speak* to me. Do you know what I mean? I know that I was an Indian in a past life. Probably a Navajo, but possibly a Hopi. I went to a psychic, and she told me that I was. But I already knew."

Mary didn't realize it, but she had already handed me everything she owned. It's hard to explain why I decided to amuse myself by going to work on her. It was partially resentment for having to be in a place I couldn't stand, and partly that exploiting weakness was a key element in how I earned a living. There was more to it, though: it was an inborn instinct to turn the tables on anyone trying to hustle me. I think I was offended that someone as unskilled as Mary would attempt it.

I asked her what had initially brought her to The Golden Palomino, knowing that she would present a sentimental tale of outsiderness—a Horacio Alger story taking the additional step back to rags, filtered through the narrative of not being as beautiful as the other women in the club, finding her true calling through jewelry making, and a paltry *saga*, as she'd put it, of destiny.

"I don't get out of here until four," she told me, "but if you want to see my jewelry, I could take you back to my place."

She paused for a second. "Unless you're married or something. I know a lot of guys are."

At that moment, the Superstar bounded up. He'd been roaming freely though the club. He was in a frenzy, grabbing at my arm.

"Charles, Charles, you gotta come with me. You're not gonna believe this."

He noticed Mary. "Oh, hiya. Charles gotta come with me now. C'mon. This isn't gonna wait."

As we hurriedly moved across the showroom, he started to explain.

"They got a *special* room in the back where they keep the chicks who are too good for most of these bozos. I picked out the best one. This is the most gorgeous girl I've ever seen. C'mon, hurry. I don't want to keep her waiting. She might be gone."

"Why did you take time to come and get me if you're so worried?"

" 'Cause you gotta *see* her. I've never seen anyone this beautiful."

I was trying to picture what the most beautiful woman the Superstar had ever seen might look like. I was virtually certain that silicon would be involved.

"There she is! There she is! Mitzie! It's me! I'm back!"

Something was wrong. My brain was unable to come up with a life trajectory that would have brought the woman before me from wherever she'd started to this desperate and negligible place.

Mitzie was the most beautiful woman I'd ever seen. It wasn't a simple beauty, although she presented herself as straightforwardly in The Golden Palomino as she might have if first encountered at a dance recital or a library or in a park. She looked you in the eye, neither defiantly nor abjectly; she connected with you.

She was small and slender, with blonde hair, caramel-hued skin, and jade-green eyes. Her features were generous but not outlandish—her eyes and mouth slightly larger than average, safely below the surgically exaggerated level beginning to make its way into pornography. Unlike the other women we'd seen in the club, Mitzie was dressed in clothes that she could have worn on the street, although they emphasized her striking figure.

Her voice was consistent with her appearance, and, amazingly, audible amid the buzzes and beeps and basslines, the elevated yelling and frenzied laughter.

She reached over to shake my hand, saying as she did, "Hello. I'm Mitzie." She then dropped her voice to nearly a whisper that was somehow still audible, and added, "Except that my name is really not Mitzie. It's Vanessa."

This came out in a surprising contralto, musical and much deeper than might have been expected. She spoke with an accent that I couldn't immediately place.

I introduced myself, then asked where she was from.

"I'm from Madrid. But I lived in Germany for five years before I came to Las Vegas."

Trying to carry on a conversation with Vanessa in The Golden Palomino seemed like trying to carry on a conversation with a nun at a peep show, assuming that you wanted to fuck the nun and thought there was a chance you'd be able to.

Vanessa seemed to be having similar thoughts about the inappropriateness of this location for conversation. She asked the Superstar and me, "Can we go somewhere after I'm done here? This"—she made a small sweeping motion—"is no place to talk."

We agreed to pick her up when she got off work at 3:00.

"We should go back to my apartment first. I'll need to let Ron know that I'm safe."

"Who's Ron?"

"Ron is my husband. But it won't be a problem. I'll explain it when you come to get me."

It was around midnight. This gave me three hours to try to figure out what was actually going on. I knew The Superstar, loopy with infatuation and untutored as to how this subsection of the world worked, would be no help. In order for him to not be in my way, I decided to ignore him.

Since she was married, Vanessa's husband either was a dupe or played an active, willing part in the equation. If he'd been a dupe, Vanessa would have left him already; he'd have outlived his usefulness. So, Ron was a hustler of some sort. Because Vanessa looked as she did, Ron couldn't be a complete lightweight.

This led to questions about why Ron would relinquish her to the vultures at The Golden Palomino and why, if his intention was to pawn her off, he'd settle for anyone associated with a place like that. While it was true that she could make a lot of money there, it wouldn't be close to the money Vanessa working with someone with street sense would get.

Vanessa either wanted to get out of her current circumstances and thought I could help her do that—I had already dismissed the notion that she thought The Superstar could—or she and Ron had some kind of setup prearranged for when she brought men to their apartment.

Unless she was being intuitive, there would have been nothing to suggest to her that I'd be able to do her much good. Going with the other option, The Superstar and I would be lousy picks for who to jack, blackmail, or otherwise exploit in any kind of bait and switch or sting.

I was looking at an incomplete picture. Going to the apartment and meeting Vanessa's husband would fill things in.

We picked Vanessa up at the Golden Palomino at 3:00. She seemed more excited than was warranted. It turned out that The Superstar had promised her that we—or I—would be able to further her career in music. I then found out that she sang.

She directed us to a bad section of East Las Vegas. Her place was a cinderblock residential motel with outdoor concrete stairways. Someone would have to be broke and desperate to live in a dump like this. How was it possible that she and Ron lived here?

Inside, the place was orderly and clean. Scratch heavy drinking or drug use as reasons for the couple's impoverished living. It being Vegas, gambling could factor in.

We waited for Ron to get home. I wondered about his being out at nearly four in the morning. Vanessa explained that they had met in Germany, where he'd been stationed with the army. She loved him, but was not happy in her marriage. She had come to America with visions of pop stardom, certain that Ron could guide her to that goal.

I imagined Ron to be some redneck fuckup from a hick town in the South, who had somehow talked a gullible Spanish girl into marrying him and moving to the States. I conveniently forgot to ask myself why a gullible Spanish girl was living in Germany.

Ron turned out to be black—a big, handsome, athletic-looking, articulate kid who seemed as ill-suited as Vanessa to living in the dive they called home.

Talking about their living situation, he seemed entirely straightforward.

"I love Vanessa, but we only got married so she could get her Green Card. She's a good person and she deserves to be happy. But she's interfering with my work. I never expected her to live with me for so long. She never intended to. Do you think you might want to take her with you?"

The Superstar, silent to this point, decided the time had come to pipe up.

"Take her with us? Why? Is there something wrong with her?"

Nobody paid any attention to him. He was in way over his head and wasn't part of the conversation.

Ron said, "It's not that we don't love each other. But I wasn't looking for a wife and Vanessa doesn't want me for a husband. We're hoping we can find someone who'll help her with her singing career."

The Superstar asked, "Do you have any tapes, Vanessa?"

"No. I don't have anything."

"Well, we gotta be able to hear you first."

I had an idea. "There's a piano in the lobby of the Imperial Palace. You can sing for us there."

"Right now?"

"Why not? There's no night or day in Vegas."

Ron said, "I've got to crash. Vanessa, you should go. Let them hear you."

On the way to the Imperial Palace, Vanessa gripped my hand. She was shaking. It was hard to know whether she was frightened, excited to be singing for us, unhappy about nearing the end with Ron, or some combination of all three.

The piano was off to the side of the nearly deserted lobby of the Imperial Palace. The Superstar knew enough to give me space. I sat at the keyboard.

"Can you sing what I play? I'm just going to play a scale. I want to get a sense of your voice and how well you sing in tune."

"Yes, I can do that."

I slowly played a C scale, starting from an octave below middle C, one note at a time. I would play the note, then Vanessa would sing it. I didn't push her voice; C to G—a little over an octave and a half.

She had a soft, rich voice, perfectly in tune, without affect. It was nothing like a pop voice.

"That's very good. Will you sing a tune for me now?"

"What shall I sing?"

"Whatever you like."

"What if you don't know it?"

"That's okay. I'll figure it out."

"May I sing a Spanish song?"

"Anything you want."

Vanessa sang what sounded like a child's lullaby in Spanish—very easy to pick up—in her unadorned way. She sang earnestly and with great feeling. On the second verse, tears formed in her eyes. By the time she'd finished, her cheeks were shiny.

"Oh," she said.

Then: "You know the song."

"No."

"How could you play it?"

"You told me how to play it."

She started crying and gripped my hand again. "Thank you."

Her singing had been truly lovely. But there was no market for it in the States.

"You'll help me?"

"Vanessa, I'm not sure what I can do. There's no audience for that kind of music here. It would take a lot of work for you to make adjustments."

"You could teach me. I could learn."

She smiled at me, still crying.

"Please take me with you. I promise I will learn."

The Superstar kept his distance. I was warring against myself without letting it show. Playing the piano was a gift, but it was hard work. It could also be a trick. The part of me I couldn't stand performed a trick.

There was nothing to be done for Vanessa. There was no real place for her in the world. That's why she was living in a dump, why she had a husband who needed to get rid of her, why she was working—or not finding work—in a glorified whorehouse.

It was why she unquestioningly went with two strangers to their hotel; why she would follow one of them anywhere based on the authority of his hands moving on piano keys and his ability to intuit what she needed him to play for her.

It would be tidy if my relationship with Vanessa had stopped in Las Vegas. But she had my number and for nearly a year at increasingly infrequent intervals would call me, asking to come to Boston. Then she gave up.

In the small lounge of the Dunes Hotel there was a setup designed to separate vain out-of-towners with showbiz aspirations from their money. A simulacrum of a Las Vegas stage was constructed at the end of the room, with "professional lighting" and "a band" provided to give the "headliner" the support they required to "perform a sensational show." The professional lighting was a single spotlight; the band turned out to be a Karaoke machine. One hand mic, cranked up to maximum volume, was handed to the performer.

In this dubious setting, the Superstar made his Las Vegas debut in front of a crowd of twenty-five rubes who, although initially apathetic, wound up being swayed by his spirited renditions of musical banalities, cheering him on while each selection was videotaped at twenty-five dollars a pop.

The Superstar had dressed for the occasion with a slimming open-collared black shirt with matching pants, a heavy gold medallion that formed his initials, and shiny black ankle-length boots—their gleam possibly an attempt at coordination with his hair and mustache, which had received last-minute touch-up darkening.

He wanted to look his best. He believed there was a good chance that there would be talent scouts in the audience. A polished and well-received performance could lead to a paid engagement in one of the "small rooms"—a kind of audition to backing up a headliner at a major casino, from there only a short hop to becoming the headliner himself.

The enthusiastic response to "my set at the Dunes" so exceeded his overheated fantasies that he instantly began to form a plan for how to use it as a springboard. It started by asking the *actual* band playing the room later that evening if he could sit in with them. Maybe they could back him on a couple of numbers.

The young kids in the band, already seasoned vets, stonewalled him by politely telling him they had a set list. The Superstar rebutted them by pointing out that he knew some of their tunes. They trumped his response, saying that the audience had grown used to hearing their arrangements. The Superstar said that quite a few members of that very audience now made up a vociferous part of *his* audience. They'd be eager to hear him again. Finally, a quick-thinking member of the band asked the Superstar if he was in the musicians' union. When he admitted that he wasn't, a nonexistent "union-only" rule was invoked, ending the Superstar's short Las Vegas career.

Getting to Crystal, Nevada, from Las Vegas by car is virtually the same as getting to Area 51 from Las Vegas by car. Area 51 in Groom Lake is about twenty-four miles farther up north—at 3:00 a.m. about a fifteen-minute drive. There will be no one else on the highway I-15 North. You will feel only the deepest, most desolate sense of remoteness. You are nowhere, heading into a vast nowhere.

If you were sane, you'd ask yourself, "What on earth am I doing here?"

It was definitely what I was asking myself as I sat in the passenger seat of our rental car with the Superstar behind the wheel. He was convinced that if we got to the legal brothel in Crystal in the dead of night the prices would be a lot lower than during "peak hours."

At one point I had tried to warn him about what he might find at the Crystal Love Ranch, but I had given it up. No matter how bad it was, he'd have to see it for himself. And now here we were, flying down the empty highway at a hundred miles per hour, seeing only tumbleweed, jackrabbits, and the carcasses of animals who'd had the bad luck to attempt crossing the highway at one of the rare times a car happened to be on it.

"I wonder if it's gonna be like one of those old Western whorehouses with a fancy bar and a piano player in the background and dancing?"

"It'll be a trailer. And there'll be guys with guns standing guard. Let's roll down the windows."

The desert gets cool at night, and the scent of sage, primrose, eucalyptus, and cactus is powerful and invigorating. The stars are vast and clear. Mostly they were distinct and individuated, but there were also milky washes of stardust covering sections of the sky. Every few minutes a shooting star would plummet from the outer reaches of the universe.

Even with this, the dominant effect was ominous. Although not given to conspiracy theories, belief in alien encounters, or mysterious disappearances, heading toward Area 51 didn't fill me with a sense of wonder. It was a place where nothing good could happen, and where any interaction that *did* take place was bound not to be one you'd wish for.

We drove and drove through the desolate moonscape, not talking much, the Superstar occasionally going through Oh Boy-isms, projecting the kinds of delights he was sure would await him once we'd reached our destination.

Eventually we turned left onto a small dark highway that we nearly missed, drove a few miles, turned right onto a pitted dirt road that we also nearly missed, and saw a few dim lights in the near distance.

The lights belonged to a compound of sorts: several trailers set behind hefty circles of razor wire that looked like deadly Slinky toys, and rampways leading to and connecting each building. Large dogs began to howl on hearing our approach. It was not a hospitable place. If anything, it seemed to send the message that no one wanted you here.

The front trailer, optimistically labeled "Bar," had a handwritten sign that read "ENTER HERE FIRST."

The Superstar and I followed the instructions and found ourselves facing two men at a bar—one behind it, the other seated at it. The bartender was a big man with an enormous handlebar mustache. The man on the customer side was nearly a giant.

We'd interrupted their conversation, and they didn't seem happy to see us. They didn't look like men who'd be happy to see anybody, including each other.

Still, the bartender's voice was neutral, businesslike.

"You here to see the girls?"

"My friend is here to see the girls," I answered. "It's a long ride from here to Vegas, so I'll drive him back."

"Two drink minimum for both of you, then your friend can see the girls. You got to buy two drinks too. Ten dollars each." He waited a second. "That's ten dollars for each drink."

"I'm going to be drinking orange juice."

"Doesn't matter. Ten dollars a drink. I don't have orange juice. Soda or water."

The Superstar asked, "Can we at least see the girls before we decide?"

"Nope. You've got to have your drinks here before moving on to the main house."

I said, "You don't mind if I just let my friend here drink my two drinks, do you?"

The bartender looked vaguely irritated. "You can do that if you want to. But I wouldn't advise it. Be too bad if he went into the main house, then couldn't do what he came to do."

"Good point. Water for me, and whatever my friend is having."

There was a jar on the bar labeled "tips accepted." I wondered whether it would be useful to tip the bartender, but the twenty-dollar tab for two glasses of lukewarm water overruled my good judgment.

The Superstar and I repaired to the furthest part of the room, and the two men resumed their conversation. I got the sense that they were now speaking for our benefit.

"They were arrogant assholes," said the bartender. "You were right to do what you did."

The near-giant answered, "Fucking A-rabs think they own everything. They don't know who they're dealin' with. They don't understand, once they're out here, they're all alone."

"This isn't the USA anymore either. This is our own country. Our place, our rules."

"There ain't nothing here but you, me, the desert, and the dogs."

They laughed. The Superstar whispered to me, "Are we gonna get out of here alive?"

I said to the bartender, "You *do* understand that we're Americans, right?"

He laughed again, and I knew we were okay. We moved over to the bar.

"It's just that these assholes own everything," he explained. "And in Vegas everyone kisses their ass. Then they come out here and they think it's going to be the same way. But it's not. Who do you think pays to put the sheriff in office here in Crystal?"

The near-giant spoke up. "And don't nobody know they're out here. So, if they get out of line, there's lots of places to leave 'em. Lots of open space in the desert."

"We had a few of these A-rabs come here four, five weeks ago. They got rough with a couple of the girls. Maybe that goes back where they come from in Saudi Arabia or Iran or wherever, but not with me and Mike." He nodded toward the other guy.

"Those were dudes who never made it back to Vegas. Fuck 'em."

"You boys ready to go to the main house?"

The Superstar looked less than ready. The talk had unsettled him. Me too. I put a ten in the tip jar.

"How do we find it?"

"Just follow the rampway up to the next building over. Got a light over the door. I'll buzz you through the gate and call to let them know you're coming. Thanks for the tip."

We made our way up the ramp to the door with the light over it. A woman opened it as we reached the tiny porch.

"Come on in, boys."

She was in her late forties or early fifties, good-looking, friendly in an unforced way, and clearly an alum who'd come up the ranks of the working women to her current position.

"You're here to party?"

"My friend is here to party. I'm here to provide moral support."

"Moral support. That's a good one. I'll have to remember it. You sure you don't want to party too? We've got some mighty cute gals."

"Thanks, but no."

"Your loss. Maybe you'll change your mind when we bring 'em out."

The woman stepped through a door, and a moment later returned with five young women, each wearing a bikini bottom and see-through negligee. They were all attractive and varied in appearance enough to accommodate a range of customers' tastes.

I was sure the Superstar wouldn't choose the black woman, although she was the best looking of the five. One of the women looked like she might be from Venezuela, and I didn't think she'd be picked either. Of the three remaining women, the one I worried most about him choosing was a perky-looking blonde cheerleader type. He'd miss seeing it, but she was clearly a hardened pro—someone who had calculated the price of literally every gesture the john would make in her attempt to force him through his bankroll before anything remotely intimate took place.

The Superstar spent a minute meeting each woman then without hesitation made the worst possible choice. Off he and the cheerleader went.

The other women said goodbye and I sat on the couch to wait for The Superstar.

I didn't have to wait long. Ten minutes after he'd entered the inner sanctum, he was back, grim-faced.

"Let's get out of here."

He strode from the trailer, head down, fists clenched, moving quickly. The dogs began their howling. The Superstar paid them no mind. Down one ramp, onto the next, and out to the parking lot he power walked, me trying vainly to keep up with him.

When we reached the car, he tossed the keys to me.

"I'm too angry to drive," he said.

I got behind the wheel and started the car. The Superstar was already hunkered down in the passenger seat, his feet tapping impatiently.

As we passed through the entryway, he said, "Three hundred dollars. And my skin never touched her skin."

I hit the accelerator, and we were on our way.

"One hundred dollars for her to put on a latex glove to wash my dick. And she barely touched it."

I was moving us as fast as I could down the small highway that'd get us back onto I-15 South.

"It was the worst experience of my life, Charles. She didn't even look at me. I was just another guy on the conveyor belt. I was so freaked out that I couldn't get hard. She offered to give me a hand job to get me ready. Another hundred dollars. I gave her the hundred, but I was still having trouble. She told me that I could feel her tits while she was getting me hard if I paid another hundred. I gave her the money, then she said I'd have to keep a handkerchief in my hand while I felt her up. It'd cost another hundred to feel her bare tits. I lost my hard-on again when she said that. I thought that maybe I wouldn't be able to perform—he pronounced it "pa-*fahm*"—so I decided that enough was enough."

A few moments passed.

"Did your ten-dollar drinks have any booze in them?"

"Not much."

"And your skin never touched her skin."

"My skin never touched her skin."

We both started to laugh. I hit the turn onto I-15 South, and we headed back to Las Vegas as the sun began to rise over the desert.

Jerry Quarry

In late 1988 I spent a couple of evenings gambling with Jerry Quarry at various Vegas casinos. Quarry appeared to have been brought to town by Joe Goossen, who had middleweight champion Michael Nunn fighting Juan Domingo Roldan in the main event at the Hilton Center.

Quarry was good company at first—bright, soft-spoken, and for the most part philosophical about his years in boxing. He was generally coherent, although it was clear that, having retired five years earlier, he needed to stay retired. I still can't figure out how any commission could have sanctioned him to fight five years after the time I knew him. Any boxing person would have spotted how impaired he was in 1988. Anyone with a working brain would have seen it from a mile away before his last fight in late 1992 after a nine-year layoff, only seven years before his death due to acute dementia.

Quarry's boyish good looks had calcified some; his neck had thickened; the dutifully combed hair was missing its earlier luster. He was still cheerful, but an air of introspection would intrude at times, and then he would become anxious or even testy.

He wasn't really a large man—and certainly a small one by contemporary heavyweight standards—and he had rounded shoulders that further camouflaged his size. But his hands were big, rocklike slabs, much like his two-time opponent Floyd Patterson's, and he projected imposing physical strength. Unlike some fighters—and despite his friendliness—he seemed like someone you wouldn't want to test too much.

As the Hilton fights grew closer, Quarry became edgy, as some retired fighters do when bell time draws near. There was a to-and-fro element to this edginess: he would snap at people, but then immediately apologize. The dealers in the Strip's casinos fared particularly badly through these mood swings. Quarry was not a good gambler, making impulsive decisions at blackjack, then suggesting to the dealers that he had been rushed into foolishly sticking or hitting on a hand. Again, he would apologize, sliding a generous tip in with his apology. Meanwhile, his gambling decisions got crazier and crazier.

His behavior also became more erratic. When I ran into him at the Hilton Casino on the day of the fight, I wasn't sure I wanted to be around him anymore. There was a dark cloud hovering over him.

Trying to steer him back to a lighter mood, I asked about his first-round knockout of Earnie Shavers. It turned out to be the wrong subject to bring up.

Quarry's face turned red and he began to shake. His voice was no more than a low growl. "At the weigh-in, Shavers presented me with a pair of yellow women's panties. Yellow. . . . Women's. . . . Panties."

His eyes narrowed to slits and he balled both hands into enormous fists that he placed too close to my face.

"Brother," he hissed, "*nobody* calls me yellow."

He glared at me as if defying contradiction. The incident had taken place fifteen years earlier, but Jerry Quarry was reliving it as if the murderous-punching Shavers was now thrusting the yellow panties in his face. There's no question that Quarry would have attacked Earnie Shavers if he'd walked in.

I was not at all sure that Quarry wouldn't attack *me*. His shaking continued even more violently, and he seemed suddenly blind to his surroundings.

To bring him back, I said, "But you took care of it, Jerry. You knocked him out in the first round. No one else—not Ron Lyle, not Larry Holmes, not even Muhammad Ali, came close to doing that."

"Fuckin' A, brother. Fuckin' A."

It still emerged as a growl, but Quarry's violent spell seemed to have passed. I wasn't going to stick around for the next one that I knew would come.

1990s

Blood

Nobody in boxing can make more money than a heavyweight who captures the public's attention. Although heavyweights aren't nearly as good as the fighters in any other weight division, businesswise that doesn't matter. If you're a manager, you try to represent heavyweights even though they're a costly proposition. Heavyweights can get title shots without first establishing their worth. Even the most improbable no-hoper fighting for a major crown will bring home a mid-six-figure payday. A high-profile champion's price tag will be ten million per fight, and often much more.

People are intrigued by heavyweights, presumably because of the absolutism attached to the bigger-is-better maxim. An undisputed heavyweight champion can call himself the toughest man in the world, and his claim will be vaguely credible if you don't think about it too carefully. A junior flyweight, regardless of his knockout ratio, will be laughed at if he calls himself "the baddest man on the planet."

I entered the heavyweight sweepstakes a few times, including once going for the ultimate sucker Powerball ticket. During the couple of zany and frustrating years that I managed him—if anyone can be said to manage Mitch "Blood" Green—he was twice offered million-dollar paydays despite his not having won a fight in seven years. To my dismay, but not complete surprise, he turned both down, forcing me to look like a chump when I had to go back to the guys who made the offers to say that it was going to be no dice.

How good a fighter Mitch Green was is a matter of debate. His ability to attract attention is not. I never went anywhere with him where he didn't draw a crowd. People always knew his name. I offered to bet billionaire right-wing head case Sheldon Adelson's similarly hennaed brother Lenny $10,000 that if his fighter, Alexander Popov, and Mitch Green started on separate sides of the block in Kenmore Square and walked the mile to Copley Square in downtown Boston, Popov would still be alone by the time he reached his destination while Green would have picked up a parade's worth of followers. Adelson had been talking big about what a splash his hapless Russian was going to make in the division, but he shut up fast when invited to put money on the table. Maybe he didn't have his brother's billions to throw away on lost causes.

Crowd gathering aside, there were not many things that Mitch Green liked to do. His two favorite pastimes were posing while talking about Mitch Green and posing while listening to people talk about Mitch Green. I don't think he preferred one to the other.

I had no luck with Mitch Green. Days after we signed our contract, he got shot in Harlem by a Mike Tyson fan he'd slapped.

Blood limped six blocks to receive a misdiagnosed X-ray taken at Harlem Hospital. The technicians had miraculously failed to notice a bullet lodged behind his femur. Weeks went by while Green walked, ran, and occasionally jumped rope, bringing his 240 pounds down repeatedly on what amounted to a split tree limb. By the time I flew him to Boston where Frank Bunch got a look at Blood's leg, the threat of amputation loomed.

Bunch rushed him into the ER and over a period of eight hours secured the femur by placing a number of large metallic pins around his knee. This bought Mitch six months of enforced inactivity—overall a happy, if boring, time when nothing was required of him other than rehabbing the damaged leg.

He was hard to keep entertained. A giant television—pre-flat-screen era—was purchased to cover an entire wall of his living room. Unless I took him out, there was nothing else for him to do but watch. He didn't read. He talked on the phone a lot, and it was important to unplug my phone late at night or risk sitting through a monologue that could go on until dawn.

Luckily, I was thinking about going into music management, and there were some rock, rap, and hip-hop musicians around most of the time. They couldn't get over having Mitch "Blood" Green hanging out with their crews.

Of all these musicians, only Garrett Dutton—better known as G Love—looked to have any real chance at success. For a brief moment, I managed him and Mitch simultaneously. Typically, I caught them both when they were least able to benefit me.

They liked each other. Blood had a sense that G Love was on his way to becoming famous, and saw himself as a street mentor to a kid who'd been born into every imaginable comfort.

Mitch suffered from a kind of verbal dyslexia that made his aphorisms come out incorrectly sometimes. He would occasionally let G Love know "not to take my weakness for kindness." If Garrett would come back with a perceptive response, Green would give him a pensive look. Understanding at some level that he'd gotten the hoary saying wrong, he'd solemnly utter, "Out of the mouth of wisdom . . . comes . . . babes."

Problem Tenants

I brought Mitch to the four-family building I owned on Broadway in Winter Hill, the area of multiunit houses in Somerville where hardworking blue-collar homeowners daily passed by places of criminal enterprise controlled by Howie Winter and Whitey Bulger. Having Blood accompany me on visits to unruly tenants went a long way toward easy dispute resolution. One look at him was all it took to get even the most truculent of them to capitulate.

The police called me after a double knifing had taken place in my building. Then my tenant, whose brother was one of the victims, called.

When Mitch and I got to the apartment, we found blood everywhere. It was on the sidewalk outside the house, on the steps leading in, all over the walls, covering the furniture, some even still congealing into the hardwood floors.

The two men had fought with knives throughout the house, then out onto the street, and finished so near death that they collapsed on the curb. Both were now in the intensive care unit of Mass General, and no one was sure if either would live.

I was there to make sure that, lease or no lease, the tenant understood that he'd be moving out immediately. I hadn't known about his brother living with him.

As Mitch Green loomed over him, the tenant described what had happened. It turned out that his brother had a long and violent history of mental illness.

His brother and a friend had been drinking heavily the previous night, then switched over to drugs, which led to an argument over who owed whom what for the drugs. Things escalated, the knives came out, and the men wound up bleeding across the sidewalk.

My tenant, looking at Mitch and visibly shaking, kept saying, "I'm so frightened of you."

He looked small, dark, and frail. I imagined his brother looked that way too until he had a knife in his hand.

"You've got to move out tomorrow."

"I paid my rent for the month."

"Tell him, Blood."

"You got to go."

The tenant shook more. I assumed we were finished here.

"I've paid my rent."

"That won't cover the cleaning costs. I'm not here to argue with you. We'll be back tomorrow. Make sure you're gone."

"I'm afraid of this man," my tenant answered, looking at Green. "I don't want to get hurt. I paid my rent. I'll clean the apartment. When you come back tomorrow, it will look like nothing ever happened here. I don't have anywhere to go. I'll make sure my brother doesn't do anything else. I have rights. I'll go to a lawyer."

"Did your brother come here from Brazil legally?"

"No. But we don't have anywhere to go. If my brother lives, I have to take care of him. Let us stay. Please. I've paid my rent. I will clean the house."

It was time to bring Mitch Green into this.

"I guess you'll have to explain to him, Blood."

"He seem like a good dude, Charle. And he and his brother don't have nowhere to go. He gotta take care of his brother. They won't start no more shit. They be cool."

This Solomonic Judgment put me in an uncomfortable position. If I got into a debate with Mitch it would make me seem indecisive to the tenant. Overruling Mitch would make him look like an underling and a goon.

I chose to "see the wisdom" of Mitch's approach, magnanimously acquiescing, explaining to the tenant that he was allowed to stay only because "Blood just vouched for you." It wouldn't be me he'd answer to if he betrayed Mitch's faith.

The tenant and his brother stayed for the month. Mitch had guessed right about the guy. I'd been wrong. The next time we went to the house, the apartment was spotless. It was quiet for the entire month. The tenant and his brother didn't take advantage of our generosity. I never sent an eviction notice. When Mitch and I returned at the beginning of the month, the apartment was empty, cleaned to a professional standard, and ready to be rented to new tenants whose arguments, if they even had them, never moved beyond low-decibel verbal ones.

Ringside for the Mike Tyson vs. Mitch Green Fight—Minus Mike Tyson—Live from the Bank of America Parking Lot

Mitch "Blood" Green had a superb memory for events that had taken place. His interpretation of those events could sometimes be a little bit subjective but always contained at least a kernel of truth.

He was particularly incisive when it came to reconstructing his fights. Mitch could re-create them round by round, exhibiting a near-total recall of every sequence of punches, every clinch, and every verbal exchange.

He did have a unique—and, as far as I know, unshared—take on his ten-round contest against Mike Tyson at Madison Square Garden in 1986.

One night, Mitch decided to plead his case for having won the Tyson fight, stepping from the car at a Bank of America parking lot in order to replicate the entire ten rounds in real time, adding commentary as he did.

For the next thirty minutes—he didn't take breaks between rounds—Mitch "Blood" Green fought his half of his ten-round fight against Mike Tyson, narrating Tyson's half too. He called it as he saw it, seldom giving his opponent credit for connected punches, while ascribing damage done from his own that didn't necessarily reflect what the judges and general audience thought they had seen.

Gradually a puddle formed beneath Green's swiftly spinning torso, jabs and right-crosses flashing out at dazzling speed, jarringly catching his opponent's head repeatedly as Tyson unsuccessfully attempted to work his way inside.

Occasionally Blood would give credit where it was due: "Okay, he hit me with a good shot there." Or, "Tyson got kinda fast hands." Even, "Mike punch pretty good." Finally, "I was talkin' to the little homo. That how he caught me with my mouth open and knock my bridgework out. He wouldn't of never did that if I wasn't talkin'."

In Mitch's telling, there was no question about who won the fight. Seeing a sweat-soaked Mitch Green standing triumphant after ten fast-paced rounds, who could possibly disagree with him?

Oh, We're in Boston

Buddha's Delight was a vegan restaurant in Boston's Chinatown, a few blocks from the Combat Zone, the city's infamous red-light district. I was in the habit of bringing boxers and musicians there despite their misgivings about trying animal-free food. Everyone who went was won over, and it was easy from then on to get them to go.

Mitch Green loved the place, although he was never entirely convinced that the cook hadn't slipped some beef or chicken into the entrees. In Boston, things apparently weren't always as they appeared.

Blood was explaining to two would-be pop stars and their girlfriends that all the food we were having was vegetarian.

"Charle don't eat no meat," he explained. "But this food is *good.*"

All the kids wanted to talk about was themselves and their hoped-for careers. Sitting through that was something Green could tolerate for a limited time before needing things brought back around to him. I'd learned the hard way what would happen if they weren't. He'd grow cranky, then demanding.

"Maaann, I need a Kanga cap. An' some new gold chains. There gotta be a place around here where we can get 'em."

One of the youngsters piped up.

"Oh yeah, Blood. There are pawns shops all up and down the street just a couple of blocks from here."

He turned to his girlfriend. "It'll be so cool to go shopping for gold chains at pawnshops in the Combat Zone with Mitch "Blood" Green. That'd be the bomb."

"Yeah, yeah, yeah," said Mitch. "What they gonna do when Blood walk in with his posse?"

I thought, *They're going to know that Christmas has come early.* Our unlikely little group made its way store by store down Washington Street, Blood basking in the attention of thugs, winos, and hustlers, the would-be pop stars grinning from ear to ear and pointing Mitch out to strangers, the girlfriends deeply bored and uneasy to be in such a perilous part of the city. I waited for the ax to fall once Green finally settled on a pawnshop.

He picked one of the usual suspects. It was a long, narrow building that was easy enough to enter but, being overcrowded, nearly impossible to get out of once you stepped inside. The clientele divided its attention between Mitch "Blood" Green, who everyone seemed to recognize, and the two ill-at-ease white women, who were novelty items in this junction of the desperate and the tightfisted.

A beaming man came tearing across from the back.

"Is this who I think it is? I atchully got Blood Green in my own shop? What brings you here, dawg? What can I do for you?"

The customers had made their choice: Mitch was now officially the star of the show. It brought out his largesse.

"I got my crew here, and I'm lookin' to pick up a few little things."

"Of course, brother. What you need?"

"I'm lookin' for a Kanga cap. . . ."

"Shoot, we run out of Kangol caps. I can't keep the dang things in stock. Soon as a shipment comes in, out it goes again. I'm sorry, dawg."

"It's cool, it's cool. How 'bout gold chains? Show me what you got."

Our aggregation was led to the front of the store where dozens of "I ain't goin' nowhere in life" chains were laid out under glass. They weren't cheap; well, they *were* cheap, but they weren't inexpensive.

"You got sets of any of them so the posse can all wear them?"

I started to signal no to the kids, but needn't have bothered. They didn't want to wear the chains any more than I wanted to buy them. They shook their heads at me, avoiding Mitch's glance. He was focused on the trinkets anyway.

"Nah, man. 'Cause I never know what's gonna come in. I only got what people bring me. But there's some beautiful chains here. Check 'em out."

I had been willing to part with a little cash until Mitch started asking about specific chains and I heard the prices. Ninety dollars here, $75 there, $165 for the "deluxe piece" displayed in the center of the tray. And there could be discounts for multiple purchases.

"I hope you know that none of this is real gold, Mitch."

"What you mean, Charle? *Naturally,* it's real gold. These are gold chains. What you think it is?"

"It's a base metal with cheap gold plating. They might even spray the gold color on."

"No, man. These are gold chains."

I turned to the owner.

"Are these gold chains? Tell him."

"Well, they got gold in 'em."

His smile was gone.

I didn't want to embarrass Mitch Green in front of the kids. And if the shit jewelry had been cheaper, I would have let him buy it. It was just too expensive. I made the guy admit that the chains weren't exactly *pure* gold.

Green got a melodramatically stricken look on his face. He slapped his forehead.

"Oh, wait a minute," he exclaimed, "I forgot. We in *Boston*! I was thinkin' we was in New York. But this *Boston*. Oh shit. I'm freakin' out here."

Two young guys entered the shop, one moving quickly toward the back of the store, the other stationing himself by the entrance. Mid-monologue, I hurried Mitch along with the others out to the street and kept them moving.

I explained to everyone that the pawnshop was about to be robbed, but it didn't slow Mitch down.

"Man, I'm totally freakin' out here," he continued. "I forgot I was in Boston. I thought I was in New York."

"And you're saying that they have 24-carat gold chains in all of the New York pawnshops, Mitch?"

"Of *course* they do, Charle. You think they get away with that kind of behavior in New York? Don't you have no sense? You a very intelligent man, but you actin' like you stupid."

Woodbridge, Virginia: It All Comes to Nothing

We had one of Jerome Peete's white-man-scaring black jailbird giants fresh from the joint ready to drive up from Tennessee for the $1,000 he'd make for two minutes of work. Then the DC/Northern Virginia area fell under a rare blizzard and we had to rely on matchmaker Eric Bottjer to come up with the right guy. His choice was solid: professional loser Bruce Johnson—8-22-1—could make it to Woodbridge from Ohio. It's true that Johnson wasn't told to fall down by anyone, but it was assumed he knew his role. His telling me he was afraid of Mitch Green, then holding me up for an extra $200, seemed to imply as much.

Mitch was entirely committed to losing that night, however, and not even Johnson could persuade him to do otherwise. Pat and Tony Petronelli, the referee, and I all tried too. Green needed only to throw a punch or two, but he stood firm in his conviction to leave his hands by his sides, allowing Johnson's increasingly purposeful punches to land harmlessly where they would. Our entreaties for Mitch to do *anything* were ignored as he embarked on his search for inner peace in the most inappropriate place possible.

In scoring a TKO victory over Mitch "Blood" Green, Bruce Johnson was able to do what Mike Tyson didn't come close to doing. I tried to get the ordinarily corruptible Virginia boxing commissioner Doug Beavers to do the right thing and accept my bribe, but he stood firmly against it. I'd always liked the rough-hewn wiseass Beavers, and I thought that he liked me. When Al Braverman told IBF Chairman Bobby Lee to rate my fighters, Lee would tell Doug and he'd do it. The only thing I can think of was that I wasn't offering enough money. But Beavers never told me that.

After the fight, I was too angry to talk with Green, while he insisted on telling me why he'd been right in not defending himself and it had been my mistake to put him in the fight. Every time he would attempt to confront me, I'd turn and walk away from him. After a while, I began to address him through other people in the hotel lobby.

"Will you please tell this motherfucker that I'm not speaking to him?"
Not surprisingly, this only added to the tension.

"You're gonna talk to me, goddamnit."

"Will somebody please tell this dumb motherfucker to leave me alone?"

"Who you callin' a dumb motherfucker, Charle?"

"Will someone please tell this dumb motherfucker that he's the guy I'm calling a dumb motherfucker?"

I kept walking away, and Mitch kept stepping in front of me.

"You better talk to me, Charle."

"Or what? You're going to punch me? Everybody knows you can't punch."

"I'm gonna show you how hard I can punch."

"Wait, let's get Bruce Johnson in here. Oh, I forgot. It's too late. He already knocked you out."

Within minutes we were standing an inch away from each other—me being reminded once more just how big Mitch Green was—our voices rising as the lobby filled with fight people and hotel guests. I knew it was just a matter of time before the confrontation would turn physical, but I needed to stand my ground. Luckily for me, that moment was when the cops arrived, ordering Mitch and me in opposite directions, cautioning us to call it a night, as the crowd dispersed.

Sparring

I've got a Mitch Green sparring story.

I have very fast hands. I don't know whether or not it comes from playing musical instruments, but it's something I've always had. I idiotically mentioned this to Mitch one afternoon.

"Charle, you got fast hands? Lemme see. Try an' hit me."

"That'd be crazy. I'm almost a hundred pounds lighter than you. Naturally I'm going to have faster hands."

"Okay, I know, I know. Well, just show me."

I threw a jab to Mitch's body. It slipped through his guard and landed effortlessly.

"Goddamn, Charle. You *do* got fast hands. Do me a favor. Show me again."

I threw a second jab with equal success.

"Ain't that a bitch. You got you some fast motherfuckin' hands, dude. One last time?"

As I began the third jab, Mitch moved his elbow a fraction of an inch, blocked my punch, and a millisecond later an enormous right fist came out of the sky and stopped less than an inch from my forehead. I swear it made a whistling sound.

"Well, maybe they ain't that fast after all," Mitch laughed.

Leon Spinks

I never intended to manage Leon Spinks. I had no interest in him as a fighter. The plan was for me to manage his sons Darryl and Cory, and to take on Freddie Norwood at the same time. Leon was to be brought in as a one-time publicity stunt to kick off the careers of the next generation of Spinks brothers.

By coming to Raleigh, North Carolina, as a favor to his kids, their trainer Charles Hamm, and me, Leon was repaid by getting monotonously beaten up over the endless course of a bullshit main event in a dilapidated and stifling arena filled with hooting rednecks, all for barely more money than an autographed photo session might have netted him.

It's not that I didn't know beforehand that Leon was a shot fighter. What I couldn't have known, not having observed him in person before, was how irreparably damaged he was. Still, even after I saw how things were, I didn't give him the kind of attention I should have. I didn't take the one or two steps that would have made a difference.

That Raleigh card was bad news for me. Because there was an overload of things to do, I foolishly pawned some assignments off on others who, like me, had not bothered to take stock of the conditions that prevailed.

As a result, aside from Freddie Norwood looking like the best fighter in the world that night—which I'd expected—everything went wrong. I managed to fix the things I had to fix—everyone who I really needed to get a win got one—but in the overall picture the fixing did more harm than good.

Things were weirdly off from the start. Leon's sons didn't make it to Raleigh. Cory had never been told about the arrangement, and somehow

Charles Hamm had lost track of Darryl. They were replaced by Tommy Spinks, a heavyweight who called himself Leon's son, but was actually the biological son of Leon's wife Betty. The only thing he inherited from the Spinks family was the ability to fuck things up.

Tommy was sprung on me as a surprise, so a local opponent had to be dug up for him. An army recruit named Ken Williams from nearby Fort Bragg, who was Tommy's virtual double and who'd never fought before, decided to give boxing a try.

Down and nearly out thirty seconds into the fight, Williams appeared to have been the right choice for an opponent. But it was 91 degrees in Raleigh that day, hotter than that in the Ritz with no air conditioning, and much hotter still under the ring lights. The effort of trying to put Williams away wound up being too much for the blubbery quasi-Spinks, and his roundhouse punches steadily wound down and down, reduced finally to exhausted slaps. In the fourth round, Tommy, with nothing left, gasping and heaving, was knocked out by something much more like a push than a punch.

Throwing his robe over his shoulders, with a demented look in his eyes, the Next Generation Poster Child managed to stagger back up the aisle, through the front doors of the theater, and onto the concrete entryway. There he collapsed and there he remained unmoving—arms dramatically thrust out in classic crucifixion posture—for the next twenty minutes as latecomers stepped around and occasionally over him on their way to the ticket counter.

The Three Paths

Once I'd made my guilt-driven decision to manage Leon Spinks, I had three options for which approach to take in picking his fights. As always in boxing, these options were determined by prevailing conditions—conditions being much more important than the nuts and bolts of boxing as an athletic competition, the who can beat whom.

By the time I met Leon Spinks, he could no longer fight and shouldn't have been in a boxing ring with anybody. This wasn't a matter of whether there was anyone he could beat. That would have been irrelevant. Even the very few bottom-of-the-barrel guys he might have eked out a win over would have hit him. And he was no longer neurologically sound enough to absorb any further punishment.

The first option was to find promoters who would pay Leon to come to their small-town venues for fights where everyone's best interest would be served by his winning. The locals would get to see a prominent ex-champion win a fight, and they could go home happy.

The miniscule payday Leon would get didn't automatically mean it would be a bad idea to take those fights. The argument in their favor was that they'd start to rebuild his winning record, let promoters see that he was active, and bolster his case for a bigger fight that would be the final payoff at the end of an admittedly overlong road.

For a fight at this level I could only expect Leon to get offers ranging from $1,500 from a cheapskate to maybe $5,000 from a novice promoter. The opponent would have to be paid at least a thousand. Although the promoter might have been willing to foot that bill using a local fighter, it wouldn't be wise to let him choose the opponent. The fight's outcome was something I'd need to control, as well as seeing that Leon not get hit with a genuine punch. So, I'd have to choose and pay for the opponent.

There's an upside to these kinds of fights. If you repeated this maneuver successfully four or five times, people would start entering Leon's name in the Foreman/Holmes Oldies Sweepstakes conversation.

And there's a downside. Leon would barely make any money and I'd be losing some. And any error in judgment would kill off the entire project.

A second option would be to offer Leon as a moderately high-priced name opponent for prospects who themselves weren't very good. At this level, I'd encounter managers who were trying to do with their fighter from one stage up exactly what I was trying to do with mine.

The fights in this category would have brought Leon anywhere from $15,000 to $30,000. His opponents—the guys beating him to move up the ladder—would likely get less, although it would depend on the circumstances.

These would be the most dangerous fights for Leon, and the ones where if you were strapped for cash your character might be tested. Vin Vecchione offered $25,000 for Leon to fight Peter McNeeley at the Boston Garden. Even though I trusted Vin and Leon needed the money, I had to turn him down.

We'd talked about having me stop the fight in the corner after the first round, claiming that Spinks had broken a rib. But I insisted there could be no head shots, and Vecchione was sure that McNeeley would not be able to hold back and confine his punches to the body.

"Chaales," Vin told me, "he won't be able to do it. Peter ain't that *talented*."

If you are going to accept fights at this level for a damaged fighter, you are morally obligated to fix them—and not just the result; you need to fix the power of the punches being thrown and where they land too.

To somehow be moved into a fight with another ex-heavyweight champion—preferably Holmes or Foreman—would have been Leon's ceiling.

I wound up getting the kind of offer that would ordinarily have taken a year or more to set up—with me spending plenty of money along the way—from an unlikely source.

I had been trying to get a foothold with boxing in Beijing through some generals in the Chinese army and a high-powered company called the Jin Wah Corporation that was tied into both the television and casino businesses. All of the back-and-forth conversation was being translated by a pleasant but thoroughly confused woman named Shin Yi Lo. In the '90s, communication between the United States and China was a costly and unpredictable nightmare.

I was trying to hustle the generals and Jin Wah; while the generals, who were a bunch of corrupt and dangerous motherfuckers, were trying to hustle me. This was where Shin Yi Lo kept getting tangled up. It was inconceivable to her that either side would attempt to take advantage of the other. And she found it unconscionable that, in the absence of a deal, no one would get paid. "I am to get *nothing* for my efforts?"

It saddened me to have to wise her up.

It was into the heart of this madness that someone called me to offer Leon a $175,000 payday to fight Larry Holmes in China. That would have been the cash-out option—the one that you'd have been building to and holding out for.

I wanted to take it, but I understood that an unrestrained Larry Holmes would hurt—and maybe even kill—Leon. The only way to accept the fight for Leon would be to come to an arrangement with Holmes.

I thought it might be possible. I'd spoken with him several times over the years, and we'd gotten along. He'd once advised me to spend my money at the roulette wheel in Atlantic City instead of "throwing it away" on Mitch Green.

I'd watched Holmes use every trick in his highly evolved repertoire to keep from destroying Muhammad Ali when they'd fought. I had no doubt about his capacity for mercy.

I also knew something important. In 1993 Vin Vecchione's heavyweight Paul Poirier had fought Holmes on *Tuesday Nights Fights* from Bay St. Louis, Mississippi. Poirier was a good regional-level boxer—a slick-box, no-punch guy who had turned pro as a 140-pound fourteen-year-old. There was no way he should have been in the ring with Larry Holmes, and Vin knew it.

Vin told me that he had spoken to Holmes's brother Jake before the fight, asking him to talk to Larry about not hurting Poirier. He promised to pull Paul out of the fight after six rounds. Given the okay by Larry, Vecchione was as good as his word, stopping the fight between rounds while a genuinely distraught Poirier argued vigorously to be allowed to continue.

So expert was Vin's seemingly heartfelt intervention that *Tuesday Night Fights* featured the stoppage in a weepy holiday season highlight clip illustrating the kindness and mercy people in the business felt toward those under their care.

I called Holmes and explained the situation, being entirely candid about everything. I reminded Larry that he had destroyed Leon when they'd fought in 1981, back when Spinks could actually fight.

"It's thirteen years later, Larry. Leon is thirteen hard years worse. If you're going to hurt him, I can't take the fight."

"How old is Leon now?"

"He's forty-one."

"Shit, none of us is getting any younger. Nobody needs to get hurt in this one."

Armed with an agreement from Larry Holmes and a $175,000 offer, I moved Leon Spinks straight into his derailment.

I can explain everything I did from this point on, but can justify none of it. I thought it would be good for Leon to score an impressive knockout somewhere other than a tank town. I connected with my friend Cleveland Burgess in DC, who put together a card at the Convention Center with Leon headlining the main event.

Nothing about the promotion was normal, starting with the promoters themselves. The company sponsoring the fight was called either Panic Promotions or Madness Connection, depending on whether you were looking at the contract or the fight posters, and was run by a couple of DC drug dealers who used the event as a fundraiser for the coke and crack mayoral candidate of choice, Marion Barry.

I had convinced Marc Machain to come in from Rutland, Vermont, to lose to Leon. The Rutland Bull wasn't eager to take the loss, but he was a friend and a stand-up guy, and he was going to be allowed to have a give-and-take fight with Leon until a "rib injury" would force his corner to stop the fight over his protests. It wouldn't be exactly the kayo I would have most wanted, but it would be an entertaining fight that would get people talking. There'd be no slipup.

And then Machain's CT scan came back bad. The DC Commission wouldn't clear him to fight. With almost no advance time, I had to get creative. I enlisted the help of John Carlo, Fernely Feliz's trainer and a real-life tough guy, who looked more like a fighter than most fighters. Although he'd never had a pro fight, John agreed to fight Leon. I had to find a way to somehow get him past the Commission by falsifying his record and providing a fake doctor's report, and then finessing him through the various local sports radio, TV show, and newspaper reporters who would have semi-insider questions.

The fake medical records were easy: Vecchione had someone at a doctor's office in Boston who'd supply them. We'd done this together before. Compiling a plausible boxing record for John Carlo took a little more doing, but I knew which heavyweights were routine losers to the up-and-coming prospects in unregulated states—places where results weren't always sent to record-compiling agencies. I was able to come up with the names of real fighters as John Carlo's victims—the "fights" taking place in Montana, Idaho, and North Dakota.

I generously gave John a 13-2-1 record with nine kayos. Boxing insiders might wonder why they'd never heard of a white heavyweight who was 13-2-1, but no commissioner was going to be sharp enough to pick it up.

As long as John didn't do anything too questionable during the prefight interviews, we'd be okay. He nailed them, saying exactly what he was supposed to say in a tone that mixed humility with determination: he was honored to fight a great former champion, he didn't come to DC to lose, it had been Leon's time, but it was now his, and so on.

I liked Leon Spinks a great deal and had deep respect for him. I recognized him to be—insofar as he was anything in mainstream culture—a figure of amusement, even of mild ridicule. Attached to any such figure is the subliminal hope that they will lose, and preferably lose humiliatingly. It was my job to see that that didn't happen. I could not have failed more thoroughly.

As expected, John Carlo flew past the Commission. So did Jimmy Harrison, who I'd arranged to bring in as Melvin Foster's opponent as a favor to Dennis Rappaport. Jimmy had been winless over the last eight years, going 0-15-2 during that time, so he was really being fed to the lions with Foster, who was 15-1-1—his only loss coming by split decision to former world champion Trevor Berbick. I felt bad for Jimmy, who I knew was going to get beaten up for his payday, so I checked in with him and his trainer Papa Ray Drayton. Jimmy's fights weren't fixed—he just couldn't fight—so there was no business to get straight; it was just a little social call.

Leon was having fun in the dressing room before the fight. Not a hint of nerves. Some drunken street person from his past had somehow sweet-talked his way in, and the two of them were laughing away, recounting happy times of their youth spent drinking Boone's Farm Strawberry Hill Wine together. The drunk told Leon that the cheap pink soda pop that would get you seriously looped, if you sat around on the stoop drinking it all day, was back on the market. A cause for rejoicing. Leon, who no longer drank, seemed as thrilled by the prospect as the drunk. His eyes narrowed in an expression of faux-inebriated bliss.

This joie de vivre was pretty much what he brought into the ring with him for the main event. He wasn't the only one happy to be there. The drug dealers from Panic Promotions had their own candidate doing the introductions for the main event. Three feet from us in the center of the ring was civic leader/crackhead Marion Barry himself, the effects of a bulky holiday sweater that would have ordinarily made him look festive and slightly avuncular compromised by his knotted brow and perplexed expression. Barry had a small piece of paper in his palm, and was almost inaudibly mouthing the words it contained. Something about those words was troubling him.

I inched closer. He was worrying a phrase, modifying its inflection with each repetition.

"The foam-ah hev-weight *chapeen*. The former *heava-weight* champ-yun. Duh *fuh-muh* hebbyweigh' champin of the *worl'*."

The mayor was working on his street voice, trying to remember how it should sound. I looked at him. He looked back, gave me a small smile and apologetic shrug.

It hadn't once occurred to me that Leon might lose. It hadn't even occurred to *John Carlo* in any realistic way that Leon might lose. We had even joked about it before the fight. He'd called me to ask, "What if I win?"

"John, you're a tough guy. I know that. But you'd have to knock him out to get the win. And how likely is it that a guy who's never fought before could knock out the guy who beat Ali for the title? I don't care how shot he is. He's an Olympic gold medalist."

John laughed. "I know, I know. He's gonna kill me. But, ya know, what if?"

Here's where I made the most inexcusable mistake of my managerial career. I said, "If you can beat him, beat him. If he can't beat someone who's never fought before, he shouldn't be in the ring."

The bell rang, and I walked from the corner to the front row, where I sat with two associates. The fighters met near Spinks's corner and Leon extended his right glove in a brotherly tap, which John Carlo accepted and returned. For some reason, Leon repeated the gesture; it was as if he couldn't make the transition from bonhomie to fight mode. John discontinued the lovefest and stepped inside Spinks's overextended right hand to land a perfect left hook that dropped Leon straight back onto the canvas where his skull cracked full force, his body laying partially outside the ropes. I told my colleagues, "The fight's over," and moved back to the corner. From there I tried to signal the ref to stop the fight. Leon just beat the very slow count, but he was completely out of it, unable to offer even a token defense. The referee, as unprepared for what had happened as everyone else was, seemed not to quite believe what he'd seen, so let the fight go on. The crowd had set up a collective primal howl of supersonic volume—screaming for the kill, laughing and pointing into the ring, yelling that the fight was fixed, with some shrieking for the referee to stop it.

Fighters either have or don't have a killer instinct. There's nothing you can do to change it. It turned out that John Carlo had a natural killer instinct. He expertly positioned Leon onto the ropes across from his corner and unloaded with a series of hard—hard even by professional standards—left hooks that dropped Leon again. I was about a foot away, and was frantically trying to signal to the ref to stop the fight. I could see that Spinks's mouth was dripping a lot of blood; it was already covering his chin. At this point, a commissioner stepped onto the far apron of the ring, wildly waving his arms to get the referee's attention. He was ignored. A towel came sailing into the ring from Charles Hamm. Nothing. It took an endless additional fifteen seconds—and ten more solid punches—before the referee emerged from his stupor and stopped the fight. Leon, stiff-legged and bleeding profusely, tried to make it back to his corner. He stumbled and nearly fell. I got to the corner as he did. He was semi-conscious, not really aware of his surroundings. The crowd, now that the fight was over, had transitioned into party time, if a party can be said to have a vicious undertone. The noise was still deafening. Leon didn't seem to know to sit down. His mouthpiece was removed, and I could see that there was a disturbing amount of thick blood in his mouth. He would have already swallowed a lot of it. His eyes were glazed. He was blinking over and over again. He was an accident victim.

I couldn't shake the crowd's horrible reaction to the knockout. It was a hateful mixture of undisguised anger, inchoate but palpable glee, and gloating.

But here's boxing: by the time the official decision was announced in the ring, I was already John Carlo's manager. Dennis Rappaport and I had already staged a confrontation in front of the cameras between John and Melvin Foster. Business never sleeps.

Indian Summer

It was an uncharacteristically hot afternoon for DC in late October. An Indian summer, I guess. I was sitting in the coffee shop of the Courtyard

Marriott, directly across from the Convention Center, talking to someone I knew. The night before had been a fucked up one for a number of people, myself included. None of us had lost money directly, but what had happened would keep us from making money.

Leon came across the lobby to where we were sitting. He kept himself at a slight distance, making his presence known, but not interrupting.

I said to my acquaintance, "Have you met Leon?"

"No, but I'd like to."

I introduced the two men. They shook hands. Once Leon had been introduced, he felt freer to talk to me.

"Mr. Farrell, I want a rematch. I do better next time. You get me a rematch?"

"No, Leon. No rematch. I'm sorry."

It was uncomfortable. Nobody knew what to say.

Leon, who'd taken a seat after being introduced, got up and started to move away.

"Can I get some money for something to eat?"

"The promotion is picking up the tab for the hotel expenses," I said. "Don't you want to eat in the hotel?"

Leon looked uneasy.

"OK, no problem. How much do you need?"

"I don't know. Can I get five bucks?"

I handed Leon some money and we watched him go outside.

The Factotum

Are we gonna make a move? Or are we just gonna sit around playing fuck-fuck all day?
—Chris Gingrow

During his short life, which ended with his falling off a bridge in Bath, Maine, while doing roadwork, part-time boxer Chris Gingrow had done all kinds of mostly stupid shit.

He was a man not quite smart enough to figure out that, in the businesses he'd chosen, you couldn't be not quite smart enough.

And so the short life. And so the roadwork ending.

❖ ❖ ❖

I met Chris Gingrow on a hot August day in Old Orchard, Maine, the tawdry seaside honky-tonk where I'd spent my early childhood summers forty years before. Pat Petronelli and I were now quixotically promoting a fight card at the Old Orchard Beach Ballpark that would feature Stanley Wright, a six-foot-eleven black man with size eighteen shoes—each left footed—who'd grown up in Portland, twenty miles away.

We were trying to pawn Stanley off as both a colossus and a young man from the area, although he was neither. Our approach was foolish enough in itself. Dumber still: why did we think that anyone in this obdurately white state would give a fuck that some really tall black guy was throwing punches above the pitcher's mound of a mosquito-infested baseball diamond on a humid summer night?

In order to waste even more of our money, Pat and I decided it would be a good idea to buy some cheap TV time on the Old Orchard cable channel. We threw together a commercial that was as ineptly set up visually as it was empty-headed narratively, tossing it out to local hayseeds who shrewdly chose to ignore it.

We had painstakingly coached Wright to refer to himself as "The Power Drill"—a misleading nickname meant to emphasize his ferocity by equating it to the efficacy of Stanley tools, the preferred household hardware of do-it-yourselfers.

The commercial opened with Wright being tended to by a scantily clad blonde stripper who was—possibly by osmosis—understood to be his "valet," his "trainer," or his "manager." Any italicized word that could be used to induce a smirk of prurient connotation would have served. "Amanuensis," though not part of the working vocabulary of any member of the targeted audience, might even have produced lurid grins, sound effects, and various tongue and finger gestures.

As Leigh Ann Cyr doted over the oddly chilled-out giant, he seemingly *noticed* the camera for the first time, doing a mild double take as, in his mentholated drawl, he began the pitch.

"Yo, everybody. Stanley Wright here. Some of y'all know me as Big Stan."

Goodbye Power Drill.

"I'm going to be fighting this kid Chris Gringo next Saturday night at the ballpark. People sayin' he's supposed to be a dangerous dude, and how he got a right hand that might hurt me. So come on out and help me whip this big white boy's ass."

I thought, "Yeah, the state Militiamen will be lining up behind you for that one, Big Stan."

At this point Gingrow stomped onto the set. Wearing a plaid lumberjack get-up and toting an ax, he looked convincingly like a rugged woodsman, but *not* like a professional prizefighter. He slowly scanned Wright top to bottom, hefted his ax, paused briefly, then spoke his one written line.

"Timmm . . . berrr."

If Gingrow had been passable in his delivery, Leigh Ann was far less so in hers. Fissiparized by the combined effects of the rolling camera and her acting responsibilities, she took a few zombie steps to within a couple of feet of Chris, thrust out her flattened hand like a crossing guard holding back a group of overly eager schoolchildren, and in a waifish voice squeaked out her only line.

"Step off."

It was horrible—so horrible that it failed on every level. Nobody would want to see Stanley Wright as a fighter. Nobody would believe that Chris Gingrow *was* a fighter. And nobody would have enough prurient interest in Leigh Ann's admittedly seductive body to pay to see it anywhere but draped around a pole. Most important, nobody would decide that it might be worth a laugh to see these freaks in person.

The commercial had cleared the fence from being so bad it was good to being so bad it was bad.

A Short Time Later

Wright was being difficult; throwing temper tantrums and acting crazy. He'd gotten into a shouting match with me before we left Boston. He'd started an argument with Pat Petronelli over some foolishness about his trunks and robe. And he'd alienated Leigh Ann by exaggeratedly staring at her ass and yelling "Bam!" in a booming voice that drew the attention of passersby. Everybody needed a little break from Stanley Wright.

After the commercial, we all took a few steps away from him. Gingrow, who had nothing to do before fight time, decided to hang out with us. He fired up a cigarette. Wright, for once showing the quick reflexes of a professional athlete, pounced.

"Yo. Can I get me one of them smokes, bro?"

Gingrow himself was quick to spot and attach himself to people and situations that might benefit him. He knew I was bankrolling the card, was responsible for paying him, that I was somehow traveling with a nearly nude stripper, and that the main-event fighter he'd be facing in a few hours worked as my driver most of the time. Chris wanted to put himself on my side. He just didn't know how to do it, or what being on my side meant. Of course, it didn't have to be my side per se. Anyone who could advance his station in life would do.

Garment Bags and Suitcases

I'd made the tinhorn mistake of briefly losing custody of my fighter, assuming that my friends receiving him down in Miami Beach shared my interest in his continued well-being. They may in fact *have* had an interest in his well-being. The problem was that it was starting to look as if they might not have had much interest in mine.

The first sign of trouble came from Tony Petronelli, a reliable guy who I'd sent to work Martin Foster's corner as well as to serve as my eyes and ears during the trip. The answering-machine message from him was ominous.

"Charles, I don't like it down here. Something . . . something don't smell too good down here."

Shortly after that, I got a phone call from Chris. He sounded relaxed and cheerful—a trusted lieutenant whose work was going well and brought him satisfaction.

"I used up some of the expense money on things we needed. I thought you'd want us to impress these guys, so I bought some matching garment bags and suitcases for Martin and me. Now we don't look like a couple of hobos."

"What about Tony?"

"Nah, Tony wouldn't take one—says he's not gonna need it. He's only gonna be in and out anyway. Me and Martin can use them every time you send us someplace."

"Okay, what did they cost me?"

"We did good. I got everything for about six hundred bucks."

"Listen, I want to hear about Martin's opponent before I accept him. And I want Tony to get a look at him.

"I can get a look at him."

"Good. But have Tony get one too. And don't agree to anything until you've talked to me again."

Some time passed, and then Chris called again.

"Henry Grooms is having a hard time coming up with an opponent."

"What happened to the opponent Henry had lined up?"

"Looks like he got knocked out less than a month ago in AC. The commission won't pass him."

"Tell them to keep looking. I'll make some calls . . . see if I can find someone."

Soon after, I heard from Henry Grooms. He was using the burnished Arthur Prysock Lowenbrau commercial voice to bear bad news and sell me a bill of goods.

"Charles, I wanted to make this call to apologize to you personally. I take full responsibility for Martin not getting his fight tonight. I am deeply embarrassed. Please give me the opportunity to make things up to you."

What did it mean? The Tampa-based Grooms was connected in Miami, a fight town with a surplus of overfed Cuban and freshly-out-of-prison black heavyweight opponents who were all looking for work. He managed to keep his own heavyweight—the small, substandard China Smith—busy and winning. Getting an opponent for Foster would have been child's play for Henry Grooms.

The logical explanation was that Grooms had used my not personally flying down with Martin as a chance to hijack a white heavyweight with a great record. It made sense. It was actually a smart move.

If it was true, it meant two things: Martin Foster hadn't fallen for whatever Grooms's pitch was, and, if he knew what was happening, Chris Gingrow hadn't told me about it. Foster hadn't either, but I was used to fighters looking out for themselves, so took no offense.

Once Foster, Tony Petronelli, and Gingrow got back to Boston, Chris couldn't wait to tell me about Grooms's perfidy. He seemed unable to comprehend that it was an abnegation of responsibility to wait until he'd returned to town empty-handed before letting me know.

This was the first time I started to think of Chris in terms of pathological or even sociopathic behavior. The disconnect that produced such a seemingly clear conscience in his now throwing Henry Grooms under the bus made me wonder. Maybe he really didn't see that, although the business of boxing is a game with almost no rules, it doesn't mean that there aren't consequences for shifting sides as opportunities arise or recede. If you show yourself to be an untrustworthy motherfucker, people will still do business with you, but they won't forget what you've done, and it's just a matter of time until they let you know it.

The One Fighter Floyd Patterson Wouldn't Train

Although he'd been an immensely popular former heavyweight champion, Floyd Patterson didn't have much to do to pass the time. He had come down a long road to dementia despite looking wonderful and speaking clearly. He had none of the physical symptoms common to fighters with the illness. You had to know him to understand how bad his condition was.

Still, at sixty-two, he maintained the training routine he had used during his time as champion, and still moved faster and punched harder than any of the heavyweights he was training. He wanted to work with fighters and, because he was a charitable man by nature, found ways to see championship-level qualities in nearly every one of them.

Talking about the inept Martin Foster, he boldly opined, "I am certain he will become the heavyweight champion of the world." And then, Floyd being Floyd—inherently conflicted and modest—added, "Or at least he'll become a top contender."

During the time I knew him, the only fighter who Floyd Patterson couldn't find a way to talk himself into wanting to train was Chris Gingrow. Because Chris frequently drove me to Floyd's place, Floyd had come to know him fairly well and was fond of him. But there were no qualities that he could invent that would allow him to see Chris as a future champion, a definite top contender, a tough journeyman, or even a decent sparring partner.

"That fellow who brings you here, the one who spars with the other guy, the one I'm training, he really shouldn't be boxing at all. He may wind up getting killed."

Floyd was temperamentally methodical and cautious. Things had to be outlined and enacted systematically, one step at a time. Not having known him earlier in his life, I could never figure out if this was an inherent part of his nature or a strategy that he'd developed to help him deal with his encroaching dementia.

Chris did a funny impression of Floyd's driving directions. He wouldn't alter his voice—the heavy Maine accent remained intact—but still managed to capture Floyd's substance and rhythm.

"Just after you get to Exit 18 for New Paltz, there's a toll booth. Slow down, then stop your car. Pay the toll."

Hearing Chris imitating him, Floyd would become giggly.

"If there's a tollbooth collector, pay him. Wait for change, if you have any coming. Count it before you leave. If you're using the machine, carefully toss your coins into the bin. If you miss, put your car in park, get out of the car and put the correct change in. When the light turns green, go."

Floyd laughed, "I didn't say that. But you will have to stop and pay the toll."

It's Fun Right Up Until Everything Stops

Being around gangsters—sharing in illegal operations, facilitating their execution—can seem like a lot of fun to someone of a certain temperament.

Contemporary Mafioso, foolish, vain men who model themselves after movie and TV gangsters, contribute to the sense that everyone involved is living some cinematic variation of the Good Life. Even what violence takes place—almost always threatened violence and tough talk—is stylistically molded after *Goodfellas* and *The Sopranos*.

When something goes wrong for real, anyone whose life will be affected by the fuckup runs the risk of missing where the shift from the imaginary to the real took place. Chris Gingrow was still having a ball at the time some people decided it was a mistake to keep him around.

You get used to good things. It doesn't take long. For Chris, focused on finding someone with a winning hand, the adjustment was instantaneous. He knew how to effortlessly insinuate himself into a crew. He could find the little jobs that weren't being done—not essential jobs necessarily, but factotum gigs geared to make those running the show feel special and important. He didn't toady. That would have been too jarring; it would have made his inclusion too obvious. It was more a matter of how he, with a few well-chosen blandishments, floated inside the circle.

Chris didn't grow soft through increased familiarity with comforts. He kept his energy, continued doing what was asked of him with enthusiasm and good cheer. He didn't turn down any job, regardless of its legality. Once he was in, he was in. He understood and enjoyed that he was occasionally called on to do dark work.

But not the darkest. Nobody was telling him to kill anyone. These people had specialists for that.

License

For some reason I never understood, Chris decided to precipitously lose over thirty pounds to come into his fight with Sulaiman Muhammad as a cruiserweight. It was a meaningless four-round fight that would pay only slightly more—$800—than Chris generally got for an opening bout, and considerably less than what he got for taking a dive in matches where no weight loss was required.

Boxrec.com lists his fight with Sulaiman Muhammad fight as occurring in Kingston, New York, but it actually took place somewhere else in New York. I had my own fighter co-headlining on the Kingston card that night but had spent the previous day at the Boxing Commission offices on William Street in Lower Manhattan with Gingrow. I was there to renew my New York manager's license. Chris was getting the routine physical required to obtain a boxer's license. My business was completed within minutes, so I walked Gingrow upstairs to his physical. It turned out to be a very strange half hour.

No doctor was present but a stylish Latina in her late forties wanted us to understand that she was "a medical woman" entrusted by the Commission to give the fighters their exams.

"Are you both here for your physicals?"

Chris and I looked at each other. I was forty-two years old and had never fought in my life.

Bright sunshine poured in from the overhead windows at the tops of the fourteen-foot-high dark wood walls. It looked like an authentic place of business. The world seemed solid enough.

"No, just the big guy here."

"Are you sure?"

Chris and I looked at each other again.

"Completely sure."

She brought Gingrow into another room. They were gone for about fifteen minutes, during which time I drank in the quality of light in the room. When they emerged, the Commission official wore a severe expression.

"He's not in good enough shape to be a boxer. I'm going to let him take his fight because he has traveled a long way for it, but I shouldn't pass him."

She filled out some forms, then send Chris off to the Commission office downstairs.

She next turned her attention to me, narrowing her eyes. I was unable to read her expression.

"Come here, I want to show you something," she said.

I moved next to her.

She patted her upper thigh. "Here," she said, "feel this."

I must have looked dubious.

"It's okay. I'm a medical woman. Feel how firm my legs are. I keep in good condition. I exercise religiously."

I tentatively squeezed her thigh.

"No, harder. You'll see. There's nothing wrong with this. I'm a medical woman. It's perfectly professional. You will find no excess skin."

Once I'd felt her thigh, she placed my hand on her stomach.

"Feel my abdomen. It's okay, even the lower part. This is not an impropriety. One hundred sit-ups every day. Feel how firm? That's how your abdomen should feel if you're in good condition. Now you. This is a professional medical procedure. It is in no way improper. You must trust me."

The woman felt all around my stomach, poking and prodding. "Very good. Your abdomen is in perfect condition. Not like the man who came in with you. His abdomen was soft."

Just as I was trying to decide whether I'd lose my manager's license if I got caught fucking an assigned official in the Boxing Commission's examining room, Chris came back, grinning like a fool because he was now a licensed boxer in New York State.

A Bad Day at the Office

I wasn't at the gym the day that Chris Gingrow sparred with Josh Imadiyi. I heard about it when Pat Petronelli called me from the hospital.

"Oh, the poor thing," he began. It struck me as an oddly feminine expression—an old timey phrase that my grandmother Betty used to use. It was always applied to children, animals, or the retarded—a term for naïfs.

'There was nobody to spar with Josh, and the kid . . . Gringows . . . that Gringows kid who Stanley fought up in Maine there wanted to get in with him. I shouldn't have let him spar. Or I should have stepped in when Josh broke his nose."

"Josh broke Chris's nose?"

"Yes. It wasn't a bad break, but I shouldn't have let it go on. The kid insisted."

"So now he's in the hospital with a broken nose."

"No. Well, yes. But also with a broken jaw."

"Josh broke his jaw when he broke his nose?"

"No. Later. After Gringows got back in the ring. He insisted. He absolutely insisted."

"Jesus, Pat."

"I know. It's a terrible thing. The kid's gonna be okay. I'm just waiting for the doctor to release him. I don't think they're gonna need to keep him overnight."

"Fuck, this isn't good."

"No, it's not good. I don't know what I was thinking. You know, Josh never gets any work. I just wanted to get him a little work."

Mother and Child

Near the end, Chris found himself shuttled into new circumstances. Jane, his on-again, off-again, occasional live-in girlfriend, gave birth to a daughter, and the trajectory of Chris's life started to shift. It seemed to be something he enjoyed, but it arrived too late, after whatever else that was going to happen to him had already been set in motion.

Jane was better than Chris in every possible way: solid, hardworking, straight-thinking, responsible, with the Down East humorless humor of a native-born Mainer. She saw what was good in Chris—he had a gentle nature, was funny and accommodating, and was semi-willing to work fairly hard. She wasn't blind to his faults either. She knew that if they stayed together—which was what she wanted—she'd be trading down.

But it could work; Jane could picture it. She was the stronger of the two, and Chris was by nature a follower—if one who occasionally had his own ideas—so she'd be able to push it through. She'd see that he got a job at the Bath Iron Works—steady employment with fair wages and good benefits—that would tire him just enough to keep him out of serious trouble. She'd make sure that dinner would be ready when he came home at 6:00. He had it in him to be a good father to their kid. Chris could put all this foolish boxing shit behind him. She knew his professional record, where the proof was in the numbers. He wasn't a boxer and would never be one; he'd lost every one of his fights except the one to Lou Turchiarelli. And it was long past time to have to listen to him brag about that victory.

Chris Gingrow wasn't violent by nature. If anything, he seemed just the opposite—both easygoing and accommodating. His degree of equanimity contributed to my ever-increasing suspicion that he might be a sociopath. If there was money or a bump up in his job description on the line, there was nothing too brutal for Chris to do to someone. He would laughingly quote the AC/DC title "Dirty Deeds Done Dirt Cheap" as his personal anthem. Having watched him box dozens of times, I still found it hard to imagine him as a professional prizefighter, but it was easy to picture him smilingly walking straight up to a stranger and smashing him across the face with a two-by-four or sneaking up behind someone to stave in their skull with a crowbar.

For much of the time I made my living in boxing, I kept all of my answering-machine messages. I knew that I might wind up in trouble someday and thought that the messages might provide some measure of protection, or at least give whoever listened to them some clear indication of who had done me harm.

One of those messages is from Chris.

"Looks like I can't come down to do it today. I got to see my probation officer. So it's gonna be next week before we can make a move."

What were we going to make a move on? Did the move get made?

Final Record

Boxrec.com lists Chris Gingrow's record as 1-7, with all fights ending in knockouts. He was actually 1-8.

He never saw the third round of a fight, and after his third fight never again saw the second.

Some of the fights he lost by first-round knockout I know to have been fixed. In hindsight, I realize that the Stanley Wright fight—where he pulled what I now recognize as a characteristic gesture of exaggeratedly shaking his head as if to clear it of cobwebs after arising from a knockdown—was one too. His flying down to Miami Beach to get taken out by Duane van de Merwe—again in the first round—may have been another.

The Factotum's Last Stand

There was an incident in the dressing room before the factotum Chris Gingrow's last fight on June 22, 1996. Chris's opponent, Charles Livingston, was 11-0—all of his wins coming by knockout. Chris, with a listed record of 1-6, was by far Livingston's best opponent to date, and one of only three who had actually won a fight. The complete won-lost record of Livingston's opponents was 3-30. Only Hector Mercedes had ever gone the distance in a fight.

It may be overly facile to describe an unnaturally muscled, excessively rubicund man as looking like a side of beef, but Charles Livingston looked like a boiled side of beef. He wore his hair in the Parris Island meringue-placed-on–top-of-the-head fashion common to Caucasian muscleheads of the period. While those white fans who were educated on boxing wisdom through the Rocky movies interpreted the look as that of a surefire future heavyweight champion, boxing people and anyone with sense knew they were looking at someone who'd be unable to throw a real punch if his life depended on it.

Chuck was ambitious, friendly, and well-spoken. He was handsome, if a boiled side of beef could be said to be handsome. Vin Vecchione was expertly moving him toward a million-dollar payday fight that Livingston would lose quickly. This financial bonanza would be followed by six-figure purses of ever diminishing amounts for fights he would also lose, interspersed with cheap wins to offset the losses. Eventually his record would be sufficiently compromised that the string would be played out and his career would be over.

Chuck Livingston had a head cold that Saturday. He'd always been afraid of fighting, but he was particularly worried that night because he felt so under the weather. Peter McNeeley had told him that Gingrow had a dangerous right hand, so Livingston came in to politely ask Chris not to hit him hard.

Chris and I were still laughing about this when Massachusetts boxing commissioner Bill Pender entered the dressing room.

Pender, the brother of former middleweight champion Paul Pender—who through the machinations of canny promoter Subway Sam Silverman had pickpocketed the title from Ray Robinson at the Boston Garden—was detested by the local boxing community. As clumsy as his brother was light-footed, this ungainly thug was envious of—and so hated—fighters. In particular, Bill Pender hated black fighters. He hated them enough so that he was later found by a jury to be guilty of discriminatory acts in contributing to the unjust cancellation of a card put together by Doug Pendarvis that heavily featured black fighters. Pender was ordered to pay a fine and compensatory damages to Pendarvis—an unsuccessful but hardworking man who, summoning up the fraternal twins Humility and Hubris, referred to himself as Don King Junior.

The first thing Pender did was brush imaginary lint off his pants, leaning forward to make sure that we saw the holstered gun stashed inside his sports jacket. Since Chris and I were the only people in the room with him, this penny-ante gesture was meant to intimidate us. It didn't. We had both had guns pulled on us by better men than Bill Pender.

He placed himself closer to Gingrow than he needed to be. "My name is William Pender. I'm the Boxing Commission in Massachusetts. I've heard about you. So I'm warning you now—it came out 'wahnning you now'—you better make a real effort in there or I'm gonna have your license lifted."

I'm not sure why I got angry, since it wasn't my business. Because my fighters had all moved past the Massachusetts circuit, there wasn't much Pender could do to me other than shoot me. I'd heard he was an officer in the State Highway Patrol, but I doubted that anyone there liked him any better than those who knew him from boxing. Imprudently, I spoke up.

"Is there something wrong with you?"

He turned his attention to me.

"Are you talking to me?"

"You're the commissioner, and you sanction a fight between an 11-0 guy who's knocked out everyone he's fought and a guy who is 1-6 and has been knocked out in every loss. And you're expecting the 1-6 guy to be competitive with the 11-0 guy? You're expecting this guy here to go to war for $500? Are you out of your mind?"

"Are you his manager?"

"You know goddamned well I'm not his manager. You know exactly who I am. Now answer my question."

"This has got nothing to do with you."

"It does now. You're saying that if Chris doesn't get out of the first round, you're going to turn it into a problem? You'd okay this kind of bullshit fight, but would start some trouble when it doesn't turn out to be an even matchup? You've got a lot of fucking nerve."

I don't know what I was thinking. I made it a point to never put myself into the middle of things that had nothing to do with me. But I liked Chris Gingrow and I disliked Bill Pender. More important, I sensed that Bill Pender was a bully—someone who could be backed down.

Gingrow told him, "I'm going to knock Livingston out, Mr. Pender. If the fight doesn't go into the second round, it's because I got him in the first."

This gave Pender his out.

"You're gonna do your best? You're gonna give an honest effort?"

"I'm going to win this fight."

"Because I'm gonna be watching you."

"Yeah," I said, "and I'm going to be watching you, and you're going to be watching me, and we're all going to be watching each other. Now are you going to let this guy get ready for his fight?"

Pender left, and Chris started to laugh.

He said, "Are you gonna give an honest effort?"

"Don't you want to let it go a couple of rounds to keep Pender off your back?"

"*Shit*, no. Fuck Pender. I'm gonna let Chuck knock me out in the first minute. Poor kid has a cold."

The Conceit That Ended Things

I wonder what brave and futile gene caused him to march so resolutely to his own end.

If you're a fucking Johnny-on-the-spot, automatically in place to do with a sunny disposition any runaround function that comes up, the chances are that people will want to have you around. If you're a little bit dumb, ambitious in a limited way, and given to wishful thinking, you're going to mistake this enjoyment of your presence for a vote of trust.

A Kid from the Neighborhood

I didn't know the voice on the other end of the line, but his name was instantly recognizable. It would have been to anyone who knew anything about the Winter Hill Gang because the caller was at the top of its food chain. His voice was quiet and surprisingly mellifluous, with only a slight Boston accent. It was a pleasant, friendly speaking voice. If not for his reputation, no one hearing him would have thought they had anything to fear.

Having done business with area Mobsters, I would have known about him anyway, but I also owned a four-family rental property on Broadway on Winter Hill in Somerville. Maybe we had neighborhood issues in common.

"Charles, I've been asked to call you to find out if you'd consider managing a fighter our friends have a lot of interest in. A kid from the neighborhood. Do you know Frankie DiOrio?"

"Very well. Frankie's a good kid. He lives on Partridge Street. I own a four-family right on that corner."

"Is that so? Small world. What's your opinion of him as a fighter?"

"He's good. Very good."

"Can he be a world champion?"

"That's a tough question to answer. *Can* he be? With the right connections, with some help? With money behind him? Or based solely on his ability?"

"Those are good questions. I can find out how they want this handled. If we want him moved along, can you help with that?"

"Yes, I can help with that."

"Good. For the moment, let me ask if he can make it just based on his ability."

"No."

"You're positive."

"One hundred percent positive. He's a fine local fighter who can beat anyone around here. That's as far as his talent will take him. I assume you want the truth."

"Yes, I want the truth. I appreciate your honesty. Okay, Charles, I'll take this to my people. You may hear from me again on this, but probably not."

"Thanks for thinking of me. I appreciate it."

"Thank you for taking my call."

I can't mention the caller's name, but if you do a little homework, you can figure it out. Although I hadn't met him, our paths had crossed indirectly many years earlier under much different circumstances in an incident mentioned in a previous section.

I never heard back from him. To be honest, I'm glad I didn't.

Santo Domingo and the Big Bet

I lost a big bet once—much bigger than I could afford. I'll never know whether I lost it legitimately or if I was scammed as I'd scammed others. If the sting and privation from the loss are now distant memories, it's not lost on me that my current debt is very close to what I would have made from winning that bet.

If I'd won it you wouldn't be reading this now. The payoff of $1,250,000 would have sent me into seclusion and lifelong retirement in the Caribbean.

The bet was presented third-hand through Al Braverman—whom I considered a most reliable source. Al had heard about it from someone he trusted, who had been offered it by someone *he* trusted. Nowadays it's not the kind of bet I'd take. I was forty then, still fairly young, ambitious, and reckless.

Braverman called to ask me who I thought would win the upcoming WBA middleweight title bout between Steve Collins and Reggie Johnson.

"It's a very even fight. It'll go the distance. Politics being what they are, Collins will probably get the decision. There are big fights to be made for him in Europe."

"But a pick-'em fight? You're sure?"

"Yes. Too close to call. 6-5, no way more than 7-5."

"What would you say if I told you I could get you something like 3-1 on Collins?"

"I'd ask you if you knew anything about the fight that I didn't know."

"Right. That's the right question. And I don't. Nobody gives a shit about either guy. But something just came over the transom—guy looking to make that bet. Friend of a friend situation."

"You don't know him?"

"No, not directly. His friend who's my friend is with us, though."

"Then maybe I'm interested."

"It's going to have to be a big bet, though. This guy's down in the Caymans or some shit, and he's not interested in anything small."

"Find out for me, Al. If it's something I can swing, I'll take the bet."

It turned out to be the outermost edge of what I could swing. I had the money without needing to borrow, but losing would wipe me out completely.

In the '80s and '90s, there was a lot of weird shit going on in Santo Domingo. It was a short jump to Haiti where even more weird shit was going on—although nothing I had anything to do with—but the Dominican Republic had plenty of action in its own right.

The guy making the bet knew people in Santo Domingo and, as luck would have it, I knew a couple of the same people. One of them was a gangster who owned a restaurant where deals were occasionally made. It was set up for me to meet the bettor's two couriers in a private back room of the restaurant where we could watch the fight. We'd have our suitcases full of money. I would be bringing my own courier.

I knew an American realtor in Samaná whose father was building resorts and marinas in the area. The realtor was a lightweight who thought it was a big deal to marry a Dominican teenager at forty, but I'd spent a couple of afternoons with the father, who'd impressed me as someone with his finger on the pulse of everything happening on his part of the island.

I asked the old man who you'd have to know to get in and out of the country while carrying a lot of money in suitcases.

"Coming in from the States?"

"The States or Puerto Rico."

"If you can, make it Puerto Rico. Fly in under the radar. People do it all the time. I can smooth things for you here in Samaná. That'll cost you a little bit with a few of the locals. When are you coming in? Where do you need to be?"

"A couple of weeks from now, winding up in Santo Domingo. But I've got guys who'll meet me wherever. They can take me the rest of the way."

I had to figure out how to get a private plane to fly my bodyguard and me onto the landing spot outside of Samaná. It did seem easier to take off from Puerto Rico than the States. I had an acquaintance who ran the operation of a large hotel in San Juan that put on boxing shows. The hotel flew high rollers in for them.

Braverman had introduced us, so I called him.

"On this bet, I was thinking of asking Pantalones for a favor. I'm going to need to fly into the Dominican Republic."

"Yeah, I know Pants."

"I know you know Pants. You introduced me to Pants."

"I introduced you to Pants? Pants checks out. He's reliable. I don't know if he can help you, but you can talk to him."

Pants could, and did, help. There was a scorched cane field just outside of Mayagüez that could be used. When the pilot saw the size of my bodyguard, he wasn't sure whether his two-seater could handle all our weight. The cockpit was crowded and uncomfortable, the trip itself was bumpier and longer than expected and we flew much lower than I thought we would, but our pilot put us down right in the middle of the second scorched cane field.

By this point at least a dozen people knew most of what was going on. That was too many, but there was nothing to be done. My concerns mostly centered around the politicos in Samaná who had to okay my arrival and whoever was being dispatched to turn over or collect the betting money.

I tallied up what would protect me from being hijacked. The civic leaders in Samaná were held in check by their ongoing accessibility. They weren't going anywhere. If they robbed me or shook me down, my friends knew where to find them.

The locals would be afraid to fuck with the powerful American developer who called the shots on that part of the island.

The couriers represented the other bettor, who had his own reputation to maintain and was answerable to the gangster who owned the restaurant where our privacy and safety had been guaranteed. The bettor would also be trackable if there were complications.

I'd brought a giant with me to carry the money and to act as my bodyguard. He was a dangerous guy, but slow to pick up signals. I would have been happier with someone more alert, but I was stuck.

My drivers in Samaná were longtime friends who had done work for me before. They were tough, savvy characters who could both be trusted. The two of them had been waiting in the cane field all day. Living on Caribbean Time, it hadn't bothered them. They laughed when they saw who I'd brought to carry the money.

"Jesus Christ! How did you ever get into the plane?"

"It wasn't no picnic, brother. Believe me."

"How tall are you? Eight feet?"

"About seven."

"I hope the car don't collapse. You are one big boy, bruto."

We made the trip across the island to Santo Domingo and got to the restaurant. There's a small but vibrant crosscurrent of gangsters who float between New York, Miami, San Juan, and Santo Domingo, so a lot of people know each other vaguely. My drivers knew the restaurant owner, who knew the guy I was betting against, who knew the guy who knew Al, who knew Pants, who knew my driver. The guys who brought us both came into the restaurant to say hello to the owner, which amplified the message that I was being looked after down here.

I'd been told that I would recognize the two couriers. That turned out to be true. Anyone would have recognized them anywhere, doing anything. If you were to walk into a place looking for two guys who you were told you'd know on sight, these would always be the two guys. The guys who'd be sent to take care of things.

They were Samoan or Fijian or Tongan. Probably Samoan, but I wasn't going to ask. One looked to be in his early forties, the other in his late twenties, but they were almost identical otherwise: both a shade over six feet, three hundred-ish pounds, wearing dark glasses, gray slacks, white open-neck untucked shirts. No-Fucking-Around uniforms. They were borderline pleasant but opaque. Their stoic competence drove home how ill-equipped my own bodyguard was.

We were given privacy in a back room where we could watch the fight. There was the requisite showing of the money, with me faking indifference in contrast to the Samoans' genuine impassivity. My bodyguard made no attempt to curb his excitement. "This is a *shitload* of money, dude," he boomed. His manic burst of enthusiasm brought him three blanks stares. At this level of operation, any expression of unchecked emotion came across as being slightly unhinged.

I was sure we'd see a good, evenly contested fight, and we did. Given that a world title was at stake, maybe the fighters displayed more urgency than they might have otherwise. Collins faded a little at the end, but, from my seat in the Self-Interest Section, it looked like a close win for him. I counted on boxing politics to nudge him over the finish line to the title, sensibly accomplishing what he might not have quite done himself.

The Samoans watched the fight with full concentration but no apparent interest, remaining silent throughout the broadcast. My bodyguard, apparently forgetting what he'd been brought there to do, left the room a couple of times to get free cokes from the bar. I would have preferred that he not do that, but to show alarm was to show weakness. When he asked if he could get me anything, I just shook my head. At least he knew not to drink anything alcoholic.

Waiting for the fight's decision turned out to not be the worst heart-stopping episode I've had, but it was a bad one. The feeling is like being suddenly suspended, knowing that everything is about to be different. It's too late to take back whatever is going to happen, and the most reliable thing you've got—your own heartbeat—has just bailed out on you.

Ed Derian's trademark was to repeat fighters' names twice when introducing them and again when announcing the bout's winner. He spared me this time, as if deciding that it was best to rip off the band-aid quickly. He let me—and presumably others—hear the life-fucking news: "The brand-new middleweight champion of the world, 'Sweet' Reggie Johnson!"

Good news. I wasn't going to have to figure out how to take my winnings from the Samoans if they decided not to cough them up. There would be no problem with the weight of their suitcases. Or mine.

Was it freezing cold in the room? I wouldn't be retiring to the Caribbean after all. Back in the States, I'd have to go back to hustling in order to pay my bills. Life would return to being semi-dangerous and semi-hard.

The older Samoan gripped my shoulder, looking me in the eyes. "Sorry," he said. "That's a tough loss."

An Alternate Interpretation of What Happened with Johnson vs. Collins

Seen at its simplest, my losing $420,000 in Santo Domingo was a case of having guessed wrong in a fight between two evenly matched combatants, where the scorecards reflected just how little there was to choose between them.

For a long time, that's what I believed had happened. I don't believe it anymore. I think I was one of ten or twelve suckers who were the victims of an ingeniously clever scam. The tip-off—and the thing that should have caused me to back out, but was the lure that brought me in—was the nearly 3-1 odds for a fight that any expert would have known was too close to call.

If the bettor on the other end had the available decoy cash to pull it off, finding ten or twelve patsies to take the bait would have brought him between four and five million dollars in winnings.

With non-punchers, neither of whom has ever been knocked out, in order to get the result you want in a close fight, you only have to buy two of the judges. I had done it many times. It doesn't require a big cash outlay.

You pick fighters who are not really connected—fighters who, as Al Braverman put it, nobody gives a shit about—in a fight without major consequences, being staged by a minor promoter. Nobody is ever going to come after you. It's a nearly perfect setup for success.

Along with my doubts about the legitimacy of the bet came a more troubling corollary question. Was Al Braverman, my closest friend in the fight business—a man who soon would save my life—in on it? Did someone offer to let him "take what you think is right?"

Al Braverman

I met Al Braverman not long after the first time he called me.

"I'm starting to hear things about you."

"Good things?"

"Good things. Enough of them so I thought it was time to introduce myself."

I'd been hearing things about Al Braverman for years. Mostly bad things, but said by the kind of people who made me sure that Braverman was someone I wanted to know.

Al had once been a very large man. Age had turned him into a small man who still seemed like a very large man. In 1941 he'd had three professional fights in three months in New Jersey and New York as a heavyweight and won them all. His third fight took place at Saint Nick's arena on the night that Billy Graham, one of the great New York fighters, turned pro.

Over the years, he'd managed and trained hundreds of fighters, some of them champions, and one of whom—Frankie DePaula—had been murdered in a Mob hit. Al was nearly the last of a certain breed—a very hard man who had principles and loyalty; a wiseguy from a time when being a wiseguy wasn't a pejorative term. He'd been in the boxing game long enough to have been business partners with Jack "Doc" Kearns, who'd been the manager of Jack Dempsey and Mickey Walker.

"Doc would place the cash receipts from our night's fights onto the table, fan out the bills, and tell me to 'take what you think is right.' We called our promotion 'Palaver Productions.' You know what that means? A bunch of bullshit."

"I know what palaver means, Al."

"I forgot who I was talking to. I'm used to dealing with riffraff."

He was a major player in the business—Don King's director of boxing and the boxing IQ behind King's operation. His bona fides may have surpassed anyone else's who still made a living in the game.

I've met five or six truly fearless people in my life. Al was one of them. And no one was tougher.

Al Explains the Sonny Liston Fixes

How fearless? How tough? Al told me that Frankie Carbo needed someone to stick close to Sonny Liston to keep him in line during the two Ali fixes. Al Braverman was the one he chose for the job. If you watch video footage of Liston leading up to the return match in Lewiston, you will see Al in the shots, directing the interaction between Sonny and the press.

Al agreed with me that Sonny Liston was the greatest heavyweight who ever lived—a major statement from a heavyweight coming up during the Joe Louis era. He thought a lot of Muhammad Ali too, but was confident that Liston would have handled him if their fights had been on the level. He asserted what I'd always suspected: Sonny Liston had taken dives in both his fights with Muhammad Ali.

About Sonny Liston and Boxing 101

Although it is widely accepted that the second Muhammad Ali–Sonny Liston was a fixed fight, their first is still thought by most people to have been genuine.

It wasn't. The real fix—the one that mattered—took place in Miami. Lewiston was just scooping up the stray chips off the table and going home.

The first fight gave Frankie Carbo and cohorts their big score while solving the problem of what to do with Sonny Liston. And it was the fight that laid the first brick to the foundation of Ali's hagiography.

Frankie Carbo and Chris Dundee were genuine fight guys, capable of and committed to staging entertaining bouts. Running shows weekly at the Miami Auditorium, Dundee couldn't afford to displease paying customers. But Carbo and Dundee also had a long and prosperous history fixing fights together, including ones with all-time greats like Willie Pep, Ike Williams, Kid Gavilan, and Harold Johnson.

Until about fifty years ago fixed fights bore little resemblance to the clumsy pantomimes we see today. Veterans could convincingly carry opponents, often engaging in a lucrative series, exchanging wins back and forth in alternating hometowns to build up the gate for a rubber match held in a large venue.

For Ali–Liston, Miami worked as a locale. Everybody made money in Miami, so there'd never been much Commission oversight.

Into the mix went Angelo Dundee, who'd made his way up the ranks after a lengthy apprenticeship with Al Silvani and Whitey Bimstein. Dundee had worked many corners for Mob-controlled fighters, and could be dispatched as insurance to serve as Ali's trainer.

Why sacrifice the single most prestigious prize in sports? Wouldn't the heavyweight champion of the world—during an era where there was only one champion, known by men, women, and children alike—earn enormous purses for his title defenses? No. Not if he was Sonny Liston, who entered the title picture already dead in the market. He had been too successful in his assault on the title, decimating every significant contender in the division. It was widely believed that no one had a chance against him. To make matters worse, people didn't like Sonny. His holding the title for a decade wouldn't have collectively brought in the money that throwing the Ali fight did in twenty-five minutes, with no taxes to pay on the winnings. In the Miami fix, those who knew to bet on the untested newcomer collected 8-1.

It was free money, but not won without strategizing. In order to maximize the payoff, specific conditions had to be set up in advance.

Liston not only had to lose; he had to lose ambiguously enough to allow the public's realistic expectation that he would win the next time.

To do that, his withdrawal in the first fight had to come from an injury, not from a perceivable difference in the abilities of the two men. It required that the scorecards be virtually even when Liston pulled out. They were: 58-56 Liston, 59-56 Ali, and 57-57 at the end of six rounds. Since Liston had done nothing to try to win—and had to work hard in the fifth round to keep from knocking Ali out—it is clear that the judges and referee had been instructed on how to score the fight.

Those who don't believe the fight was fixed often point to the fifth round to dispel the notion that it was. Why would Liston's corner put a caustic substance on their fighter's gloves to blind Ali if Sonny intended to lose?

What happened after the fourth round is a red herring. Liston's cornermen would have looked suspicious if they hadn't tended in the traditional way to the cut and swelling that had shown up under their fighter's eye. Liniment used on cuts inadvertently gets on fighters' gloves, and occasionally winds up in opponents' eyes. Fighters deal with it without too much difficulty. The eyes tear and the substance is washed out.

But as he walked back to his corner at the end of the fourth round with his eyes burning, Ali, a yokel fast learning the ways of the world, paranoid about the competing factions whispering in his ear and not knowing who to trust, panicked, convinced that a plot was afoot. He wanted to stop fighting.

Angelo Dundee knew that Liston was set to quit in a round or so. All he had to do was get Ali off his stool and push him back into the ring at the start of the fifth round.

Sonny knew how to do the rest. He made a show of going after Ali, but looped his punches, missing some and pushing others. One of the great finishers in boxing history, Liston idled, waiting things out until Ali's eyes cleared so that he could get back to the business of losing his heavyweight title.

I know about the Ali–Liston fixes because reputable people who were involved, people who knew Liston well, and someone who fought both men twice told me things about them.

Al Braverman, who was directly involved with the fixes, gave me the fight details. For me, he's the Rosetta Stone. Two of Liston's St. Louis cronies, one a sometime sparring partner named Charles Hamm, the other a great fighter himself, Adolph Pruitt, said that Liston had told them he threw the fights. Johnny Tocco, the legendary Las Vegas gym owner and boxing sage, told me that Liston had said the same to him. And Floyd Patterson confided, "Clay couldn't punch at all. He had no power. And Sonny Liston took a hell of a punch. I don't know about the first fight, but I'm sure that Sonny took a dive in the second."

If Liston had beaten Ali, Ali couldn't have become Ali. He could still have become champion eventually, but the defining early image of who Ali is—the beautiful and untouchable youth, destined for immortality—would not exist. That would have changed boxing history and, more importantly, culture—not just US culture—as a whole. Ali's losing to Liston would have reconfigured the world as it is today.

There are a lot of emotional, historic, cultural, and iconographic reasons for not wanting to believe the truth about the first Ali–Liston fight. I've litigated the case more times than I ever intended to. It's a fool's errand. People's minds won't be changed.

This never gets mentioned, but Liston's last fight was a knockout win over Chuck Wepner—Al Braverman's fighter. Nobody would have known better than Al what Liston would have done to Wepner in a real fight.

Why did Al Braverman take the fight for Wepner? He took it because it had been fixed for Wepner to win. The problem was that Liston—never a very convincing dive artist—was unable to find a way to lose.

Liston's win over Wepner was a more serious transgression than was generally understood. Half a year after the fight he was murdered in his Las Vegas home for fucking up people's plans and costing them a lot of money.

Al Braverman owned an antique shop on the ground floor of a building on East 69th, a quiet, tree-lined street. He and his wife Renee lived one floor up.

One day, talking about Liston with Al in his office, he stepped out briefly and came back with a warm-up jacket.

"Here," he said. "Throw this in your kick."

Stitched on the upper-left-hand corner were the letters L-I-S-T-O-N.

"This is real?"

"That is real."

"I don't know what to say."

"Don't say anything. It's not like Sonny's going to come back to wear the fucking thing."

Al could get my fighters rated in the IBF just by making a phone call to Robert Lee.

"Bobby," he'd say, "I'm going to put Charles on. He's got three names for you. You can work out where they should go."

I never knew whether I was talking to Robert Lee Senior or Junior. But my guys' names would be in the next ratings. Fernely Feliz got rated after his third pro fight.

Even if he no longer kept his ear to the ground about up-and-coming fighters—he relied on me and a few others to keep him informed—Braverman had extraordinary instincts for assessing talent.

I brought a videotape of Fernely Feliz's first pro fight to New York, sure that Al would sign him with DKP right away. Feliz seemed like a can't-miss prospect, already exhibiting the slick, unhurried moves of an experienced professional. Fernely was good-looking and spoke fluent English, so it would have taken very little to develop him into an enormous gate attraction. With Don King promoting him, he would become the first Hispanic heavyweight champion.

Al popped the tape into the player, watched Feliz for a minute, then nodded. "Got a little muttsky in him, doesn't he?"

"What are you talking about? He looks sensational. That was his *first* pro fight."

Al put up a placating hand. "I'm not saying he's not talented, Charles. Don't get excited. He's very good, shows a lot of promise. He's just not the bravest guy in the world. That's okay. We'll build a wall around the kid. Don can use him."

History proved Braverman right regarding Feliz's heart. He folded in his two most significant early fights. He could have won both easily.

Don King never did wind up signing Fernely Feliz.

Not everything Al Braverman did for me pertained directly to boxing. He saved my life once.

The Mob had a contract on me and I was hiding in Puerto Rico. Worried enough to not be thinking straight, I was starting to consider extreme measures. I first went to Vin Vecchione, who had taken over fixing their fights from me. Then I told Al about my problem with New York.

Al said, "And you say they got a heavyweight? I assume he's a white kid?"

"Yes, he's white."

"Can he fight a little?"

"Not a lick."

"Does he at least look like a fighter?"

"He looks like a movie version of a fighter, minus the good looks. He's got big, jacked up muscles."

"They got any legitimate beef with you?"

"No. There was a problem. I took care of it. No harm was done."

"I haven't forgotten that I still owe you on the McNeeley thing."

"I got paid for that."

"By the other side. I still haven't done anything for you on that."

Braverman thought about it for a minute.

"Let's bring them in. I'll talk to them. We'll work something out. They know who I am?"

"Oh yeah, they definitely know who you are."

"Then nobody will have to waste time explaining to them why it'd be good if they talked to me. I'll arrange for a sit-down."

Two weeks later, I was in Al's office with the four men I feared most. They were seated. I remained standing. I'd arrived at East 69th many hours earlier, hiding from view in the coffee shop across from the office. I waited to see if anyone had brought bodyguards or drivers who'd be armed. I watched for parked cars where no one got out. If I saw anything questionable, I was going to slip off. Even though I had great faith in Al, I wasn't sure this was a situation I'd be walking away from. After putting myself out of reach and being invisible for the better part of a year, I'd allowed myself to go straight into the lion's den, suddenly an entirely hittable target.

I was surprised the Mob guys all seemed wary too. I represented no threat to them, and assumed they knew that. There were four of them, and I was alone. I knew I was safe in Al's office. It was what might happen on the street afterward that scared me.

Braverman gave us all a hard look.

"There's no reason for this to be any more complicated than it has to be," he said. "I'm calling for a truce. Peace is good for business. I'm prepared to give your fighter a promotional contract with DK Productions. We'll be able to move him. I haven't seen him yet, but I understand he's an aggressive kid. That's good. An aggressive white kid, Donald can always use. We'll just slot him in.

"Charles is to be left alone. Understood? If something happens to him, your kid won't be welcome anywhere in the world. I want that clear. He won't get fights and he won't get rated. If he does manage to get a fight, you'll wish he hadn't.

"What's done is in the past. Nobody here is going to talk about it. Charles is with us. He doesn't want to have to watch his back for the rest of his life. And neither do you. We've all got better things to do, so let's move on. I'm done. Any questions?"

The guy I'd had the biggest problem with turned to face me.

"Charles, you know some people are starting to breathe down everybody's neck, don't you?"

"I know that."

"I mean, I know nothing happened and that you don't know nothing. But you don't say anything if somebody talks to you, right?

"Talks to me about what? Some of my fighters were on the same card as your fighter a couple of times. That doesn't mean anything."

"Right, exactly. That's what I'm sayin'."

"That's what I'm saying too."

"And it ain't gonna change?"

"Now you're starting to insult me. Do I look like Sammy?"

Everybody laughed.

They all stood up, we shook hands and hugged, and were friends again.

Even so, turning the tree-lined corner of East 69th Street after leaving Al's antique shop, my back involuntarily clenched. But nothing happened. My car was where I'd parked it, so I drove away.

❖   ❖   ❖

Al Braverman was one of the two men—the other was Don Elbaum—who brought Don King into boxing. He was rewarded with a lifelong position as director of boxing for DK Productions, and entrusted to make deals, including ones for Mike Tyson's fights.

We had an arrangement. Whatever my fighters were to receive on a Don King card, there'd be a second check for an additional 50 percent sent directly to me. My fighters didn't need to know about that check. I was to kick some of the second check back to Al in cash. How much? "Give me what you think is right." A tradition continued.

I'd always tell my fighters about the second check—Al would say, "What are you, a fucking idiot?"—and split it with them after taking out Al's cut. I'd then fly to New York to hand-deliver his share as a gesture of respect. We'd go across the street to the sunny luncheonette, have coffee, and Al would pick my brain about who King should think about signing, who to match his guys up with, and which fighters should be avoided as opponents.

I Get Stuck with the Best Fighter in the World

In almost any field, representing someone who was the best in the world would be a good thing. In boxing, that's not necessarily so.

The boxing public knows Freddie Norwood primarily from his 1999 HBO win over all-time great Juan Manuel Marquez. Norwood was still a terrific fighter at that stage, but nowhere near the unbeatable junior featherweight he'd been four or five years earlier.

During the time I managed a prime Freddie Norwood, I couldn't give him away. From the start it was clear that Norwood wouldn't be an easy sell, but I was unprepared for how completely stonewalled I'd be in my attempts to move his career. For once, I'd taken a chance on managing a great small fighter with no sellable backstory instead of a big ordinary one who I could spin a line of bullshit about.

I'd hoped that being able to okay any opponent at any weight up to junior lightweight for any insulting offer would get the ball rolling for Freddie. The idea was to make it easy for matchmakers to use him, while reducing their list of excuses for rejecting him as an opponent.

Nobody could bitch that "he wants too much money." There'd be no whining that "he won't come up a few pounds" or "he won't travel."

None of it. You want to stiff him on the payday? Be my guest. He needs to fight a guy who enters the ring with twenty pounds on him? That bigger body is just going to make more noise when it hits the canvas. Fly him to some faraway place to take on a hometown kid who has friendly judges and a caring referee? Freddie has his up-to-date passport and the fight will never make it to the scorecards.

That's not to say I didn't get phone calls. Boxing being what it is, the people who dialed my number assumed the answer on my end would be no. When it wasn't, they had to do some frantic tap dancing to get out of the proposals they'd made.

That dance was a standard two-step most of the time. Sometimes, if they were trying to save face, it would become a waltz, one-two-three, then out.

Step One: "I'm surprised you're taking the fight, Charles. Let me call Toledo's people to tell them that Norwood is in."

"They're going to back out."

Step Two: "I heard back from them. Looks like Toledo can't get below 132."

"Norwood will still take the fight. But they're going to back out."

Step Three: "I guess they figured that Norwood wouldn't agree to take it at 130, so they went with someone else. Sorry they wasted your time. We'll try to make the fight in a few months."

"We'll be looking forward to your call."

Networks didn't believe that Norwood's style was marketable. This kind of racially mediated determination had long been used in boxing to marginalize great black fighters who were defensively adroit and offensively efficient. Norwood was part of a dwindling list of Black Code fighters.

Black Code fighters had honed their techniques down to pure essence, winnowing away all extravagant display. Not only did you have to be a sophisticated fighter to master the style, you had to be sophisticated to appreciate it. Defined more by subtlety than bombast, the aesthetics of Black Code fighting floated over the heads of most viewers and commentators alike.

Years after Freddie Norwood's time had passed, Floyd Mayweather Jr. employed a similar style on his way to amassing more money than any fighter before him. Tellingly, his wealth came not from the style, but from his ability to *talk about* the style as part of his multitiered negative public-persona marketing. The style itself didn't help promote Mayweather at all, but his *telling* a credulous public about it convinced people that they were seeing, as he put it, "The Best Ever."

Floyd Mayweather Jr. was unquestionably an excellent fighter. But no serious student of boxing history has him anywhere near Mount Olympus where Ray Robinson, Harry Greb, Roberto Duran, Sam Langford, Henry Armstrong, Benny Leonard, Ezzard Charles, Willie Pep, Tony Canzoneri, or Mickey Walker hang out.

In person, Norwood had a talent for making people dislike him. He had a Jack Johnson-ish mouthful of elaborate gold grillwork that alienated white matchmakers and TV producers: it was too ghetto and too dismissive. He was selfish and opportunistic—traits that he didn't go much out of his way to hide. He and I got along, though. I understood that, other than Charles Hamm and Adolph Pruitt—both older fight people from St. Louis who had no power to do him any good outside the ropes—nobody was going to help him.

Pruitt, who died at seventy-nine in January 2019 had been a terrific junior welterweight who mostly had to fight bigger guys in order to get work. He taught Norwood the deepest tricks of the trade, and Freddie's boxing suffered when he signed on with Kenny Adams, a celebrity trainer whose fame came from assisting Pat Nappi in "training" Olympians.

Pruitt was the conduit from Henry Armstrong, who managed him, to Norwood—contiguous generations of elite Black Code fighters.

It was hard to get anyone to spar with Freddie in Brockton. The two best local fighters near his own weight, Israel "Pito" Cardona and Edwin Santana, never came back after one session with him. There was a light heavyweight, Steve Detar, who trained out of the gym—a hard worker with a fifty-fifty pro record—but even he wouldn't get in the ring after Norwood floored him with 14-ounce pillows while wearing headgear.

"It's embarrassing as fuck," he told me by way of explanation.

Finally, I hit on a plan that would put Norwood's name into every boxing conversation. I gave away his services to three matchmakers for three separate televised fight cards on three different networks, all to take place within a span of six weeks. It was a steamrolling maneuver designed to force him down the public's throat while making him the mandatory number-one challenger for a world-title fight.

Norwood's fights would be calibrated so that the first one—USA's *Tuesday Night Fights*—wouldn't go more than a couple of rounds. The next—*Top Rank Boxing* on ESPN ten days later—would take Freddie a little deeper into the fight. Three weeks later, he'd face Manuel Medina for the NABF title at the Great Western Forum, with the winner to get a shot at the IBF crown. Medina was a very durable fighter, but he was made for Norwood. The fight would go eight or nine rounds, and Freddie would look sensational in every one of them. He'd either bust Medina up or give him a bad enough beating that the referee would have to stop the fight.

It was a slave's deal: $1,500 for the first fight, $3,500 for the next, and $12,500 for the one with Medina. After that, Freddie, as mandatory number-one contender, would fight and beat Tom "Boom Boom" Johnson for the IBF featherweight title.

Then we'd hijack the title.

There are a lot of ways a fighter can hold a title. If he's a favored son from some remote republic lucking into a title by beating a strategically rated opponent with a record of kayo wins over guys making their pro debuts, he can clutch his belt for dear life, never trying to unify it. If he's a popular champion, sooner or later the exigencies of big money will force him to try to win all the belts.

But if he's a great champion no one will pay to see, he must ransom his title. He needs to be the one standing in the way of a popular champion unifying the title.

Norwood would be that great champion that the marquee champion would be forced to take on to make the final jump from popular boxer to superstar. Except that nobody could beat Freddie Norwood at this stage of his career.

Two of the three guys I spoke to in order to get Norwood on TV—Brad Jacobs and Ron Katz—were angry about my putting him on competing shows; Alex Sherer at the Great Western Forum got it completely. Since his program would be the last broadcast, it actually did him some good that Freddie was getting so much exposure just before his show.

"Let's hope that he doesn't get cut."

"He won't. We'll see you in a couple of months."

The brilliance of my parlay caused my head to swell. I was picturing what deals could be made for Norwood after he won the IBF title. That he was making a total of $17,500 for three televised fights didn't bother me at all. It was what had to be done to bring him to a championship. It didn't occur to me that Freddie might see things differently.

"I ain't fightin' for that kinda money."

"It's what you have to do to get a title shot. There's no way around it."

"Man, that's no money for them fights."

"I know that. But it puts you in the public eye, and it makes you the mandatory number-one contender. Once you win the title, everything will change."

"I ain't doin' it."

Nothing would convince him to take the fights. I couldn't manage a fighter who wouldn't let me manage, so that phone call ended things between us.

Freddie Norwood did eventually become WBA world featherweight champion. He called me in Puerto Rico to ask if I'd be his manager again. He had the title, but he wasn't making any money.

I passed. How he was seen by the public was now set in stone; he was no longer the fighter he'd been when I was managing him; and he was too unwilling to let me do my job. The prognosis wasn't good. My saying no wasn't personal. I'd always liked Freddie Norwood.

Tyrone and Mr. Farrell

Tyrone Booze only called me Charles when something really important was up with him. Otherwise, he'd call me Mr. Farrell. It bothered me.

"Tyrone, why do you insist on calling me Mr. Farrell? Can't you just call me Charles?

"You get you respect."

"I respect *you*. I call you Tyrone. We're friends, man. We're family. You don't want me calling you Mr. Booze, do you?"

"Nah, man. It ain't like that. You an older gentleman."

"I'm eight years older than you. You calling me Mr. Farrell and me calling you Tyrone doesn't seem right. It makes it sound like I'm the master and you're the slave. It sounds like we're not equals."

"I don't think we're not equals. It ain't like that. You just deserve you respect."

"Well, I respect you. But I'm not going to call you Mr. Booze."

"Good. I don't want you callin' me Mr. Booze. Call me Tyrone."

"Okay. Then call me Charles."

"Nah, I'm gonna keep callin' you Mr. Farrell."

"Okay."

Tyrone Booze and I were in line waiting to be seated at a restaurant in New Paltz, New York, on a brisk late autumn afternoon. The restaurant was a sun-filled rustic ski-lodge imitation with an open fireplace crackling in its center; the clientele consisted mostly of local college students decked out in bulky sweaters and parkas. It was a cheerful white person's kind of happy place.

Tyrone Booze was himself a very cheerful guy—gregarious and engaged. Being around white people didn't throw him off his game.

Two young women were in line directly ahead of us waiting to be seated, their sporting equipment taking up space around them.

Booze has a deep, mellifluous voice that swoops up into a disbelieving falsetto "whaaat" when he's incredulous. It's a musical voice he uses to good advantage. Tyrone also has a small, round head, intelligent, amused eyes, and sloping shoulders that tend to hide what a big, powerful guy he actually is. Even though he's one of the toughest motherfuckers in the world, nobody is afraid of Tyrone Booze.

"And what are you two ladies doing in New Paltz today," he asked the women. He smiled his open, ingenuous smile. His dimple showed up when he did that. He had spent a lot of money on his dental work.

The women smiled back.

"We came here for the spelunking."

Booze's smile faded.

"Oh," he said. His forehead creased. "Well, we niggers don't get into none of that kinda weird shit."

The woman quickly sought to reassure him.

"No, no. Spelunking just means exploring *caves.*"

"Well, we niggers don't get into none of that kinda weird shit neither."

His smile was back.

A Career in Dinner Theater

At Gleason's earlier in the day, Booze had looked terrible sparring with Martin Foster. He knew it, and knew I knew it. It made him defensive during our eighty-five-mile ride back to New Paltz. An uneasy silence hung in the air as he drove too fast down the New York Thruway, periodically glancing over at me. I pretended to focus on the scenery on the highway; he, on the exigencies of transporting us to Floyd Patterson's place. As the absence of conversation grew longer, tension built.

Finally, Booze broke it. "How I look in there?"

"What do you want me to say, Tyrone?"

"I thought I looked pretty good."

He knew that was bullshit.

"Really? Based on what?"

"I was slippin' all his punches. Makin' him pay, coming right back over the top."

"It looked to me like he was catching you with everything."

"Nah, nah. You don't know what you was lookin' at, Mr. Farrell. I was pickin' off everything on my gloves or movin' my head. He wasn't catching me with nothing."

"Maybe it was just ring rust."

"Weren't no ring rust. I was outboxin' him."

"That's not what I saw. And it's not what judges would have seen."

"You didn't know what you was watching."

"Okay, have it your way."

Tyrone had begun accelerating the car alarmingly while he spoke. I snuck a peek at the speedometer; we were doing ninety-five. Booze grew silent again. Some time passed.

"Mr. Farrell, are you afraid to die?" It sounded like "dah."

"Yes, I'm afraid to die. I'm afraid to die and you should be too."

"I ain't. I ain't afraid to die. I die right *now*."

Booze seemed oblivious to the fact that he was still picking up speed. We must have been going a hundred miles per hour.

"Mr. Farrell, you got a gun on you?"

"What the fuck, Tyrone. No, I don't have a gun on me. You know that."

"If I can't fight no more, I'm ready to die. I ain't afraid."

"Well, look, man. Maybe I wasn't paying close enough attention when you were sparring with Foster. I think you were doing some nice little things in there, really subtle moves. You're right; you looked good."

"I looked like shit. And if I can't fight I ain't got no reason to live."

Booze had taken his hands off the steering wheel and was driving the car with his knees.

"Don't talk that way, Tyrone. You're a world champion. You will be one again. You got Tina and the kids. You've got a beautiful family and millions of friends. They all love you. You've got a nice house. And you can still fight. You've just been off a while. It'll all be fine."

This caused Tyrone to bury his face in his hands while still driving a hundred miles an hour with his knees. The car started to drift in and out of our lane a little bit.

"Would you mind putting your hands back on the wheel?"

Tyrone's shoulders began to shake as wracking sobs escaped from behind his clenched fists, which were still covering his eyes.

I inched against the passenger door. There was no way to jump from the car onto the side of the highway. I wouldn't have a chance.

From the driver's seat, there came the sound of steady wailing; Booze's shoulders were now shaking uncontrollably.

"Ain't no use," came his muffled voice. "Ain't no reason to go on."

'Fuck it,' I thought. 'I'm going to die in a suicide-homicide with a fucking *cruiserweight* who only won the *WBO* title.'

I looked over at Booze to try to reason with him one last time.

He had taken his hands away from his face. He was laughing.

"What the *fuck*, motherfucker."

"Nah, man. I was just playin' with you. Everything's cool."

Tyrone, in complete control, held the car at a steady seventy-five, never budging from his lane.

I was so mad that I wouldn't even look at him.

"Aw, c'mon, Mister Farrell. You ain't gonna talk to me?"

We drove in silence for a short time. Then Tyrone reached into the center console and picked up an imaginary microphone. He lifted it to his mouth and began to croon, adopting a smooth, bland Robert Goulet baritone.

"Tyrone love Mr. Farrell. Tyrone would never do nothing to hurt his manager. Mr. Farrell is the greatest manager in the world."

He went on and on, chorus of praise after chorus of praise. I ignored him for as long as I could. Finally, I couldn't help myself.

"Tyrone, have you ever considered a career in dinner theater?"

He gave it some thought.

"Do it pay good?"

I got Tyrone Booze a gig as Riddick Bowe's chief sparring partner in Big Bear, California. Working with Bowe gave Tyrone—a career-long "away" B-side fighter—a real taste of what it was like to work under conditions where someone was looking out for you. As the heavyweight champion, Bowe was bringing in tons of money for HBO, so everybody was bending over backward to give him and his manager Rock Newman anything they wanted.

Booze loved being in Big Bear. He'd call me and say, "Man, you can't get no higher in boxing. Now I see what it's like to be at the top. This is beautiful."

He liked Bowe and Bowe liked him, so the camp was sunny and playful for the most part. The only problem was that Bowe hated being away from his family and, now wealthy beyond anything he could have imagined, had lost his incentive to fight. He was also a really big kid who loved to eat; his weight had ballooned up to around 300 pounds since his last fight.

During one of his calls, Tyrone said, "Don't tell nobody, but Riddick's gonna lose to Hullafield this time. He don't have the hunger to go to war the way he's gonna need to with Evander. He's real *talented*, and he's better on the inside than any big guy I ever seen, but he don't want to fight no more."

One afternoon, Bowe's disinclination to be in camp flared up and he got a little cranky with Booze during a sparring session, taking a cheap shot at him. Tyrone got low, charged, dug into Bowe with his shoulders, and flipped him up and over, depositing the champ on his ass in the middle of the ring.

Tyrone Booze might have been a hired hand, but he was nobody's errand boy. The incident caused no problems in the camp, and none between Booze and Bowe, but it did produce an unlikely consequence. It prompted Eddie Futch, the champ's trainer, to give me a call.

Futch was over eighty years old at this point and on the verge of becoming a boxing legend. He was a very good trainer and a genuinely wonderful man.

I was surprised to hear that he wanted permission to train Tyrone Booze.

"I see something in him. I think he could be turned into a very good fighter. He's never had the benefit of good training, and he's been matched improperly. Would you let Thell Torrence and me work with him?"

I'd spoken with Torrence many times and admired him greatly. I was also impressed that, unlike most of boxing's power players, Futch had the decency to ask for my consent to let him and Torrence train Booze.

Since Tyrone Booze would never be a box-office attraction, I couldn't see what was in it for Eddie. But I was happy to have him take over Tyrone's training. If Booze could stay in Vegas, he'd have great conditioning and sparring, be able to fight for good money on Bowe's undercards, and benefit from the connections Futch had made and the wisdom he could impart.

Futch took Booze on because he liked having him around. Tyrone was too old a fighter to undergo a complete remake, but he was teachable. He paid attention. He was incredibly smart. And he was tough in ways that other boxers and trainers would recognize immediately. He'd fought the most dangerous light heavyweights and cruiserweights of his era and had never been off his feet, with the exception of the one time he did some business in South Africa against Johnny Du Plooy, joining a good-sized club of American contender-level victims who liked the Johannesburg and Sun City paydays.

The one thing that no one had ever done for Tyrone Booze—and I doubted that Eddie Futch would have any luck—was teach him how to punch hard. It was bewildering that he couldn't. He was built like a puncher and he threw his punches correctly, using proper leverage, putting his weight behind the shots, following through, and adding combinations. Yet, when he hit them, they didn't go. There's an adage in boxing that "punchers are born, not developed." It's been my experience that the saying is true.

The apex of Booze's in-ring toughness came from his twelve-round disputed split-decision loss to Bert Cooper. Cooper was a drunk and a drug addict, a good-natured nonstop partier who happened to punch harder than almost anyone who ever lived. Early in his career, he'd been mentored by Joe Frazier, who modeled Cooper after himself, even bequeathing him his own "Smokin'" moniker. But Bert Cooper punched even harder than his nickname-sake.

Fighters knew about Bert Cooper. He may have been easily discouraged, often out of shape, and able to be outboxed, but—to a man—he was the opponent fighters least wanted to have to get in the ring with. Eddie Mustafa Muhammad once told me that when Bert Cooper hit you, "Your head would spin around like that girl's in *The Exorcist*."

On the night Cooper fought Tyrone, he was in perfect shape. It was one of the last times he'd gotten himself down below the cruiserweight limit so that he could defend his NABF title. Booze was never in jeopardy of being dropped in the fight, and he was never actually *hurt* in the sense of feeling any pain.

"Bert Cooper's punches don't feel like normal punches. I been in with a lotta hard punchers, but it wasn't the same. When Bert Cooper hits you, you in the Twilight Zone."

Two decades after the fight, Tyrone Booze still had nightmares of being trapped in the ring with Bert Cooper.

Nobody wanted Tyrone Booze to win the WBO cruiserweight title. That included Johnny Bos, his putative agent. Booze knocking out the previously undefeated Britisher Derek Angol in Manchester upset a lot of people's plans. The cruiserweight division was going through a hot streak in Europe in 1992 and there were lucrative matchups to be made between fighters from Great Britain, Germany, France, and even Norway. Fighters from the States were sometimes brought in to lose in order to add prestige to the Continentals' records.

Johnny Bos was a brilliant boxing guy, and he and Booze were friends. But Johnny's gig was as the elite supplier of opponents to Europe, where his reputation for dependability was ironclad. On the whole, he didn't tell his fighters what to do. His matchmaking ability was nonpareil; he'd send guys who could go rounds, but wouldn't be able to win. Occasionally, he'd send ex-champs who *could* win if they wanted to, but the promise of ongoing paydays combining with vacations would help them decide that there was no benefit in it.

It was easy to lose overseas. If fights went the distance and you didn't win at least nine rounds, you wouldn't get the decision. If you were rocked by a punch, the referee would step in to stop the fight for your protection. If you were on the verge of knocking out your European opponent, the bell would ring early or you'd be disqualified for landing a low blow, rabbit punch, or some other infraction.

Tyrone Booze had played the going-to-Europe-to-lose game successfully once before, handling Magne Havnaa fairly easily in Denmark on his way to losing a split decision.

As a reward for his international diplomacy, the WBO sent Tyrone back to Europe, this time to England, so he could repeat his earlier performance, now against Angol.

The problem was that Derek Angol was a stiff. The judges could make sure he got the nod if his fight with Booze went the distance, but he couldn't manage it. In picking Tyrone as the Brit's opponent, Johnny Bos had exercised due diligence: Booze was tough and skilled, but he couldn't punch. As it turned out, you didn't have to punch very hard to knock out Derek Angol. The next two top-ranked opponents he fought—Akim Tafer and Massimiliano Duran, neither any kind of puncher—both did it.

The WBO and the European promoters who they kowtowed to were now stuck with a champion they didn't want but who they'd have to pay until they could get rid of him, something they knew they'd be able to do soon.

Meanwhile, Booze flew back to the States, to an agent who'd barely speak to him, so outraged was he by his client's disloyalty. It busted up what had been a good friendship.

Three months after winning the title, Tyrone was back defending it in a career-high payday against local bad boy Ralf Rocchigiani in Germany. Rocchigiani was a fighter much like Booze himself—he couldn't be knocked out and he couldn't punch; it was tacitly understood that he'd likely take the title by decision in his adopted arena in Charlottenburg.

It didn't happen. Booze outboxed Rocchigiani so completely that he got the decision. This required promoters Klaus-Peter Kohl and Universum to up the ante to a *new* career-high payday to entice him back to Germany, where he then lost his title to Markus Bott, putting an end to their Booze problem.

By the time I managed him, the WBO cruiserweight champion was none other than Tyrone's old ring freund Ralf Rocchigiani. I smelled money there. It would make great economic sense to have the WBO, in recognition of Booze's status as their former champion, put him in their ratings—I'd already gotten Tyrone his one requisite legitimating win—then have him go back to Germany to take on a guy he'd defended his title against.

The smart move would have been to play the decision straight down the middle: to give Booze the decision along with the title if he legitimately won. There would be a mandatory ninety-day rematch clause in place. In the rematch, it was understood that the WBO could steal Tyrone's title back even if he appeared to beat Rocchigiani. Tyrone Booze wasn't a baby; everybody would make money, and no one would get hurt. If their second match this time around was controversial enough, they could go again, affording Booze one last good payday, after which he'd leave the WBO alone.

This was a no-brainer to everyone concerned. Rocchigiani's people were on board with it. I assumed that the WBO president Francisco "Paco" Valcárcel would understand boxing well enough to be too.

I was wrong. Paco and I had met and taken an instant dislike to each other. I doubted that our inconsequential mutual antipathy would hold up doing business with Tyrone Booze.

Again, I was wrong.

Clearly, he harbored a grudge against Tyrone Booze—and maybe toward Johnny Bos—for fucking him over, even though his tinhorn organization picked up sanctioning fees for Tyrone's title defenses.

I pointed out the financial wisdom of what I was proposing, but he ignored me.

"Mr. Booze was not a distinguished challenger for the title," he began, "and he was not a distinguished champion. . . ."

"He beat the guy who you've got holding the title right now," I interrupted.

"That may be, but he hasn't done anything recently to warrant inclusion in our ratings."

"Okay. What would it take to get him rated?"

"I don't know. We would have to see. We would have to evaluate."

"By 'we,' do you mean 'I'?"

"Yes."

It wasn't a shakedown: he was still piqued that Booze had won the title in the first place. Valcárcel was a popinjay: a pipsqueak dictator who wore a small, impeccably maintained mustache and favored boutonnieres with his three-piece suits. He unfailingly added "Esq." to his signature. If you didn't appeal to his vanity and ego—or weren't in a position to bully him—you'd never get anywhere with Paco. The WBO wasn't ever going to cooperate with me or with Tyrone Booze.

With nothing for Tyrone Booze to do that would make him money at cruiserweight, it was impossible to hold him back from eating his way out of the division. By the time he had his last pro fight in 1998—a decision loss to Jesse Ferguson after I'd stopped managing him—he was up to 235 pounds. From there he kept going, plateauing at nearly three hundred, somehow still not fat.

Somewhere along the way while managing him, I had to make decisions about just how far he could go. Initially, the idea was to have him win back his WBO cruiserweight title, but that wasn't going to happen. The WBO was out to get him, but there was also the issue of his weight. I had serious doubts that he'd ever get down to 200 pounds again. The question then became what could be done for him at heavyweight. Not much, I concluded.

We were friends, though, so I felt obligated to try to set some wheels in motion. The first item of business was to get him a few quick kayos to put him back on the boards, and to try to reconfigure his image as someone who could occasionally knock people out.

I had to give some consideration to what kind of fights to get him. There were plenty of heavyweights he could beat legitimately, but few he could knock out. I'd talked with light-heavyweight contender Iceman John Scully about it. Scully, Tyrone, and former welterweight champion Marlon Starling had come up through the amateurs together in Hartford.

"Ice, I don't get it. His punches look like they should do some damage. He throws them right."

"I know. But he never had any power. I used to spar with him in the amateurs when I was only a junior middleweight. He could really fight, but I never felt his punches at all."

"It doesn't make sense. He puts his weight behind them."

"I know. I could never understand it."

The first time I brought Tyrone Booze to Raleigh, North Carolina, to get him a knockout, his opponent, even knowing that he wasn't required go past one round, refused to fight a world champion. Pointing out that Tyrone was "an *ex-champion*" did no good.

North Carolina doesn't have its own boxing commission, but the commissioner brought in from South Carolina was my old friend Bobby Mitchell, soon to be sent to a federal prison for fixing fights. It made no difference to him who'd be standing—but not for long—in the corner opposite Booze's.

Armed with that information and Tyrone's disarming grin and unimposing physique, the two of us made our way through the crowd, looking for oversized men—be they military, gang member, construction worker, or jailbird—ready to earn a thousand dollars for a minute's work.

We almost scored one after twenty minutes of searching. A tall, rangy, very big and bedraggled biker, part of a color-wearing gang, was agitating audience members in hopes of provoking a fight. He was drunk. The bikers had assured us that he was the toughest member of their gang.

"Want to fight my guy here? I'll give you a thousand dollars. You don't even have to fight back."

Booze gave the biker and his friends his most innocent smile. It really *was* a heartwarming thing to see.

"You want me to fight this dude for a thousand dollars?"

"I want you to get in the ring with him for a thousand dollars. It's up to you if you want to fight him, but I don't recommend it."

"So you're gonna give me a thousand dollars even if I fall down the first time he hits me?"

"I'll give you a thousand dollars even if you fall down *before* he hits you."

The biker glared blearily first at Tyrone Booze, then at me. He smelled a rat where there was no rat.

"Fuck *ye-ew*," he yelled at me.

"What's the problem? You don't really have to fight him."

The biker thrust his flushed face into mine.

"Ah said fuck *ye-ew*! What you gonna do about it?"

"You want to fight me now? How about just fighting the big guy here so you can make money?"

The guy was so drunk he couldn't focus.

"And ah am tellin' you fuck ye-ew. I'm 'bout ready to kick yore ass."

Booze said, "If he does, do I gotta give him a thousand dollars?"

I smiled at the biker. "You're not going get a chance to kick my ass. See, the guy you're afraid of is a world champion, and I don't think there's any way you'll get through him to reach me. But, you know, it's understandable that you're scared of him. You're not a fighter."

I was hoping maybe that'd goad him into taking the bait. I should have known better. The guy would have fought me for free, but he wouldn't take a grand to fall over before being hit.

I would have made sure that Tyrone Booze got in one real shot anyway, just because I didn't like the biker.

I called my friend Marc Machain to see if he'd agree to take a kayo loss in a fight that'd be mostly real, but with a fixed ending. He didn't much like it.

"I can't beat Tyrone Booze. So just let me fight him."

"I would, but he needs to start getting knockouts on his record. I don't think Tyrone can knock you out. And I can't afford having him busted up if you bang heads or break his hand on that hard head of yours."

Machain laughed. "I know. I got a hard head. Shit, it's too bad though. It'd be fun to fight him. I'd give him a good fight."

"What if you both agreed to not quite go all out? Would you let me have it stopped five or six rounds in? It would be my ref or I'd put Tony in your corner. Something like that?"

"Aw, I wish you'd just let me fight him. I'd like to see how I'd do."

"I can't afford the risk. Take the fight, Marc. You'll be able to find out how you'd do. You can test yourself a little, and you can test Tyrone. Just make sure things don't get out of hand. And understand that it'll have to end after five or six. You'll have fun."

In the end, Marc Machain agreed to take the fight. It was a great reminder to me that you can take measures to get the result you want in a fight, and the guys can go into it having agreed to what will happen—both acting in good faith—but fighters, at some level, really do love to fight, and sometimes that overrides everything else.

Sometime during the first round, after some vigorous sparring as predetermined, Tyrone and Marc found themselves getting high on fighting in front of an audience after their lengthy times away from the ring. Neither said anything to the other, but they banged gloves hard at the bell. That signaled that a real fight was now on. They silently agreed to share the joy of not pulling their punches.

It was a little rougher than it should have been, but I wasn't particularly worried. Marc Machain wasn't good enough to beat Tyrone Booze. My concerns were ones I'd voiced earlier: accidental damage from a head butt, a broken hand, or the fight going the distance. It was a terrific fight, though. The crowd loved it. I can't say I didn't enjoy watching.

Marc Machain was short for a heavyweight— five feet seven, at most— and stocky, with short arms. He was physically strong. The only way he could fight was to get low and come barreling in, throwing wild punches meant to land wherever he was lucky enough to connect. He would be routinely peppered with counterpunches, which he mostly ignored.

Even though Tyrone Booze was no puncher, he was getting plenty of free shots. Machain added to their power by marching full speed straight into them. It's easy to catch a fighter like Machain with a solid uppercut, and Booze did in the second round, the punch producing a very satisfying knockdown.

Theoretically, I could have had Tony Petronelli jump into the ring at that point. It would have upset the crowd but served the higher function of getting Tyrone an early knockout win.

I decided that Booze would probably replicate the knockdown later in the fight. It would allow the audience its satisfaction. Booze could use the work. The fighters themselves were having fun, and that was worth something. I could improvise; I'd find a time to pull the plug.

The fight, although one-sided, remained a barn burner. To unsophisticated viewers—as the members of the Raleigh crowd mostly were—it looked as if Machain, with his snorting, rip-roaring, swinging for the bleachers style, had a "puncher's chance" to win. But Marc wasn't actually a puncher, and his shots were so telegraphed that any good pro would have avoided them. Booze, for the most part, did that easily enough, but he was just sufficiently ring-rusty to occasionally get caught. It produced the misimpression that the bout was a give-and-take affair.

I was beginning to grow concerned that there'd be no early exit opportunity—meaning that I'd have to invent one—when Booze again caught Machain with an uppercut as Marc heedlessly waded in. The punch dropped Machain, but didn't hurt him too badly. I didn't care: I nodded almost imperceptibly to Tony Petronelli, who was in the ring in a flash, signaling that his fighter had had enough.

Machain, caught up in the ruckus, momentarily forgot that this was what he'd signed up for.

"Aw, *no*. Tony, Tony, no . . . don't stop it. I'm okay. *Please* don't stop the fight. I'm havin' fun!"

We'd all had fun. And now it was time for the fun to stop.

And for more fun to begin. Within seconds of the stoppage, the two fighters were hugging in the center of the ring, basking in the enthusiastic crowd reception, and eagerly talking their way through the fight. Their conversation continued as they showered, dressed, and made their way to the Denny's across from the Ritz Theatre, where both fighters ordered double helpings of everything off a menu featuring a toxic and life-shortening combination of grease, fat, salt, and sugar. In their giddiness, food dripped from their chins onto the fronts of their shirts. It would have been hard to find two happier men in Raleigh, North Carolina, that night.

I knew some things about Tyrone Booze. I knew he had the balls to go into hostile territory and take on the house against any opponent. I knew that he had an uncanny sense of self-preservation. He would check out the terrain, then carefully set up conditions that would keep him safe. He *never* got blindsided. When he fought or trained on the road, he brought along more personal shit than seemed possible—three or four huge bulging duffle bags' worth—constructing a temporary home that provided him with some semblance of familiarity and security.

Knowing these things helped me understand how Tyrone Booze got run over by a garbage truck.

His boxing career over, his entrepreneurial venture, Smart Fighter Institute, going nowhere, his radio shows bringing in no cash, Tyrone took a job in the Parks and Recreation Department in his hometown of Clearwater.

I wondered why. It didn't pay anything. Tyrone could have made much more as a personal boxing trainer. City employees did get benefits; maybe that's what he was thinking about.

Tyrone had only been on the job a short while before his legs were backed over by a garbage truck slowly driven by a friend and fellow municipal employee. Both legs were broken. He was listed as being in stable condition at the Mease Countryside Hospital in Clearwater.

I instantly thought of the nearly consecutive fights Tyrone Booze had taken for paydays—the ones where he faced Eddie "Flame" Mustafa Muhammad, Dwight "The Camden Buzzsaw" Qawi, Evander "The Real Deal" Holyfield, Nate "Mr." Miller, Tim "TNT" Broady, and "Smokin'" Bert Cooper. Especially Bert Cooper. And that thought led me inevitably to another one.

Booze picked up the phone when I called his room at Mease. He sounded out of it, but he knew me.

"Am I still your manager?"

"Yeah, yeah, Mr. Farrell. You always gonna be my manager."

"Then I'm in for a third. That's the way it works. What are you looking for? A million? Million and a half?"

Tyrone chuckled at the other end of the line.

"Don't make me laugh, Mr. Farrell. You crazy."

"You get run over by a garbage truck, and I'm the one who's crazy? I see what you're doing. I want in on it."

"Mr. Farrell, c'mon, man, don't make me laugh. I'm s'posed to be restin'."

"Okay, Tyrone. Get some rest. I just wanted to check up on you. I'll try to make it down to Clearwater. But don't think you're fooling me."

"I'm serious, Mr. Farrell. I can't be laughin' like this. I gotta go back to sleep now. You crazy, man. Thanks for callin'."

A couple of years ago, Tyrone had a stroke. He was still in his fifties at the time—an age where you wouldn't expect it to happen to a lifelong athlete. But his weight was high, he ate a lousy diet, and he'd spent decades being hit in the head by some of the hardest punchers in boxing—all of them big men. That he always went the distance undoubtedly exacerbated whichever of his health issues was boxing-related.

The stroke left him partially paralyzed and able to only speak haltingly, with great difficulty enunciating. I called him a couple of times, but he was struggling to talk during our conversation and I sensed that I was doing him more harm than good by keeping him on the phone.

A mutual friend was diligent in staying in touch with Tyrone. He would call me with updates.

"It's painful," he'd say. "I can't understand him a lot of the time. He asks about you. He always says you're crazy. You should call him."

I should. But I don't. Experience has taught me that you can't be a part-time friend to fighters. Their lives are so chaotic and their concerns so exigent that checking in only once in a while just adds to their disarray. This goes to the intrinsic paternalism of boxing relationships—an imbalance that perpetuates how boxers are seen, even often by themselves, as needing to be looked after and taken care of. It's a working model that, during the time when the fighter's career is still ongoing, benefits everyone in the business other than the fighter himself.

Fighters create what are often fictions about their managers. Every fighter I've ever managed has insisted that I am rich and that I have an impressive education. Neither is true. I'm about $1.4 million in debt. That makes me poor. And I've yet to manage a fighter—including the two who couldn't read or write—who didn't get further in school than I did.

Nevertheless, the manager-boxer dynamic is so firmly established that it often resists refutation even in the face of clear evidence.

"You a very rich man, Charle," Mitch Green would tell me. "You a very educated man."

He'd say that despite often being at my home, which was a late-nineteenth-century white elephant that was crashing and burning on a daily basis. He'd see me using credit cards to pull cash from ATMs—a suicidal move that only someone in deep financial trouble would ever consider. Sometimes, when even his most wishful thinking couldn't connect me to having money, he would alter his statement to, "Well, maybe you ain't got money *right now*, but you *had* money. And you *gonna* have money again. You just gotta fake it 'til you make it."

Tyrone saw things similarly.

"I know you very wealthy, Mr. Farrell. You got houses in Boston and here in Florida on Davis Island and down in Puerto Rico. I know how expensive those are. You dress good. And you talk good. You got any Jew in you?"

A lot of fighters will give you whatever they have. Because you know this, you feel obliged to reciprocate.

The thing is, they never have anything to give.

You can't reciprocate an act of generosity that never does—and never could—take place.

Once a fighter's career is over, and he falls on hard times, you think, "Fuck, this is hopeless. There's nothing I can do to help." You retreat rather than face conditions as they are. It's a pretty gutless thing to do.

That's where I am with Tyrone Booze. I love him; he's my friend and he's family, but our trajectory is entirely downhill. He's one of two fighters I've been friendly with—although I didn't manage Marc Machain—who left identical voice messages on my machine after not hearing from me for a long time: "Mr. Farrell, you don't love me no more?"

It's funny, and they meant it to be funny. But it's not something you want to think about for too long.

You can't be a part-time boxer. And you can't be in the boxing business part time. If you box, and you're not in the gym every day doing the many things necessary to keep yourself sharp, you will lose and you will almost surely get badly hurt. If you are in the boxing business and are not in the gyms and on the phone and, nowadays, online all day, every day, you will get left behind, lose all your money, and almost surely get badly hurt. The commitment to box or to be in the boxing business precludes doing anything else.

When I made my living in boxing, I worked fourteen to sixteen hours days. I'd sleep for four hours a night, still ready to take any calls that came in during those hours—which they did. When I got out of boxing, I was instantly left behind. I still watch a lot of boxing, but there are people—even people who don't earn their living at it—who are much more up on what goes on in the sport than I'll ever again be. I no longer get early tips about an unknown fourteen-year-old junior flyweight destroying seasoned pros in some gym in Nicaragua or Honduras or Thailand. No former champs call me to let me know to get some money down because they're flying over to Germany or Denmark to take a dive in the fourth round.

Being out, I can no longer take on the weight of caring for fighters. I've got problems of my own to deal with, and those are the only ones I have room to focus on.

I can't say if I was a good friend to the fighters I managed, but I know I can't be a good friend to them anymore. Without the potential to earn something back as a result of the friendships—as horrible as that sounds—I can no longer afford the luxury. This means that I'm letting Tyrone Booze go. That's a difficult thing to admit.

"I Done Some Things for Some Guys"

Before I met him, I assumed that Vin Vecchione—who I knew of only through hearsay—would be just one more New England bumpkin bringing along yet another bumbling local heavyweight. The guy wouldn't have any money. He'd be suspicious and provincial, with a vastly inflated notion of his fighter's talents. He'd be the kind of dope who, if he managed to scrounge up money to bus in opponents, would soon pick the wrong one, so that his efforts would come to nothing.

By the time Vin helped me off with my coat, linked his arm into mine to escort me to a booth of the small diner in Whitman and see that I was comfortably seated, he had already begun to clarify how things were going to be.

"Look, I been hearin' about you. You got an undefeated white heavyweight. I got an undefeated white heavyweight. Our two undefeated white heavyweights ain't never gonna fight each other, so we might as well get along."

I instantly understood how wrong I'd been about him. The better we got to know each other over the next few years, the more I recognized how intricate the blueprint for *his* undefeated white heavyweight was, especially when placed against the conventional plans I'd made for mine.

At the diner, I listened to a true boxing guy unspool a vision. It was clear and systematic; it was also profoundly creative, since it had to be done without the benefit of capital. Vin may have been quick to ask for and accept favors—as I found out—but he didn't rely on anyone to make his plans for Peter McNeeley take form. He knew how to do everything himself.

There are a couple of ways to be a true boxing guy. Some know everything about what happens once two fighters step through the ropes, but nothing about the business that brings them there. Vin didn't know shit about boxing.

His legitimacy was achieved from the opposite end of the spectrum. Vin understood boxing's tides: the relentless economy that always began in the grimiest outposts.

He was capable of following a trickle from the leaky backyard plastic wading pool that was the Whitman Armory—where his palmed cigar undoubtedly poked the hole in the pool's side that got the leak started—watching where the trickle went, and tracking the tributaries as they flowed stream to pond, pond to lake, lake to river, all the way out to the ocean—where he was meant to swim all along.

It would be easy to imagine that someone as driven and autocratic as Vin Vecchione would be impossible to be around. Anything but. Bundled in among the items on his to-do list was "have some laughs." Spending time with Vin was a blast for everyone lucky enough to have done it. He was the best storyteller ever, and nobody's money was any good when he was around—even if he had to borrow that money from you so that your money wouldn't be good when you were around.

Over the first of our countless shared pots of bad coffee, he gave me the detailed projections for Peter McNeeley's career. It was the kind of step-by-step blueprint that, without a prodigious bankroll, could only be implemented by someone with every old-school trick firmly placed in his arsenal.

You had to be careful. You had to fix as much as you could and unfailingly guess right about the rest. You had to do favor after favor, file a mental inventory of who you'd helped, and occasionally call in those markers to keep the ledger sheet straight. When I first met Vin, he hadn't yet, as far as I could tell, out-and-out fixed any of Peter McNeeley's fights. That meant that he had been right twenty-two straight times on behalf of someone who was always at the precipice.

He managed to do this while remaining invisible except to those few who needed to be able to see him. Being able to pull off this now-you-see-him, but now-you-don't trick was difficult to execute because it required sending very advanced signals.

Two essential elements were really no more than wisely deployed props, both right out of Central Casting. Vin always wore his scally cap and would never be seen without a stogie, lit or unlit as the law allowed. These visual cues, when put together with his strong Boston accent and fractured grammar, marked him for most as a primitive—uneducated, coarse, probably Mob-connected, and untrustworthy.

The kinds of affectations that New York fight guys used to mask their fraudulence, Vecchione used to allow his authenticity to remain uninvestigated. He didn't *want* outsiders to know how legit he was. Caricature suited his interests well; he could be overlooked and underestimated. This was not unlike Don King's decoyed hair and vocabulary. As was true with King, Vin was seldom not the most intelligent person in the room, taken lightly by people who couldn't see what their underestimation of him would cost them.

Of all the knee-jerk assessments people made of Vin, only the Mob-connected part was entirely true. When I asked about it, he gave me his inimitable deadpan.

"Chaales, I done some things for some guys."

Maybe because of its understated accuracy, it's still the funniest sentence I've ever heard. Its only rivals are *other* sentences from Vecchione.

Things hadn't been easy. Vin still had a bullet lodged in his back, picked up while running from two hitmen in a dispute over money. Visited by Feds for questioning in the hospital while still in critical condition, he assured them that the attempt on his life had just been "a case of mistaken identity."

Once I'd become friendlier with him, I pressed him on what doing "some things for some guys" consisted of.

He sighed wearily, as if indulging an inquisitive and possibly slow-witted child. "Chaales, I used to be sent to locations in Revere or Chaalestown to pick up old caahs, and I hadda drive them caahs out to the *maashes* all the way down in New Jersey. I'd go at night when traffic had thinned out and there weren't too many people on the roads. Drive safe, stay under the speed limit, keep to the center lane. Drop off the caahs after checkin' to see that the coast was clear."

In what I came to learn was a characteristic gesture when he was fucking around, he draped a heavy hand over my arm, dropped his voice, and looked theatrically to his right and left to make sure we were alone.

"Chaales, sometimes I got the feeling I wasn't the only guy in them caahs."

Over time he'd moved away from earning his living by doing "some things," and it appeared that whatever enmity had existed with the Mob had been cooled out, but Vin still had his connections. I came to the conclusion that these associations were no longer business-based, but more in the nature of some of the small favors that Vin would do—goodwill being a valuable commodity in the boxing world.

"There's a place somewhere for young Peter," he'd tell me. "It's haahd to say what it's gonna be. But believe me; someone's gonna have some use for him at some point. I just gotta keep him busy and keep him winning."

Until I got to know him, I harbored the misconception that Vin saw more in McNeeley than actually was there. I was wrong about that. One of the things he told me was that "Peter's not the most *talented* kid out there." To his way of thinking, talent could lead to problems; it invited insubordination. What he wanted was a fighter who would do what he was told, no questions asked. Preferably someone who was smart enough to understand that Vin knew how to maneuver him through the ranks, but dumb enough to think that he could actually fight a little. Vin needed someone aggressive and fearless, so that even losses, when they inevitably came, could be spun to advantage.

And he had one further requirement: his fighter must be white. "Other guys, they get to go to bars, have a few laughs, a couple of drinks. Me, I'm searchin' for big, young, well-built white guys. How fucked up does that sound?"

He didn't know at the time where Peter McNeeley's payoff would come from, and he meant to keep him undefeated until it did, but he wasn't naïve.

"Look, I realize mistakes can be made. Peter might lose a fight or two. That's not necessarily the worst thing. A guy's undefeated, you're never sure about him; maybe he's better than you think. A careful manager might steer clear of having his guy fight him. But if you see a coupla losses on his record to guys he's supposed to be able to beat, you know he's safe. If I move Peter to 36-1 or 38-2, I'm gonna get them calls."

He did get them. He didn't take them; they would have resulted in sure losses for McNeeley, but not for the kind of money that made desecrating his record worthwhile. Vin was going to hold out for *the right* calls.

I was something new to Vin Vecchione—a boxing guy who didn't seem like a boxing guy. As much as he didn't want people knowing his business, what he was trying to pull off was too brilliant to let come to pass without a witness. It had to be someone who Vin trusted and whose intelligence he respected, and I got the nod.

Vin was an inveterate late-night caller. The magnitude of his grand design would get to him; he wanted someone to help him work things out aloud, which meant for the most part listening to his monologue. This strategic play-by-play would always start without any greeting.

"You know me," he'd begin—the words slowly drawn out like the beginning of a well-rehearsed comedy skit already familiar to its audience—"Wouldn't you say that I'm pretty cute?"

I would then get a detailed account of either some play he'd set up or how he'd avoided a perilous offer that would have jeopardized Peter's progress.

"I cahn't explain these things to most guys," he'd tell me. "They think this is about *boxing*. About two guys fighting each other so you can know which guy beats the other guy. So I get this call from Katz. He wants me to put Peter in with David Tua. With David Tua."

"Yeah, I got the same call for Martin Foster. Five thousand dollars."

"I got offered a little more than that. Katz says to me, he says, 'Why ain't you gonna take it, Vinnie? He's undefeated, your guy is undefeated. Let's see who's better.' Like we're a couple of . . . what you call them guys? Sportsmen."

"Tell him you'll bet him on who wins. You can take Tua."

"At least I'd have a shot at making some money."

It was hard to know what bothered him more: that people in the boxing business would be dumb enough to make an offer like that or that they'd disrespect him enough to think that he might actually take it.

We were in North Carolina getting wins for our heavyweights when Top Rank's East Coast matchmaker Ron Katz called to offer McNeeley a televised fight against Joe "The Boss" Hipp.

It was the opposite of the Big Call Vin was waiting for. Joe "The Boss" Hipp was a Blackfoot Indian from Yakima, Washington; a fat, quick-tempered, out-of-control southpaw drunk who no one wanted to fight. He was impossible to knock out, could punch, and was a genuine roughneck, using head and forearms in addition to his fists. Hipp wasn't too particular about where his punches landed either.

Vin and I were standing on the balcony of his motel room, soaking up the warm Raleigh sunshine, killing some time before the evening's card. Katz droned on and on, seemingly unwilling to take no for an answer. I could dimly hear his voice, hectoring on the other end of the line.

Vin would never accept the fight for Peter, but he was getting a kick out of letting Katz spin his wheels. He was laughing to himself, periodically raising his eyebrows at Katz's wheedling.

Meanwhile, the price kept going up. At one point, Vin stifled a laugh. "I'm sorry, Ron. I didn't catch that last thing. Could you say it again?" He put the phone up to my ear.

". . . saying that I don't understand what the problem is. After all, he's just an *Indian*."

From that day on, whenever an absurd proposition was offered to Vin or me, we would use the code phrase "After all, he's just an Indian" to characterize it.

Eventually, Ron Katz, frustrated by his inability to get the fight signed, raised the offer beyond what it was actually worth—somewhere in the $50,000 range. Vin didn't have a dime. I was footing the bill for McNeeley's fight—covering plane fare for him and Vin, paying the opponent, and kicking in an additional thousand to Peter to make him feel like a professional. Fifty thousand dollars was a lot to Vin at the time—I was keeping him in walking-around money during the trip—but he never gave a thought to taking the fight.

And then Vin's years of waiting, preparation, and going without paid off. I found myself in the small office of the antique shop with Vecchione and Braverman at the meeting that set Mike Tyson–Peter McNeeley in motion. I even bought Vin the airline ticket that got him there.

All of those years boiled down to one Wiseguy 101 play between two savvy operators. Although later other interesting developments came directly from the conversation in Al's office, the terms for the Tyson fight itself could not have been simpler. The purse would be a modest $700,000, of which $100,000 would be illicitly siphoned off as a thank-you to Braverman. Vecchione and McNeeley would split the rest evenly. The 50-50 split was in violation of existing laws relating to licensed boxing managers, who were entitled to no more than one-third of their fighter's purses. This was a nonissue to Vecchione, who had earned his half, and to McNeeley too.

Before the Tyson fight, Don King decided it would make sense for his fighter to go straight from prison to the heavyweight title. The WBC champion was the wayward Oliver McCall, an unhurtable monster King could only control to a degree.

McCall was generally agreeable, but given to sudden bursts of perceived injustice that might at any moment violently awaken him from his default in-ring passivity. When he decided to put someone away, he'd do it. McCall was also a drug addict—something that only added to his volatility—and much older than his advertised age.

He and King had done business before and the promoter must have thought that they could do more. Tyson would fight McNeeley, not McCall, for the WBC title. It was a safer fight—since Oliver could knock out the rusty and disenchanted Tyson if he chose to—and a more marketable one. Further, if the unthinkable happened and Peter beat Tyson, it set up lots of opportunities for King—ones that wouldn't be there if McCall took his cash cow out of the picture.

King reasoned that the road ahead would be fraught with problems with McCall involved. At any stage, for any reason, Oliver had the ability to upend everyone's big plans. Was the heavyweight title per se, fractured and devalued, worth that much? Or would Tyson's return to the ring be the richest boxing match ever, irrespective of who was in the other corner?

Although the Oliver McCall–Peter McNeeley WBC heavyweight title bout had been announced, signed for, and the occasion for a blowout gala in the penthouse at 30 Rock, the fight never took place.

I had been at the fete with Vin Vecchione, Peter McNeeley, Tom McNeeley, and Al Braverman. When I saw Peter on the dais with McCall, my first thought was, "Nobody will ever believe this."

Don King must have come to the same conclusion. He pulled the plug on the fight, moving McNeeley straight to Tyson.

Although signing for the Tyson fight would bind fighter and manager to a three-year self-renewing contract with Don King Productions, it was tacitly understood that once that fight was over—assuming that McNeeley lost as expected—Vecchione and McNeeley would be free to make what they could of the opportunities it opened up.

In the months leading up to the fight, I heard from Vin almost every day. Some nights there were two or three phone calls, with Vecchione testing out ideas, voicing worries, providing training updates, telling funny stories. When I was on the island and unavailable, he was given to leaving short, cryptic phone messages.

"Chaales, I seen something on TV about that Huey Long down theyuh in Louisiana. You don't think they'd let a guy like that stick around, do ya? See ya."

He sang, "Help . . . I need somebody. Help . . . not just anybody. Help . . . I need a friend."

I had to fly into Boston from Puerto Rico a couple of weeks before the fight. I was in some legal trouble that seemed orchestrated to lure me back to a reachable spot. There was an indictment, and it had me nervous. Without going into detail, if the witnesses against me showed up, I was fucked. If they didn't, the case would fall apart. They didn't show up, the case was dismissed without prejudice, and I wound up with some free time to kill with Vin, who was preparing to fly his crew out to Vegas.

We had lunch at the Braintree Holiday Inn Express. Too much was going on, but Vin was handling it, listening to offers, accepting and rejecting, making side deals for everything imaginable, bringing in experienced, reliable sparring partners to build up McNeeley's confidence, and figuring out what all the Vegas angles might be.

He was philosophical about his fighter's chances.

"I'm not saying he's gonna win, Chaales. It's gonna be short and explosive, one way or the other. I'm sendin' Peter maachin' right out after Tyson. Nobody knows what Mike's got left. We might be catching him at the right time. He ain't been in the ring in years, and he wasn't what he'd been when he got sent away."

I said, "If he wins, he'll make more money than any fighter in history for the rematch."

"And even if he *doesn't* win, there are gonna be things for him to do."

Just before we headed our separate ways, we sat in Vin's car in the Holiday Inn parking lot. Boston was going through a heat wave, so we kept the car doors open while the air conditioning kicked in.

I was thinking about how much was on the line for Mike Tyson. Peter McNeeley was the safest opponent imaginable, but the only sure results in boxing come from fixed fights. Tyson was a billion-dollar industry.

"Vin, has anyone come to talk to you?"

Vecchione looked theatrically to his left and right to see if anyone was within earshot, then whispered dramatically, "Chaales, close the door."

No one had talked to Vin. McNeeley was so lightly regarded that he was allowed to do his worst. I flew back to Puerto Rico. I was going to be stuck watching the fight on my twenty-foot Outer Space rotating satellite dish.

A strange thing happened. The day before the fight I got a phone call.

"Our friend wanted me to let you know that a million-dollar bet got placed that the fight wouldn't go ninety seconds. He thought you'd find that interesting."

"I do. Please tell him that I appreciate his letting me know."

"I'll do that."

There was nothing I could do with the information. It was too late, and I was in too remote a place to take advantage of it.

As the world knows, the Mike Tyson–Peter McNeeley fight ended abruptly at the 89-second mark when Vin Vecchione stepped into the ring to force an automatic disqualification. His explanation was that he was saving his fighter. That may well have been true, but I knew it wasn't the only thing he was saving.

I got paid well for the Tyson–McNeeley fight. Not the kind of paid that a few others were, but Vin took care of me generously. He remembered that when times had been lean, I'd helped him.

Over the years, I've read a surprising number of articles where upright citizens who can tell you what's right and what's wrong lambast me for not showing "remorse" at having been rewarded from the Tyson fight. I can assure them that I have felt a lot of remorse: it still breaks my fucking heart that I didn't have time to get a huge bet down from the tip I was given.

Taken for a Ride

I had fucked up. I had trusted in the good sense of a man I didn't know too well on the basis of a couple of things he'd done right for me. And he had fucked up, so I had fucked up.

The guy was a veteran matchmaker who had fixed thousands of fights. He knew his business. But he was a small-timer, so maybe he couldn't see past the immediate tiny score. He'd pocketed $1,000 that he was supposed to give someone to fall down in the first round, trusting that the fighter's ineptitude would produce that result on its own.

Minutes before the fighters were brought to the ring, I got a bad feeling. It wasn't the jitters that always accompany fixing a fight. This came from some subrational part of my system. I thought, "You better take care of this right now."

I couldn't find the matchmaker, so I poked my head into the loser's dressing room. The designated victim was sitting forlornly on a bench, gloved up but seeming unready. The boy was white trash—a tall pasty kid with no visible muscle—simultaneously scrawny and flabby. He had a thinning thatch of bleached-out hair and terrible acne. There were bags under his eyes. He looked less like a fighter than a high schooler who'd knocked up his fourteen-year-old girlfriend and was trying to fix it by working nights down at the 7-11.

He was attended by a black sharpie wearing an ornate pimp's hat—an unnecessary artifact of one exploitative profession transposed to another. Because he didn't factor into the decision-making process, I didn't bother talking to the fighter.

"Does he know what to do?"

"What you mean what to do? Do he know how to fight?"

"No. I already know he can't fight. Did the matchmaker go over things with you?"

"What you mean?"

"He didn't pay you?"

"Pay after the fight."

"How much?"

"Seventy-five-dollar a round. Three hunnit dollars."

"And that's all you're getting?"

"That's all."

"Stay here. Both of you. Don't go to the ring. Don't leave this room. Wait for me. You hear me? Do not leave this room."

I found the Mob guys ringside. With their expensive suits and upscale warm-up jackets, lumpy bodybuilder physiques, and deep salon tans, they stood out among the sea of sleeveless T-shirts.

I told them, "We've got a problem. The guy didn't fix the fight."

"We don't got a problem. *You* got a problem."

The guy I dealt with most stood up, threw an arm over my shoulder to draw me in, and opened his jacket. Firmly resting against his side was a holstered gun. He barely made an effort to hide it from those standing nearby.

"Charles, you'll fix this thing or I swear to God we're gonna kill you. Then we'll kill that cocksucker, kill the faggot promoter, and kill everybody else. I'll put the bullet in the announcer's head personally. Fuckin' take care of it. We're relying on you. You got about five minutes."

"I'll handle it. Sit tight."

He withdrew his arm.

"We ain't going nowhere. I didn't fly all these people out here to go home without getting what we came for. You better make this right, Charles. I don't wanna hear no more bullshit."

My first stop was to the box office where the promoter and announcer were making last-minute preparations for the show.

"We have to hold up the show for a couple of minutes."

Michael Buffer was a sanctimonious pretty boy whose success was based on one idiotic catchphrase. He looked put out. That was his default expression when he wasn't in front of a camera.

"Hold up the show? For how long? Why? Who are you?"

"I'm the guy who's telling you that we're holding up the show."

From the auditorium, "The Star-Spangled Banner" began playing over the loudspeaker system.

I found the matchmaker in the back of the auditorium. He was a dishonest, furtive, chain-smoking little weasel. A lifetime of obsequiousness had twisted his body into a perpetual question mark. He knew boxing. He could bring opponents who'd lose. He could fix fights. He could work a corner and stitch up cuts. He was a low-level jack of all unsavory trades. We'd done business in the past. I'd never liked him but until that moment things had gone fine between us.

I dragged him into the intended loser's dressing room, and then cleared everybody but the fighter and the sharpie out.

"You didn't tell him what to do."

He gave me a wheedling smile. Then he coughed. He fished around his shirt pocket for his cigarettes.

"It's a one-round fight. This boy cain't fight a lick. He cain't beat nobody. Your kid's sure to knock him out in the first round. Guaranteed."

"You didn't pay him off. My guy can't fight a lick either. Right now, he's back in his dressing room throwing up. If this hillbilly even looks at him wrong, he's going to keel over. I'm not even sure he can walk to the ring. You weren't paid to bring in a stiff, you were paid to fix the fucking fight. They're about to come in here and kill all of us."

"I'm telling you it won't go but one round!"

I turned to the sharpie.

"Take off that fucking hat."

"Say what?"

Precious time passed while my brain went on strike. Then I woke up.

"In about one minute, some men are going to come in here and shoot all of us. They're going to shoot your fighter, me, and this fucking piece of shit. And then they're going to shoot you. Now take off your hat and listen to what I'm telling you."

I turned to the fighter and started giving him instructions. He was not to throw any punches. He was not to move far from his own corner. He was to back into the ropes when hit. And he was to go down the second he felt a punch land on his face.

He swallowed hard. He blinked.

"No, sir. I cain't do that."

"You're going to do it. You have to do it."

"No, sir. I maybe ain't much of a fighter and I heard he come down from New York. He's prob'ly gone beat me anyways, but I cain't just quit. My family's here. They come to see me fight. My mother is here."

I pointed out that they'd rather see him lose than see him dead. But he wasn't buying it.

He clamped his mouth shut tight and nodded his head vigorously. He began to shake. Then he burst into tears.

"He's some kinda big amateur star from up in New York. Prob'ly kill me anyway." His voice was no more than a whisper.

I was reminded that some people were too dumb to live.

"Yeah, he would. But we're never going to find out."

I turned back to the matchmaker.

"Pay him. Give him everything you've got in your pockets."

"Well, course some of that's the gate receipts. And some's my own money. Plus, what you give me."

"That's your problem. Empty your pockets."

It came to about $1,800 that I had him hand over to the fighter's now-hatless attendant. I told the matchmaker to guarantee the kid four straight wins after tonight's fight.

And then I thought of something else. I told the kid, "You don't have to fight under your own name. Make up a name so you won't have the loss on your record."

I made the mistake of asking him his name, then telling him to come up with a new one.

Seconds passed. He began panting. He stared off into space. His shoulders slumped. It was too much for him.

He kept coming up with names that were the same as his real name, with one letter changed. Mike Jones turned into Mike Bones or Ike Jones.

He was breathing in ragged sobs. He wouldn't look at me. He kept at it, nonsensically coming up with names that were silly rhymes of his real name.

"Okay, forget it. I'll think of a name. Come with me."

I brought the three clowns out to the parking lot. Most of the customers were already in the building. The few who weren't witnessed an odd sight.

I told the fighter to put his hands up. He started to go into a tentative fighting pose. As he did, I hit him in the stomach as hard as I could. I'm no puncher, but he was very soft. He made a noise of surprise. What made people think that they could be fighters? I punched him in the same spot again. It moved him back slightly.

"This is what's going to happen. Back up when you get punched. Do not punch back. Don't even *start* to punch back."

He nodded. I punched him in the face as hard as I could, badly splitting his lip. He hadn't seen it coming. He was no fighter. I hoped that the punch might hurt him enough to make him worry about what a real punch would feel like. He blinked and backed up another step.

I turned to his now-hatless keeper. "You see how it works? Third punch, throw in the towel. Toss it in high and make a show of doing it. Yell something as you throw it. Make sure it lands in the center of the ring where the crowd can see it. Step into the ring if you have to. You understand?"

"I understand."

I rushed back to the box office. Pretty boy was where I'd left him.

"We're changing the name of the fighter in the first fight."

He looked down at his notes.

"Which one?"

I told him. "He's fighting under a different name. Doesn't matter what. Think one up."

Buffer instantly came up with a good one, throwing in a nickname.

"A nickname? Motherfucker. I didn't think you had it in you."

From there, I went to the loser's dressing room and told the now-hatless sharpie to wait five minutes, then bring his fighter to the ring.

I got the loser going, and then went back to the Mob guys at ringside.

"All set. Bring your kid out."

"The guy knows what to do? You're sure?"

"Positive."

"Stay right here. Don't go nowhere."

"No, let me get right up under the other kid's corner. I want to be where they can see me."

"Okay. One round, right?"

"One round."

If you didn't know that the Mob kid saw himself as a condemned man walking to the gallows, his slow procession to the ring would have seemed impressive.

"I Got the Power" rattled the foundation of the old arena. A black hood covered the Mob kid's head. He was flanked by a somber entourage of large men. The group took a half-dozen steps in unison, then paused. The audience grew more agitated, sensing that something unusual was taking place. The local fighters didn't have entourages. They didn't have entrance music or wear hoods. They didn't look so scary.

By the time the Mob kid entered the ring, the crowd was primed for something horrifying to happen.

Although he was a tiny heavyweight, the Mob kid, with his steroid muscles, plastic bulk fleshing out his pectorals and traps, looked massive next to the Loser. Both fighters kept their eyes glued to the canvas during the referee's instructions.

The bell rang. In a blind animal panic, the Mob kid tore out of his corner throwing punches wildly. He trapped the Loser on the ropes and flung undirected haymakers. From just beneath the corner, I could hear both guys hyperventilating. The Loser may have genuinely sagged against the ropes, clearly caught by surprise. The noise in the arena was deafening.

Half a dozen punches landed on shoulders and arms before the first clean blow struck. It landed with full force, legitimately snapping the Loser's head violently back as a white towel sailed high over the top rope and fluttered to the center of the ring.

The referee jumped between them, grabbing the beaten fighter around the waist with one arm while pushing the winner away with the other. Exactly seventeen seconds had elapsed from the opening bell.

The crowd was in an uproar—a howling mob. It had all looked very real. If I hadn't set it up myself, I wouldn't have known.

I rejoined the Mob guys. I received kisses from every one of them, including the two who less than a year later would receive the contract to kill me. Tears streamed down their faces even as they all laughed hysterically.

"You really made your bones tonight, Charles. You handled things the right way. This was the first step. But we gotta lot of big plans. Did you fuckin' see him in there? He did it! I couldn't believe it. He was an animal! He nearly killed that kid."

Another one in the group said, "Yeah, yeah. I hope the kid's okay. Jesus, we just about took his head off. He's got an awesome killer instinct."

"I know. Unbelievable. Charles, is that kid gonna be okay?"

It was as if they believed what they'd seen was real. Maybe they did believe it.

"I think he'll pull through. The ref jumped in on time."

"Yeah, it's a good thing he got right in there. Thank God for that. We coulda had a fatality."

'Well,' I thought, 'you got that right.'

On and on they went. They were convinced that they'd brought the next Mike Tyson down from New York City. Better than Tyson in their view because Tyson was a nigger.

The New York Mob got what they wanted.

The Loser earned more for a few seconds of work than he'd ever again make in his sorry career. Presumably the sharpie got his hat back.

The knockout broke the existing record for the shortest fight in the state's history. The local sports pages gave it a good write-up the next morning.

And people were fooled into thinking that the Mob kid could actually fight.

Under the circumstances, everyone should have been happy with the night's result and let things go at that. But the Mob wasn't what it had once been. At some level they realized that they didn't know what they were doing, and it short-circuited their systems, leaving them looking for others to blame.

Still, I thought I was off the hook, and got busy with my other fighters on the card. I didn't think that my friends from New York would start building up resentment toward the matchmaker within minutes of their victory celebration.

After cementing my last fighter's win, I started to go back to my hotel room. I was pulled aside.

"We can't let this thing go. We gotta do something about that little cocksucker."

"Why? The fight went perfectly. Even better than it was supposed to. Just let it go."

"Nah, we can't do that. We can't let him get away with making assholes outta us."

"He didn't get away with it. And you didn't look like assholes."

"No. Because he got caught."

"Right. Because he got caught."

"But he hasn't paid for being caught. He's gotta pay."

"He paid $800 of his own money. That's a lot of cash for a guy like that."

"That's not how I mean, Charles. We wanna talk to him. Go get him."

That's when I understood that there was a chance that they might wind up killing me. Not for what I had done wrong—although I admittedly *had* done something wrong—but because I'd witnessed something that caused them embarrassment.

I found the matchmaker across the street at a restaurant where the fight crowd hung out after the card. In a town where most fights lasted one or two rounds, it wasn't unusual to see the winner and loser of a fight amiably chatting together at the same table.

The matchmaker was sitting with the promoter, the promoter's much older wife, who sometimes bankrolled his cards, and a group of their society friends out for a night of rubbing elbows with colorful lowlifes.

I motioned for the matchmaker to come with me. He picked up his fork and pantomimed that he was still eating and then he gestured to the others at the table. He was busy at the moment.

It was the wrong thing for him to do. The gesture made me angry. I approached the table.

"Don't let me interrupt your dinner. You don't mind if I borrow our friend for a few minutes? He and I have some business to discuss."

The matchmaker threw the promoter a pleading look, but the promoter was a predatory little son of a bitch. He had a survivor's instinct to cut a wounded animal loose.

"Wanna borrow our friend, do ya? Yeah, I guess we can spare him for a while."

It took the matchmaker a long time to walk the length of the restaurant. He knew I was bringing him to the Mob guys, and he knew they might kill him.

"Charles, please. He only gone one round. He got his money. I'll never do it again. Talk to 'em. The kid I picked cain't fight. You seen he couldn't fight."

"I told them. They don't care. Let's go."

"I'm scared. Cain't you tell them you couldn't find me?

"You know I can't do that."

The fact was, I didn't want to do that. As much as I didn't want the matchmaker killed, I felt no sympathy for him.

He'd been foolish and had made things tough for me as a result.

Even with that, killing him made no sense. No damage had been done. The matchmaker's losing his own money, added to being scared out of his wits, seemed like appropriate compensation for the nonsense he'd tried to pull.

The Mob guys didn't think so. They were waiting for us in a van outside. The side panel door was open. I didn't want to see any of them, but the one I least wanted to see was in the driver's seat with his window rolled down.

One of the men got out of the back seat and motioned for us to get in. Another man was in the rear seat. That made four.

We got into the van, and the guy who'd waved us in followed and closed the door. That was it. The driver rolled up his window and we pulled away. They had the matchmaker direct them how to get out of town. He cooperated. I'd seen that before; people trying to save their own lives stopped fighting those who might kill them. I'd never seen it work.

The matchmaker was now visibly shaking. He looked small and old and used up. I managed to keep from shaking, but I understood how the matchmaker felt. The Mob guys bringing me along was a bad sign.

One of the men turned to the matchmaker.

"You thought we were gonna let you get away with this?"

"No, sir. I'm sorry. I tried to pick the right opponent."

Nobody said anything. I began to think that this really was going to be the end. The silence frightened me more than anything else. The matchmaker would try to say something, to get them to listen to him, but the four men paid no attention. They didn't look at him. Periodically they'd talk among themselves, saying inconsequential things. They even laughed. That was the most unsettling part. It was as if the matchmaker and I weren't there.

We drove for about twenty minutes. We left the city and the road became quiet. It was the middle of nowhere. The van smelled like sweat and cologne, aftershave and the matchmaker's tobacco. It smelled like angry and terrified men. It was horrible.

The guy in the seat with us said, "We don't let people screw us. It doesn't happen."

He addressed the rest of the men in the van.

"What do you think we ought to do with this piece of shit?"

Nobody said anything for a minute. Then the man in the front passenger seat said, "I don't think there's anything you *can* do with a guy like this. You can't reason with him."

We had pulled over. It was the middle of the night and the highway was now empty.

The matchmaker started to talk.

"I know I done wrong. Please. I'll never do nothing like that again. I picked a kid who cain't fight. I shouldn't have done it. I should've done what I was told. Please don't do nothing to me. I'm sorry."

His shaking was noticeable. He smelled very strong. This was it. If it was going to happen, it was going to happen now. There was humming in my ears, a pressure. The men looked hazy in the darkened van.

"Charles says we should let you go."

"Yes, sir."

"Get out of the van. Charles, stay inside."

The matchmaker got out. The man in the back came over the seat and got out of the van.

"Walk away from us. Take ten steps and stand there. Keep your eyes facing forward."

The matchmaker tried to walk but his legs buckled. He steadied himself and walked ten steps. I watched from the open panel.

Nobody said anything. Nobody did anything.

"Get back in the van."

One of the men who'd stepped out climbed over me into the backseat. The matchmaker got in, followed by the other man. We drove back into town. When we got to the hotel, they let the matchmaker out.

The man sitting next to me said, "We'll take you to your hotel."

"It was smart to let him go. You made your point."

"No, we didn't. This isn't over."

The New York crew were bad guys. They could never be trusted; no one was safe around them. They'd do dangerous and reckless things out of stupidity, vindictiveness, and deep insecurity.

But I was a bad guy too. And I didn't just stop being one overnight. I fixed three more of the Mob kid's fights before deciding that nothing good was going to come of it. I pawned him off on someone else, who insisted on being paid up front before each fight.

I had done the right things in the end: the Mob kid had won all of the fights I made for him with first-round knockouts; the fight fixer I moved him over to was highly skilled and equally successful at getting him kayo wins. After some time had passed, I thought the fuckup with the matchmaker was over.

I should have known better. One of the Mob enforcers—a guy who liked me—left a phone message. He needed to tell me about "a few things." I should "await" his call at 10:00 p.m.

My phone rang at 10:00 on the dot. There'd been talk about me bad-mouthing the Mob guys. I said it wasn't true. I had no opinion of them. I didn't talk about them. He said that they'd heard different and that I better be prepared.

"Are they sending you?"

"Yeah, it looks like it. Me and the other guy. 'Cause they know I don't want to do it. But if they tell me to, Charles, I'm gonna. I'm just lettin' you know. Maybe you oughta talk to them first."

I didn't do that. It wouldn't have helped. I heard unnerving things from people in the business. One of the Mob guys foolishly called and left threatening messages. Killing me was now in the pipeline. I took off and went into hiding, first to La Romana in the Dominican Republic, then to

Puerto Rico. Through the factotum Chris Gingrow, they found out what country I was in. They just didn't know where.

I was on my coffee farm at the top of the highest mountain in Las Marías. My horses were in the barn. My dogs were in the house. At night, the only sounds came from the wind, the coquís, an occasional rooster crowing, and the howls of Satos calling between one mountain and the next. The sky was full of stars. I liked the air up in the mountains.

Life on the Farm

I had spent my life wanting to be left alone. Nothing made me more reassured than living on the top floor of a building that had a dead bolt on a solid oak door at the bottom of a long flight of stairs.

After the age of fifteen, I had shown poor judgment in every line of work I'd chosen. A teetotaling introvert, I spent my early professional life as a public performer in venues where everyone drank and comradery was a necessity. I made that bad decision worse by playing in Mob clubs. I had become a gangster even though I didn't have a tough bone in my body. I gambled at things like poker despite being unwilling to do the necessary study into percentage probabilities and not having the requisite ice water running through my veins. I had some talent for managing fighters, but I wasn't cut out to deal with the pettiness, insecurity, and general vindictiveness of the minions you had to talk with to get anything done.

As I turned forty, I decided to become a citizen instead of remaining outside the law. I started buying houses.

Within a couple of years, I had about $3 million—maybe $10 million in today's market—of real estate along with nearly unlimited credit because of my loan-to-value ratio and because I'd bought the first two houses in cash. I also had about $1.5 million in mortgage debt, beautiful (but old) houses that would need constant maintenance and repair, and a landlord's ongoing crises over unpaid rents.

I had to come to terms with paying mortgages, income tax, and real estate taxes. If I didn't pull in $20,000 a month, I wouldn't be able to cover my bills. Living outside the law, I could do it. As a citizen, everything would have had to go right for me to earn that much.

But everything was not going right, and I piled problems onto problems. I got back into boxing with the kind of commitment that requires spending money, adding to the amount I needed to bring in every month. To help make the income from boxing required to cover my expanding expenses, I got involved with various criminals who were in—or were trying to get into—the business.

As Vin Vecchione would have put it, "I done some things for some guys."

And so, I also started looking for places to escape. There'd come a time when something bad would happen, either through my own mistakes or because of the ineptitude and insecurities of the Mob guys. I could feel it coming: I had another couple of years before the roof caved in. I needed somewhere where I'd be impossible to find.

I considered a number of countries: Costa Rica, Belize, and the Dominican Republic; a guy was selling a small private island off the coast of Honduras, but that would have been unmanageable. I got as far as having an offer accepted on a farm in Samaná, before realizing that it wasn't feasible to buy it. There were too many restrictions for traveling in and out of the Dominican Republic.

I wound up looking for land in Puerto Rico. I might have liked the Dominican Republic a little better, but I could come and go in Puerto Rico as easily as I could going from state to state in the U.S. And what I did with my money there was my business.

I rented a house in Rincon, from which I checked out various properties and fincas. Nothing seemed quite right. I wanted a lot of land and a lot of privacy. I actually almost bought a farm in Las Marías, but backed out of the deal when I discovered that the singing from a nearby church carried all the way up to the house. The realtor let me know that there was another bigger, cheaper farm for sale less than a mile away, higher up in the mountains.

She told me, "It's a working coffee plantation, but nobody wants those anymore. They don't make money, the work is really hard, and it takes a lot to maintain them. It's cheaper than the place you almost took."

We drove up to the top of the mountain, went down then up a long, bumpy private road bordered by acre after acre of orange and avocado trees with coffee plants lower down in the fields. It was one of the most beautiful places I'd ever seen.

The owners were a married couple named Santa and Nego. Santa spoke a little English; Nego didn't. He had been born, raised, and schooled on the farm, growing up in the little shack at the foot of the driveway—a small building that now had stalls for three horses. When the realtor told Nego what I did for a living, he asked her to ask me if I knew "Abdullah Boochee" personally.

I liked the place—although the house itself was barely acceptable—but wasn't sure I wanted to buy it. Nego took me by the arm and led me out onto the balcony of the second floor. The entire western half of the island was laid out in all its verdant luxury. We were only a couple of miles from El Yunque, Puerto Rico's rain forest. I'd never seen so much green. It would be eternally heart-stopping. Weather patterns were clearly delineated; one part of the island would be sunny; there'd be a thunderstorm in another. Desecheo Island was visible forty miles offshore. You could see Rincon, Mayagüez, Aguada, Maricao, San Sebastián, and more. The road at the foot of the property snaked circuitously through the mountains; trucks that looked no bigger than toys slowly labored up and down them. Roosters crowed in the distance. Satos barked and howled. There was an ice cream wagon on the road. Its nursery-rhyme theme tinkled faintly in the warm breeze.

Nego looked me in the eye. "Muy tranquilo," he said solemnly. He squeezed my arm empathetically. Nego was a fine, fine salesman. I bought the farm for the asking price then and there.

La Lotería

For a short while I managed a fighter who should have been the first Hispanic heavyweight champion. For a short while the cosmos was in the kind of alliance that not only would have made that possible—it might have even made it easy. But the cosmos is ever-shifting; if you don't make your move at the exact moment that it's propitious, the planets start to shift and you're left with nothing but a small pile of space debris and a bunch of backseat drivers saying, "I told you so."

❖ ❖ ❖

Fernely Feliz sat on a bench across from the main ring at Gleason's Gym, casually wrapping his own hands. Al Gavin had offered to do it, but I didn't want anyone hearing what I was going to say to Feliz.

It was a Saturday early afternoon, and Gleason's was packed with fighters, trainers, managers, and various hangers-on. The fighters were mostly there to work. Everyone else was hustling—jockeying for position, trying to get noticed, looking for employment or advancement.

I was talking quietly with Feliz, carefully laying out exactly what he should to do as he glanced toward the ring where the Russian heavyweight was shaking out in preparation for their sparring. The Russian had an impressive amateur pedigree and would go on to win a version of the heavyweight title a few years later, but I wasn't worried about Feliz handling him.

"Nod your head like I'm telling you something about the guy. Now look at the old guy standing beside the fighter and laugh a little bit, but not too much."

The Russian heavyweight was going to be a breeze for Feliz because he had Tommy Gallagher—the old guy being laughed at—training him. Tommy Gallagher, who had lurked around the periphery of boxing a long time, exemplified why anyone who believed New York to be the cutting edge of anything was either *from* New York or had wandered in off the cornfields of Kansas with a price tag still attached to their hat.

New York was where an ersatz thug like Jimmy Breslin could become an institution; where Cus D'Amato would be mistaken for a wise old man instead of spotted for the chickenhawk he was; a place where Bert Sugar wouldn't be told to please shut up for a second and to take the fucking cigar out of his mouth in a public place; where Rudy Giuliani would be the mayor instead of locked in a padded cell.

New York boxing prospects were no longer up-and-comers, tough guys, slick technicians, or big punchers. New Yorkers were soft and pampered, given signing bonuses, and trained by frauds who couldn't teach them anything.

But the knee-jerk perception that New York was still a major fight center had yet to fade in the 1990s. This overvaluation was a glaring market weakness that nobody seemed to notice, but one I could take advantage of.

If my fighters could flourish in New York, beating the natives in the gym, my trainers outthinking their trainers in the corners—if I could get my guys rated fast while the New York managers struggled, it would be assumed it was because we were singularly great. That wasn't necessarily the case. The New Yorkers just sucked.

New York trainers were vulnerable to emotional pressure too. There weren't many available spots at the top, and the guys who were getting the high-end play were all technically shaky. It made them a touchy and easily rattled bunch.

Establishing favorable conditions was more important than being able to fight. Favorable conditions were all about constructing various atmospheres—making yourself look bigger or smaller than you really were, untouchable in ways that you really were not, vulnerable in ways that you really weren't. It was about pressuring others into behaving rashly.

Much like Cus D'Amato, Gil Clancy, Kevin Rooney, and Teddy Atlas—the Lollipop Guild who rhapsodized in tough-guy Bowery Boys Brooklynese—Tommy Gallagher was much admired by the press as a New York type and by young TV producers as possibly the new Burgess Meredith. Entertainment-business opinions aside, Gallagher was a guy you'd want to see in the opposite corner.

As Fernely was watching the Russian with feigned amusement, various factions within the New York boxing community were watching Feliz. I had started stacking the deck for him around Gleason's and other strategically designated spots, planting the seeds that he was a can't-miss prospect, already too good for anyone in the division. People who mattered listened when I assured them that he would become boxing's first Hispanic heavyweight champion within the next eighteen months.

I won't name the Russian fighter who sparred with Fernely that afternoon because he was managed by a friend of mine. But Gleason's was packed, so a lot of people saw what happened.

When the bell rang, Feliz stayed right in the pocket, either expertly picking off each his opponent's punches or moving his head to avoid them. With each miss, he would land his own hard jab. Fernely didn't have unusually fast hands, but he understood where to place punches and he didn't waste motion. He was also not a terribly hard puncher—the guy he was sparring with had a lot more one-shot power—but rather a jarring one, delivering combinations solidly in unpredictable sequences with pinpoint accuracy, double hooks to head and body with an uppercut following them, straight right, feint, another right, using jabs for leverage and range. In aggregate, they had a discouraging effect.

Knowing how to fight isn't necessarily about being fast or punching hard; knowing how to fight is knowing how to fight. Within a minute of the opening round, the difference in skill level between the two fighters was apparent to everyone watching.

Gallagher began yelling instructions from the corner, immediately echoed by a translator. Initially, Tommy seemed under control. What he was telling his fighter would have made for good television if you were a fan of Rocky or "The Contender" series, but it was tactically useless.

"Back him up! You be the boss!"

The things I yelled to Fernely were tactically useless too in pure boxing terms, but achieved their purpose. I wanted Tommy Gallagher to see that people were laughing at his fighter, which meant they were laughing at him.

"Easy work, Fernely. Have fun in there."

Feliz went about doing the things that would make him look good while making the Russian seem plodding and foolish. It wasn't the same as beating an outclassed opponent up, but it had the same resonance in the gym; the onlookers *thought* the Russian was being beaten up. Tommy Gallagher thought so too and after a while so did the fighter.

Things looked bleaker and bleaker as the round passed. The Russian began loading up, missing by increasingly wide margins, and Fernely started to really lean into his counters, snapping his opponent's head back. Tommy Gallagher began to unravel in the corner, yelling louder, no longer looking for translation.

"What the fuck is *wrong with you?*" He was really screaming. It was embarrassing and funny. "Fight him. *Fight him.* Back him up!"

The tirade—very audible to everyone in the gym—continued between rounds. The Russian fighter had no idea what this maniac was yelling at him. He kept looking at the translator, hoping for some assistance. Both Russians looked miserable.

The Russian Mob guys from Brighton Beach were watching with what I took to be veiled interest. They never got involved in anything that wasn't their business—and the Russian fighter wasn't one of their stable—but they didn't look happy seeing Gallagher abuse a fellow countryman.

It was essential to pull the plug on the sparring at the precise moment when Fernely had inflicted the most possible damage and when things between the Russian and Gallagher had degenerated to their most chaotic—before there was any chance that the fighter could land a lucky shot in desperation.

That moment took place just as the third round was coming to its triumphal or demoralizing—depending on your side of the fence—close.

Feliz was starting to bust up the Russian, who was making the mistake, in his confusion, pain, and—finally—anger, of beginning to actually *look* at the idiot who was hectoring him while pacing back and forth between both sides of his corner. Whatever he was yelling no longer sounded like language. It was gibberish.

I timed things to stop a few seconds before the bell.

"Fernely," I yelled up, "Close it down. That was the last round."

The bell rang. Fernely and the Russian hugged and Feliz left the ring. I lowered my voice, but made sure it was still audible.

"No reason to keep going. You were starting to hurt the kid, and you can't learn from someone at that level. We've got to find you better sparring."

It was all bullshit, of course. The sparring had done him a world of good. But how it redounded for him outside the ring would be even more useful. Those three rounds were going to set in motion a wave of talk. By the end of the day, the word of what had happened would have made it through boxing's communication network. My answering machine would be full of propositions and a range of offers before I got back to Boston.

Because Al Braverman would place Fernely Feliz with Don King Productions and get him rated almost instantly with the IBF, I could turn every offer down. I'd do it politely, having actual conversations that would allow me to disseminate information. People would pass along everything I said.

The goal was to make Feliz the most talked about heavyweight prospect in the world within three or four months.

It was hard to believe that Fernely had had only one pro fight. His ability to discourage an opponent by combining solid, well-placed punches with total economy of movement, along with an impassive countenance, was something that was almost exclusively the domain of experienced, cerebral fighters.

Not only had Feliz only had one pro fight, he'd had almost no amateur ones—something I was always quick to point out. I wanted to send the message to people in the business that he was a savant—one of those rarest of boxers who was *born* able to do uncanny things in the ring.

"*He* can't even explain how he does it. He just does everything right. He *sees*. He'd beat Holyfield or Bowe right now."

This was the kind of statement that real boxing people, impressed but not unduly swayed by what Feliz had done at Gleason's, would correctly regard as ludicrous.

It didn't matter. I could get away with it in New York, the East Podunk of Big Cities. But people in other cities, hearing that the word was coming directly from The Big Apple, would confer legitimacy on it.

Vin Vecchione Warns Me about Fernely Feliz

Things were on track with Fernely Feliz's career, but he was paranoid and skittish. Vin Vecchione didn't like him from the start.

"I know this Feliz is a lot more *talented* than Peter. He's probably more talented than any of the heavyweights out there. But this is one treacherous little cocksucker, Chaales. He bears watching. He's never gonna be grateful for all you done for him. And I ain't sure he won't stab you in the back down the line. With someone like Peter, I never have any doubts—he's gonna be with me 'til death do us *paaht*."

"I don't trust him either, Vin. But I know how to promote him. And he's a hell of a heavyweight. I can get people to jump on board to move him. King will take him right now."

"Yeah, I know all that. But everyone's gonna be in this kid's ear. You ain't gonna get a minute's peace. I understand why it's tempting to take him under your wing. I'm tellin' you, you'd still have a better chance of gettin' your money back if you came in with me on McNeeley. I ain't sayin' that Peter would beat this Feliz if they fought. The thing is, McNeeley ain't never gonna fight Feliz. And King or Arum, or maybe one of them sick, vengeful bastards like Katz or even nice guys like Floyd Patterson or Pat Petronelli—guys who believe this shit is *real*—are gonna throw Feliz in with one of these black animals one day just because they don't have your insight, and the kid ain't gonna come out alive. As soon as he leaves your *protection*, that's exactly what's gonna happen to him."

We were talking in the ticket office of the Whitman Armory, where Vin had extended me the use of the place so I could get wins for Feliz and John Carlo, each of whom had knocked out their friends in the first round.

It wasn't as if I didn't see treachery in Feliz. We had even had a parking-lot altercation earlier in the evening not long before he was scheduled to fight in the show's opener. He and his friend, a Colombian who fought under the implausible nom de guerre "Brian Palmer," tried to hold me up for an extra $200 apiece.

I was angry enough to bluff them. "I'm going to go to my car for your money," I told them. "and to get my gun. I'll bring back your $200, then shoot both of you in the face. Or you can just take the fucking money you agreed to. Your choice."

I didn't have a gun in my car or anywhere else. Either Feliz or Señor Palmer could have left me in a heap in the parking lot. But there are things you can't allow to have happen. And there were plenty of guys in the Armory that night who would have loved to shoot Feliz and his black Irishman pal for behaving like assholes.

Nobody got shot. No one except for the newly minted Brian Palmer got beat up—and that was by Feliz himself, in the ring, gratuitously. But the attempted heist reinforced Vecchione's word of caution. More important, Fernely's reaction to my offer to shoot him, along with a comment he made later in the evening, caused me to reevaluate his chances for becoming a major player in the heavyweight division. When confronted with an ultimatum, in the face of what were clearly overwhelming odds in his favor, he backed down. When I mentioned that to him after his fight, he told me, "Charles, you had the face of the devil when you said you were gonna shoot us. The devil's face came where your face had been. I'm not afraid of no man, but I fear the devil."

He was kind of laughing when he said it. But only kind of.

I started to understand at this point that Feliz, although he might still make it to the heavyweight title, wouldn't be able to do it solely on his boxing ability. His character flaws and fears were too evident. Other fighters, especially those with nothing to lose, would read his body language and take liberties with him. In order to be brought to a championship, Fernely would need a vehicle—management, promotion, and the right matchmaking—and a forum—a dependable television outlet— that together would bring the proper narrative to his particular skills. The proportion of inside-the-ring to outside-the-ring work would have to be recalibrated. Less work for Fernely, more for me. I was reminded of Al Braverman's observation that Fernely had "a little muttsky" in him.

I was a skilled judge of fighters, but maybe Al saw something that I had chosen to be blind to. Although he had looked good in his debut, Feliz had failed to put Muhammad Askia away. Askia was a novice cruiserweight who wound up his career without ever having won a fight. It would have been better if Feliz had capped his two first-round knockdowns with a cinematic kayo. Instead, even with nothing to fear, he'd eased off and let an opponent with no weapons go the distance. Although real boxing professionals would know they were seeing a precocious and gifted heavyweight, Feliz's reticence might have kept them from being completely gung ho over him.

Not that that mattered much. Serendipity and hard work had already placed me in the epicenter of conversations and meetings that, if parlayed properly, would gain Feliz an escort through the rope barriers directly into boxing's VIP room. Braverman's role as majordomo for Don King, along with my not having to be reminded to share the wealth, gave me an enormous advantage over nearly everyone in the business.

King moved into the equation through a serpentine arrangement where, through Al Braverman, I served as the conduit between him and Wayne Huizenga. My unlikely introduction to the billionaire mogul was made by way of some bad guys I was associated with in New York City, Boca Raton, and South Beach in Miami. There was another liaison between the bad guys in New York and Huizenga. A rich devotee of La Dolce Vita from Boca Raton had also worked his way into the mix, and King would soon find ways to take advantage of this thrill-seeker.

Being in the center of this aggregation was factionally awkward and dangerous, but it offered me unlimited opportunities if I could hold onto my spot as a much-needed facilitator and the "real" boxing guy of the group.

Braverman could only help to a limited degree. I understood the ways that cagey small-timers like me might find their way on board in the early stages of an operation; the understanding among the major players being that they didn't have the know-how to put the pieces together themselves. The small-timer had the vision, provided all the brainwork and legwork, brought together all the principals, and was responsible for getting the show on the road. From an interested remove, the powerbrokers watched all this, learning whatever they could—although what they learned was never more than a tiny part—then iced the luckless motherfucker out of the picture.

It was my job to not let myself become that luckless motherfucker.

I had my method for how stay on the inside, although it was one that ran contrary to accepted practice. The trick was to give your vision away to the very people who wanted to steal it. Tell them your ideas, explain the ingenuity of those ideas, then allow them to benefit from them as if they were their own. After that, you scare the shit out of them.

I told three of the New York Mob guys, "I'm not being a wiseguy and I'm not trying to insult you. What I'm doing for you is something I can do all day, every day for anyone who pays me. I will never run out of ideas because I understand this business in a way few people do. I can tell you who can fight and who can't; and I can let you know who has the potential to become a star—which isn't the same as knowing who can fight.

I'm giving you a free sample, and not a small one. You can steal the information and then get rid of me. But it's important to bear in mind that tomorrow I will have a fresh set of ideas while you're wondering what to do next. You won't know how to use what I've given you. That's just how it is. You'll ask me to come back and I won't do it, even though I'm no tough guy.

I'll let anyone take advantage of me once. That helps me learn about the people I'm doing business with. Nobody can do it twice. I'm telling you this now because I believe you're smart enough to pay attention. It's much, much better to keep me around, pay me what I'm worth, let me build my stable, and benefit from what I know. It's up to you, of course."

I knew the speech would work in the short run—it always did—but that its shelf life was limited. I had my fingers crossed that there'd be enough time for me to become manager of the first Hispanic heavyweight champion before cupidity and ego caused them to let the whole thing blow up. Because, whatever else I saw, I saw with complete clarity that they were going to fuck it all up in the end.

Dinosaurs Roam Miami

Just crafty enough to keep from being crushed under the feet of the slow-moving behemoths who'd sent for me, I wound up first at the home of the Dolce Vita guy in Boca Raton and then at a hotel right off the water on South Beach. Don King hadn't met with Wayne Huizenga yet. The advance teams consisted of the New York guys, Huizenga's executives, some television personnel, and me. King would come in later if all went well at the meeting in Huizenga's South Beach offices.

There seemed to be an unwritten law that to step onto South Beach you had to be young and beautiful. Everyone had big dreams of opening a hot disco or the hippest late-night tapas bar on the beach. The beautiful youngsters didn't know it yet, but they were for the most part dinosaur food.

The New York guys were brontosauruses who saw themselves as tyrannosauruses. As large as buildings, with comparable speed and brainpower, they were locked into their conviction that might made right, despite dimly receiving signals—unsettling ones that they found difficult to process— that things were going on around them that they didn't understand.

The locals were the smaller, faster-moving, faster-thinking predators who were in the process of replacing their dumber brethren. They didn't understand that, despite their superiority, they were still fucking *dinosaurs*, on their way to extinction too.

Other than sharing a putative common goal, all that held the two groups together was their commitment to various men's colognes and hair products.

I'd come to Miami armed to the teeth. I'd be able to explain to Huizenga's people the direction boxing was going, and how a quickly growing Hispanic demographic, when combined with high-quality TV outlets, an identifiable local venue filled with enthusiastic fans, the name-brand recognition that Huizenga's sports and entertainment affiliation conferred, and the savvy development of fighters—focused specifically on the journey to the heavyweight title of a charismatic Latino contender—could bring untold wealth to whoever was prescient enough to put these things into play.

There was more: I'd tell the group about how, partially through design and partially through good fortune, we'd assembled exactly the right people in the right place at the right time to be able to mount a campaign that would revolutionize how boxing was packaged and sold. We had the technology. In Don King, we had boxing's leading promoter. In Wayne Huizenga, we had the world's most prominent sports and entertainment impresario. We had a built-in Hispanic fan base who until Fernely Feliz came along lacked the vehicle for claiming the heavyweight championship of the world—the greatest prize in sports—for their own. And, in me, we had someone uniquely suited to put all of these components together.

Although I couldn't say it, we also had an enormous albatross that I needed to misrepresent as being yet another part of the winning combination. The New York guys, in their enthusiasm, were loaded with harebrained ideas that they kept giddily bringing up in conversation.

"What do you think of the idea of tag-team boxing?"

"Boxing is the ultimate individual sport, Tom. I think it'd be unwise to tamper with that."

"Okay, okay. But how about at least team boxing, where the winner is chosen by which team has the most points? Like a boxing league. We could have playoffs at the end of the season."

This was the weight that was bearing down on the back of my neck. And the bearers were guys who carried guns and were easily insulted. I couldn't say, "Tom, at least as it's perceived by the public, boxing's most treasured aspect is its sentimental glorification and elevation of the individual. Everything about boxing militates against the notion of 'team.' Fans' identification with specific fighters as men who have accomplished greatness *on their own* is a characteristic almost unique to the sport. Why on earth would you want to fuck around with such an obvious winning formula?"

Instead, I'd be forced to use flattery: "That's a very challenging concept, Tom. But it's way too advanced for most people. It'd be far over their heads. Maybe sometime down the line, after we're established, we can begin to implement an idea this groundbreaking."

I knew the New York guys were liable to pipe up with this kind of foolishness right in the middle of the meeting. I was worried that Huizenga's execs—most of them themselves young jocks with insecurity problems connected to issues of masculinity—might go all-in on ideas that would immediately torpedo any promising project.

"Yeah, yeah. We could have really cool team jerseys made! We could wear 'em too!"

"We could even do a kind of corporate thing, where we all walked the team's fighters to the ring. That'd be *cool*."

"Oh man, I can see it now; 'Huizenga's Howitzers' or 'Wayne's Warriors.'"

This kind of thinking was how the dinosaurs would be wiped out by cataclysms they never saw coming. I had to figure out how to keep everyone in their exact lane while giving them the impression that we were involved in a vigorous exchange of ideas.

What did I want out of all this? A guaranteed contract with a mid-six-figure annual salary and control over choosing which fighters the new company signed and who'd they'd be matched up with. A tiny ownership percentage. And I wanted to manage the first Hispanic heavyweight champion of the world.

There were concrete ways to make it happen, some of them contrary to how I generally did things. In signing fighters who could really fight and who had some charismatic quality that could potentially elevate them into the celebrity mainstream, I didn't intend to fix any of their matches. I wasn't going to put them in with stiffs either. The House wouldn't win all the time. We would find narratives that included a safeguard where it was possible to maintain credibility even through occasional losses. If audiences got used to seeing good fights with uncooked results and competent judging, they would remain interested in the product.

Two meetings took place on consecutive afternoons. They went better than I would have thought possible. I was able to light a spark with Huizenga's people and the New York guys, and I had the good sense to let them fan the flames themselves, bouncing hyperbole back and forth, becoming increasingly certain that they had a can't-miss proposition.

"This is a *home run!* We've got the right team to make it happen," one of the New Yorkers predicted.

"And Charles has the fighters?"

"Charles has the fighters. Wait until you see this Feliz kid."

Huizenga's right-hand man asked me, "When can you set up a meeting with Don King?"

"Right away. I'll call him and find out when he's available. We'll do it here? He's in Boca most of the time these days."

I flew back to Puerto Rico. A couple of days later, I got a phone message from Al Braverman.

"Charles, I know you're in Puerto Rico as you told me, but I want you to get ahold of me some whichaway. I'm setting up this thing with Don. I'm setting it up for Monday or Tuesday, probably in Boca Raton. He knows the principals. I had a good talk with Don, and I'm gonna set it up, you know what I mean. I'm setting it up for Monday or Tuesday, but you gotta get in touch with me. I gave him the rundown. We'll sit down, and we'll see. They tried something before, but they never succeeded. Now, through Al Braverman, they're gonna get the shot. And you, naturally, 'cause you've got the people. But he only wants to talk to Wayne Huizenga, that Richie Wright guy, maybe one or two others. He don't want no bullshit. He don't want to speak to no underlings. People that can close. So that's the whole thing. Charles, try and get back to me."

I was down in Rincon when the phone rang a day or two later.

"*Mistuh* Charles Farrell," boomed the voice on the other end, "How's my man today?"

"That'd be up to you, Don. Do we have good news?"

"Ha-ha-ha. We have *fabulous* news, brother! We have the *best* news! We have the best *possible* news! Can you get to a meeting in Miami this afternoon?"

"I don't see how. I'm hours outside of San Juan. Then I'd have to catch a flight."

"I'll send my Learjet. Where you at?"

"I'm in Rincon. The closest airport is Mayagüez. No way they'd be able to handle a Learjet."

"No way they could handle a Learjet. Well, look here, that's alright, brother. I'll take the meeting myself. You ain't gotta be there. Al told me how you set all this up. I'm lookin' out for you, Charles. I got you covered."

"I know you do, Don. I'm just sorry I can't be there to see it."

"Me too, my brother. It's a *beautiful* morning here in Miami."

Later that night I got a call from Braverman.

"The deal's off. Everything got fucked up."

"What? How is that possible? It looked perfect."

"I know, Charles. But Don hit the roof when he got to the meeting."

"Hit the roof about what?"

"Who the fuck knows? He just started with, 'You white motherfuckers think you're gonna make a fool out of Don King? You cocksuckers. You're gonna try to run Don King outta the boxing business? Who the fuck do you think you're dealing with?' He scared the shit out of everybody in the room. He stormed in, was there for ten minutes, then stormed out. White cocksucker this, white motherfucker that."

"How'd you find out?"

"That Richie kid—Huizenga's guy—told me. He was still shell-shocked."

"Al, why would Don do such a thing?"

"I don't know. But Don King never does anything for no reason."

"It seemed like such a good deal."

"It did to me too. But there's some component to it that we're not seeing."

"Jesus, if you figure it out, please tell me what it is."

"Will do, Charles. Will do."

It took me a little while to see it. When I did, I understood that I was still in kindergarten. Throughout the whole setup, I was thinking about what I needed to do, as the smallest player in the game, to keep from getting pushed out by the bigger players. I knew it was inevitable that they'd get around to it.

King immediately understood that in the end this was a two-man game, and that *he* was going to be by far the smaller player in it. He figured out that, once Huizenga got things up and running, *he'd* be the one to fall under the ax.

King never intended to be partners with Wayne Huizenga. He needed to keep Wayne Huizenga *permanently out of boxing*. He decided to create an atmosphere so toxic and unbalanced—to paint a picture of a world so impossibly unpleasant to negotiate—that Wayne Huizenga would never even *think* about revisiting it. King wanted the field to himself.

King had let a number of people unwittingly do his prep work for him, in their own time and at their own expense. He then swooped in at the last second and taken care of business. He didn't even need to catch a Learjet to do it. The ride from his place in Boca to Huizenga's corporate office in South Beach took about ten minutes. I'm sure he had a driver.

Adiós to a Manager

I began to see the writing on the wall with Feliz. He genuinely had all the talent that I ascribed to him—far more than any of the other young heavyweights coming up through the ranks—and he could have been molded into a highly marketable fighter, but he wasn't temperamentally suited to the task. I had a vision for what Feliz could become, but Fernely didn't share it. His goals were more modest. Once I understood that, I knew where he'd wind up.

If you were a heavyweight fighting in the U.S. and you weren't with Don King or maybe Bob Arum, you were more or less relegated to dealing with two other promoters—Cedric Kushner and Gary Shaw. They served as conduits for up-and-coming or down-and-fading heavyweights, with Shaw working as a kind of junior-level Kushner. Kushner, a crafty and intelligent eccentric South African, produced a desperate-sounding television series called the "Heavyweight Explosion" that gave the big guys routine chances to, for very small paydays, knock each other out of the championship sweepstakes.

There was a method to the former rock promoter's madness, however: Kushner's greatest hope was to sign a heavyweight who, after fighting his way to the top on the TV series, might be seen as a no-threat defense for whoever held the championship. Kushner then kept his fingers crossed that his fighter would have the night of his life. This had actually happened for Kushner when Hasim Rahman had knocked out Lennox Lewis. Unexpectedly, Kushner held some real cards for a minute. But while he was gloatingly contemplating his power play, King swooped in on the new champ with a bag of cash.

I had provided Feliz with his opportunity after one fight to be promoted by King, but his chance evaporated when he stalled signing. Through his early career, I paid his utility bills and gave him walking-around cash. I covered the costs for bringing in opponents whom I picked. I booked him as a well-paid sparring partner, gaining him valuable no-risk experience. I was putting in time and money under the assumption that Feliz would commit to signing a contract with me.

When he finally *did* commit, it wasn't to me. Looking to find a level where he was comfortable, he signed with Gary Shaw.

I could tie both of them up through an injunction so that Shaw would eventually throw some money my way. I called Shaw's office, explaining that I was Feliz's manager. I threatened tortious interference.

Shaw, who had made his living mostly in the hotel business in New Jersey, sounded reasonable.

"I don't want to take someone else's fighter," he told me. "Send over a copy of your contract, and I'll either pay you to release him or I'll let him go."

I had a lot of paperwork on Feliz; I could establish significant expenses; I had letters from him asking for money and referring to me as his manager; I had videos of myself in his corner and standing with him during television interviews; there were receipts for airline tickets and paid bills, but no legally binding contract. A judge would award me something if I sued, but it wouldn't amount to much. My lawyer sent faxed copies of all the paperwork to Shaw anyway. It was a weak hand, but the one I'd been dealt.

I didn't hear back from Shaw's office. I hadn't expected to. I made a few calls to him, again threatening an injunction, an impending lawsuit for tortious interference, and other forms of courtroom mayhem, but they didn't work. Nowhere is talk cheaper than in boxing. Everybody knows that.

That's when I saw the future. Fernely Feliz wasn't going to be the answer to anyone's prayers. Fernely Feliz was a *problem*. I could tie up a year or two of my life pursuing my legal claims in court and wind up with ten or twenty thousand dollars if I was lucky.

Or I could watch him go, knowing that the only time he'd see a high-five-figure payday in his entire career was for a fight he'd lose. Shaw would ship him over to Kushner—who wouldn't see anything worth developing there—and he'd get beat in an undercard fight on a "Heavyweight Explosion" show.

I stopped calling Gary Shaw's office, and waited for the inevitable. Which, being the inevitable, happened.

Y Adiós a Una Perspectiva

Fernely Feliz's decision loss to Oleg Maskaev at Madison Garden in a fight where he showed more interest in not being hurt than in winning severely cut into his marketability. It also defined him. His TKO loss to John Ruiz on HBO three years later finished him as a fighter anyone would care about.

Feliz should have handled Ruiz—as he should have handled Maskaev—but Ruiz's manager Norman Stone saw to it that he didn't. Effectively ending the fight before it started, Stoney pointed to his own heart during the referee's instructions at center ring, shook his head sadly as if delivering unfortunate news to a doomed patient, and told Feliz, "No haaht. Ya got no haaht."

Feliz might have had a hard time deciphering the Boston accent but when he walked back to his corner, Stoney's message was completely internalized. He knew it to be true. It was now only a question of finding the excuse he needed to quit. The excuse he came up with was that he was being fouled but unjustly getting no assistance from the referee. And quit he did, in his corner after the seventh round as his trainer Don Turner looked on in astonishment.

The Ruiz fight ended any possible consideration of Fernely as a prospect to be cultivated. Unhurt, he had quit in front of millions of viewers on HBO, boxing's premier forum. His potential to be a star was over.

In boxing, when one door closes, another usually opens up. Although Feliz would never *be* one of them, he was quickly invited into the company of heavyweight stars as a sort of adjunct. The rest of his professional life would be spent primarily as a valued sparring partner to German and Eastern European heavyweights—some of them world champions—providing quality work as they prepared for major fights. He would also lose ten- and twelve-round decisions to many of them, never in danger of being knocked out—Ruiz was his only kayo loss—but never trying his best to win. Interspersed between the losses were insignificant wins over easily defeated opponents to serve as the ballast needed to maintain a credible winning record. Feliz was paid well for both the losses and the wins—more for the losses—and a kind of gentleman's agreement had been reached between Fernely and the leading overseas promoters as to what could be expected of him.

In the end Feliz was able to make a good if unspectacular living in and around boxing. He bought a house in Danbury, Connecticut, some property in the Dominican Republic, and dabbled in auto sales and running his own gym. He raised his family. His son, Fernely Jr.—also a heavyweight—is about to turn pro.

It's a long way from the superstardom I'd had in mind for him, but Fernely Feliz left boxing whole, with his health intact, his head unrattled, and some money in the bank. It didn't occur to me until a number of years after his career was over that maybe this was all he'd had in mind for himself from the beginning.

La Isla del Encanto: Tres Historias

Mofongo
Mofongo is a Puerto Rican dish with fried platanos as its main ingredient. Platanos are picked green and fried, then mashed with salt, garlic, and oil in a wooden pilón. The goal is to produce a tight ball of mashed platanos that will absorb the attending condiments. Most dressings and mixtures include broth, garlic, and olive oil.

At El Jibarito, they thought I was crazy for having them make mofongo sin carne. It made no sense. "How can you have mofongo without pork," the woman behind the counter asked me. "That's what gives it its flavor."

"I don't eat any meat."

"Okay, but at least lemme tell him to put some chicken broth on the side for it so it's not too dry."

"I don't eat any kind of meat, including chicken."

"Okay, okay. You don' eat no fish?"

"No."

"It's gonna be too dry. Lemme give you some garlic mojito to put on it. That don' have no meat of any kind. Completely vegetarian."

It's true that even good mofongo is very dry. It's really a double-fried paste that's exceedingly dense and, on its own, actually has little flavor. The first time I tried it I couldn't understand what all the fuss was about. But I found myself wanting it the next day. You couldn't eat it by itself; the trick was to add it to helpings of maduros, fried yucca, and habichuelas con arroz with lots of salsa. At that point, its function became clear. I got used to having it while seated at the outside terrace at El Coche, overlooking the Caribbean, timing my meal to catch the enormous sun dropping down over the sea, turning the water briefly from aquamarine to red-orange.

A Miracle in Rincon

I was staying in a house on the beach in Rincon. It was a small and somewhat charming place with tiled floors, white walls, and a flat roof you could sleep on if you wanted to watch the stars or hear the waves crashing. One morning I woke to a herd of cows grazing in the front yard. They had wandered out of their pasture next door. I led one of them back, she mooed sweetly, and the rest of the girls followed, masticating peacefully, their hips swaying as they were brought home.

Although in many ways a typical Puerto Rican pueblo, Rincon had one unique characteristic: the Caribbean Sea produced monster waves on the town's beaches that drew a yearly pilgrimage of world-class American surfers to the area. As a consequence, the locals all spoke English fluently. The surfing crowd was a major boon to the economy. People from the town liked the chilled-out surfers, but they didn't socialize with them.

The Church still played a major part in the locals' lives, and the town square overflowed with worshippers on Sunday mornings and holidays. One day a miracle occurred. The statue of the Madonna, prominently on display in the corner of the altar, had begun weeping sometime during the previous night. The suffering in the world must have weighed heavily on her, because she wept steadily throughout the morning. By afternoon the lines waiting to see her had spread down past the town square. Everyone talked about it. There were a lot of people crossing themselves, some already weeping even without having yet seen Mary at it. Having been raised around carnivals and tent shows, I was eager to get a look at what all the ruckus was about. I'd seen long shots before, but no bona fide miracles.

Because I was white and knew to wear a suit when respect was called for, I was mistakenly taken to be pious and important, and got gently pushed to the head of the block's long line.

On this hot afternoon in Rincon, shoehorned in near the altar, among the perspiring, crying, and whispered susurration of prayer, I saw a Madonna who was the unfortunate victim of a plumbing malfunction. For others, it was a miracle; for me it was an invitation to call in the parish handyman.

I was impressed by how the church officials, while neither confirming nor denying, had transformed a maintenance liability into a healthy money-making enterprise that somehow strengthened the conviction of the Faithful. Where I perceived the display as stemming from rusty water serendipitously dripping from a faulty pipe, worshippers saw tears of silent suffering. There was a parable in it somewhere.

Wild Dogs and Two-Headed Calves

By the mid-1990s, right and wrong or good and bad as they related to anyone's actions—even my own—had become too complex a moral issue for me to judge.

Serious men wanted to kill me. They'd traced me to Puerto Rico through information given to them by someone I thought to be my friend.

I felt pushed into a corner. At fourteen I made a decision to never kill any living being, and had kept to it. But I understood killing someone before they could kill you. And I knew where the men lived.

In Las Marías I was reminded of my early education in Old Orchard, where I got used to things not being where I thought they'd be, where floors would suddenly give way and I'd slide down a chute in the dark only to land in a room of mirrors, each mirror presenting its own distorted version of the truth, so all I could think was, "How do I get out of here?"

You could never be sure of what was real. In Las Marías I finally understood that I didn't control even my tiny part of the world I lived in. In Las Marías I was reminded that walls weren't solid. Nothing was ever solid. There were no mountains high enough in areas remote enough reached by roads secret enough to keep you from whatever would be.

Those who loved you most might be the ones who'd finally rip you limb from limb. Those you'd saved so they could live might belong to a tribe more primal than any you could know, and their first obligation might be to that tribe.

Ten dogs lived with me on the farm—six brought from the U.S. and four Satos, the wild dogs who roamed the island. Three of the wild dogs I'd had from when they were puppies, found tossed in the tall weeds by the side of the road and left to die. These dogs were family. I loved and trusted them all. The wild dogs protected the farm.

Then something in the household dynamic changed, and Mabel, second to Perdita in the Sato hierarchy, took up against Lila, a domesticated dog. Mabel was joined by her brother Cheo in Lila's pursuit, and what had been a peaceable habitat fell apart.

I was sitting on the back porch when Mabel attacked Lila. I grabbed Lila, who was petrified and already badly injured, and put her in my lap. Instantly, Mabel came after me, ripping my calf open. Cheo joined her, and my leg was suddenly being torn to shreds. Perdita then rushed over. I had adopted Perdita as a young pup fending for herself on the beach in Rincon. I assumed that she was attempting to rescue me, but she too sunk her teeth into my injured leg. Perdita was a pit-bull mix and capable of doing great damage. Only little Dinah, the lowest in the pecking order, refused to join the attack, walking off into the yard and shaking.

I was trying to protect Lila, who the wild dogs were still trying to reach, while defending myself. I punched Cheo in the head, which backed him off, then did the same with Mabel. Perdita came in for the kill, and I grabbed her by the jaw and pried her mouth open, holding it until the pain made her stop being aggressive.

The attack was over. My leg was in bad shape. The dogs who bit me saw the blood covering my calf and pooling into the dirt and started to whine. They frantically began licking the wounds, distraught over the harm that had come to me. They had moved past what had caused it.

I wasn't mad at my dogs. I still loved them as much as before. I didn't punish them. I let them lick my wounds until they calmed down. They were blameless. But the attack changed everything.

I had to make existential sense out of what had happened. There was an easy way to see it: a pack of wild dogs had reverted to their nature and had banded together to attack someone who wasn't a member of their pack. But they were my family. We would sleep in the jungle together, jumbled together in a big pile. Then, when it counted most, they'd sided against me.

I thought I had reached some kind of equanimity with animals. Insects didn't sting or bite me. The only exception was when I had inadvertently stepped on a tarantula while walking through the jungle barefoot. The tarantula wasn't injured, but it did bite me. I managed to put it into a box and move it to safety in the jungle. The tarantula bite wasn't anywhere near as painful as the dog bites, which had gone right through my calf muscle.

When you live outside the law, it's a good idea to not trust too many people. You have to make prudent decisions about who's with you, and whoever is with you has to be trusted unreservedly. These decisions define who you are and everything you do. Bad judgment doesn't just jeopardize *how your life is lived, it can cause you to question who you are in the world, and what that world actually consists of.*

My dogs attacking me at a time when I was already under siege upended the planet for me. If the nature of a thing—and the dogs were acting in accordance with their nature—runs contrary to what you believed it to be, and some of your worldview is based on that belief, the earth falls out from under you.

Things went further haywire. Niño and Bosko, two of my house dogs, died violently one night, convulsed by a mysterious horror.

Briefly it looked as if Bosko might be saved if he could get help in time. I managed to reach our vet in Mayagüez.

Mayagüez is close to Las Marías as the crow flies, but there is only one winding mountain road most of the way. It's treacherous—barely able to accommodate two-way traffic and requiring frequent pulling over to let oncoming trucks pass. No matter how experienced you are, the drive will take you forty minutes.

During that forty minutes Bosko died. I brought his body to the vet. What took place at the vet's office is one of the most mysterious experiences of my life.

The vet brought me to the parking lot of the small hospital. A farm van was parked there. Inside the van was an adolescent two-headed calf held upright in a kind of sling.

The calf had been born on a local finca, and the farmer believed that its remaining alive and healthy was a blessing and a sign from God.

The calf was beautiful. It was whole and placid and trusting and unafraid. Its four eyes were luminous and angelic. In my despondency, I thought I might actually be looking into the face of an angel.

The calf gazed directly into my eyes and silently told me, "I want to live."

I want to live. Animals will die if they must, but their lives, no matter the conditions, have meaning to them. Their lives have meaning beyond themselves. Their vitality—and vitality is a bestowed gift—connects them to each other and to us.

Ruby and Betty believed in messages and signs. In love and tribute, I tried to believe in messages and signs.

What the two-headed calf showed me was, by itself, simple. But almost nothing exists by itself. I'd received a lifetime of messages over the past few hours. What were they? I didn't know. I still don't know. I've spent the last twenty-five years trying to figure them out.

If we are all connected, aren't we all a tribe? Or are our tribes determined by some chemical primacies too arcane to understand, readable only to those belonging to them?

I soon had to leave Puerto Rico to save my own life. I went to New York City to meet with the men who would have otherwise killed me. While I was away Mabel killed Lila.

Lila was a friendly, gentle girl who only wanted to play.

I should have stayed in Puerto Rico. Why was my life any more valuable than Lila's? I could have stayed on top of my mountain where I would have seen those Mafia motherfuckers coming from a mile away. I should have looked after my own instead of looking after myself.

Cultural Coexistence: Brockton and the Petronelli Gym

If you were of a certain temperament, spending late afternoons in the pleasantly shopworn Petronelli Gym, a few blocks from Brockton's economically bereft business district, was emotionally satisfying and spiritually refortifying.

The gym's moneymaking years had passed; whatever stars it was going to produce had come and gone.

Pat Petronelli was my business partner and putatively served as trainer to several of my fighters, although I wouldn't have dreamed of letting him actually train them. His son Tony, who had been a good junior welterweight in his day, ran much of the actual operation at the gym. There wasn't much left to operate.

At the Petronellis', there was always time; the months, and eventually years, drifted by. The restaurant on the ground floor of the gym, dark and comfortable, remained open solely for the use of Goody, Pat, Tony and their fighters and guests. Once in a while, there'd be a short excursion to one of the local take-out joints, inevitably causing a debate between the Italian and black factions of the gym. Pat Petronelli would tell me, "Freddy Nah-wood likes that breaded catfish, that soul food. Personally, I don't care (*cay*-yuh) for it."

There were cultural differences of opinion that moved beyond the culinary. Guido Petronelli would occasionally visit his brothers in order to sit in a folding chair near ringside observing the fighters training and sparring. One afternoon Stanley Wright elected to engage in one of his desultory sessions poking at the heavy bag—an activity that required loud musical accompaniment.

Comfortably settled in a few feet away, Guido leaped to his feet when he heard Wright's boom box blasting, "Gonna fuck her in the ass, gonna fuck her in the ass, gonna fuck her in the ass."

"What am I *listening* to?" he wailed. "This can't be *music*. I can't believe the words coming from that machine. My God, what am I *hearing*?"

"You hearin' the future, baby, "Stanley calmly explained, pacifically continuing to paw at the big bag.

The Petronelli brothers had hit the lottery with Marvin Hagler, all three men becoming richer than they could ever have imagined through the champion's middleweight title defenses against Roberto Duran, Thomas Hearns, and especially Sugar Ray Leonard. But neither Pat nor Goody had a clue as to how to manage a fighter.

Vin Vecchione wanted me to move my stable from the Petronelli Gym over to his place in Whitman. He would tell me that Hagler himself was the brains of their operation.

"Look at you," he'd say. "You've only been in the business a couple of years. You know more than all them guys combined."

For me, that didn't matter. The Petronelli imprimatur still carried a little hard-core juice, and their gym was a solidly functional place to train fighters. I knew how to manage without anyone's help, and I had Adolph Pruitt to train Freddie Norwood, the only one of my fighters who was at all educable.

Attaching Norwood to the Petronelli name drew the parallel between his No-One-Will-Fight-Him situation and Marvin Hagler's during his pre-championship run to the title. It might speed up Freddie's route to the top if Pat Petronelli could go to Arum and tell him, "I got you another Marvin Hagler, Bob."

I'm sorry that Pat and Norwood rejected my proposed nickname of "Little Marvelous" in favor of "Lil Hagler." It made Freddie sound more like Marvin's wife than the smaller Second Coming of a legendary champion.

I found myself spending most of my afternoons in Brockton. I had other businesses to take care of, but after overseeing the training of my own fighters I found myself staying there, hanging out, gabbing with Pat and Tony and whoever was around.

Don Elbaum showed up out of the blue one afternoon. I had no idea how he got to the Petronelli Gym or why he was there. Even though I knew Elbaum to be alive somewhere in Pennsylvania, seeing him in the flesh was like happening upon some animal you assumed was either mythical or had long gone extinct.

Elbaum, ageless, with his great bison granite head with its lacquered, improbably ebony mane combed back in classic wiseguy style, was a living gargoyle; he looked terrific—instantly recognizable as the last of those genuine articles who understood boxing from the deepest ground-level sources to the pinnacles of its power structure. It was he, along with Al Braverman and Lloyd Price, who had ushered Don King into the boxing business some thirty years earlier. I felt in the company of a penny-ante legend.

The Petronelli Gym was already mostly a place of the past, one that created the right atmosphere for men with broken noses, scarred eyebrows, busted eardrums, and damaged voices to tell you about the times they'd had, and where you'd want to stick around to find out what they had to say. I was fortunate to be able to listen to Don Elbaum and to add him to the short list—Hank Kaplan, Al Braverman, Johnny Tocco, and Adolph Pruitt—of older boxing sages from whom I could really learn something about my business.

When Pat and I did business together, we never talked money—not that there was that much to talk about. We co-promoted a card in Old Orchard that drew so poorly that we didn't have enough cash from the gate receipts to pay even the out-of-town fighters.

Pat asked, "How short are we?"

"Looks like between five and six thousand dollars. I don't have that kind of money on me."

"We can pay our own guys once we're back. Let's take care of the local kids and the opponents who come in from out of town so the Commissioner doesn't come down hard on us. Walk me to my caah, Chaales."

Pat's Cadillac was parked at the far end of the parking lot. When we got there, he reached under the dashboard, pulled out a revolver and a wad of hundred-dollar bills. He counted some out. There were plenty left.

"Okay, here's my two thousand. Do you have enough to cover yours?" This came out "yaws."

"I'm good, thanks."

Pat carefully returned the revolver and what was left of the hundreds to their hiding place, and we walked back across the parking lot to pay the locals.

❖ ❖ ❖

Pat floored me one day by telling me a secret that, had I not known him, I would have found impossible to believe.

"You know that Marv, Goody, and me started out with a handshake deal. There was no signed contract. Later, when Marv started getting million-dollar paydays, we never changed it. Finally, when he was about to fight Ray, I said to him, 'Marv, do you think we should all sign something for this fight?' It was a lot of money. And Marv says, 'Why? We've trusted each other so far, and we're doin' okay.' Even for the Leonard fight we never did sign a contract. His whole career, we never had a contract with Marv. Everything was done on a handshake. You're the only one I've ever told that to."

Two Short, Stupid Conversations

Robbie Sims asked me to talk to his brother Marvin Hagler about buying him a house. Closing out his boxing career, bored, broke and with little to do, Robbie was trying to come up with suitable ways to begin the next phase of his life.

The $2 million he'd earned as a fighter were gone, largely as a result of his own gullibility. Robbie was particularly susceptible to any get-rich-quick scheme linked to the music business. Although still flirting with some misguided ideas along those lines, he'd also hit on a plan to pick up an investment property around his home in Brockton.

Two serious impediments were that he had no money and a terrible history of not paying his bills.

A car dealer who had owned a sneaker store in Brockton in the 1990s told me that Robbie held the store record for the most bounced checks.

Nobody would lend him money even if he could have put together the down payment on a place.

I spent days with Robbie, helping him on his fool's mission of looking for rental properties. The whole obsolete, crack-addicted city of Brockton was practically being given away. I'd passed on taking 102 units in three buildings of bank-owned two-bedroom condominiums for free, nearly suckered into taking on the responsibilities that went along with an unending disaster of drug dealing, gang warfare, random murders for a multitude of reasons sensible and not sensible, 102 units of no-pays, and real estate tax assessments of well over $2 million. The realtor who brought me through the condos took a loaded pistol from under his dashboard before we walked through them. He kept it in plain sight throughout our tour.

You had to be very savvy to be in the real estate business. Robbie Sims didn't know shit about real estate.

"Charles, talk to Marv for me. He's in town. You'll know what to say."

I hadn't talked to Marvin Hagler in a few years, and I never really knew him. I was close with Robbie and Buster Drayton; Pat and Tony Petronelli were very good friends. I'd only started spending time at the Petronelli Gym toward the very end of Marvin's career, at that point still more an observer of the boxing business than a participant.

Hagler was living at the Ritz-Carlton temporarily when I called him. I was surprised by how heavy his Italian accent had gotten. His regional inflections were complex—a blend of Newark, Brockton, and Milan.

"This-a house, how many windows it is gonna have?"

"I'm not sure which house Robbie has in mind, Marvin."

"I see. I see. What color is he a-gonna paint it?"

I wondered if Marvin was fucking with me.

"Does that make a difference?"

"I'm tryin' to a'pitcha it in my mind."

Vin Vecchione had told me that Marvin Hagler was the real brains in the Petronelli organization.

Sims and I were talking about Roberto Duran. Both he and Marvin had decisioned him. Then I thoughtlessly came up with the dumbest boxing observation ever made.

"The thing is, Duran really couldn't punch at all at middleweight."

Robbie, who'd had to go ten hard rounds with an old and over-weight Duran to win a split decision, gave me a quizzical and slightly disgusted look.

"Who told you that?"

I loved Brockton despite its being a dangerous fucking dump, riddled with crack addiction, street crime, senseless violence, and five-dollar hookers. I felt strangely at home there. The place wasn't without its Twilight Zone episodes, though.

Adolph Pruitt walked into the gym laughing, a sheepish-looking Freddie Norwood lagging behind.

The usual crew was lounging around in Pat's office.

"We was in a hold-up," Pruitt told us.

Pat said, "You got held up?"

"No, *we* didn't get held up. But we was in a liquor store that got held up."

"Just now?"

"Five minutes ago. We comin' here from there."

"What happened?"

"I just taken Freddie out for his run, we go get me a little taste and Freddie pick up a soda. I'm in line, and this dude run in, got a gun, say to the guy give him all his money. I ain't see Freddie, so I know he crouched down somewheres. And I'm laughin', thinkin' 'my little tiger gonna be a hero an' save everybody.' I'm lookin' around, lookin' around. No Freddie. Then I see him layin' on the floor and he ain't movin'. I'm thinkin, 'Oh shit, that dude shot Freddie.' But that ain't it. When Freddy seen the gun, he just fainted away."

Everyone but Norwood started laughing.

"So, your little tiger let you down?"

Pruitt nodded solemnly. "My little tiger let me down."

I almost bought a house in Brockton. It was a twenty-room mansion that had been built for a shoe baron who owned some of the many shoe factories that were the town's claim to fame until Rocky Marciano and later Marvin Hagler showed up.

In its day, the Victorian had been a showplace. Like everything else in Brockton, it had fallen on hard times and been pillaged. It was now a rooming house broken into cell-like units that provided depressing habitats to marginal characters.

I brought Mitch Green along for the realtor's tour. Blood would be living there, after all. During our walkthrough, an old woman latched onto me, grasping at my suit.

"You won't turn me out, will you? I've lived here for forty years. I got nowhere to go. Please don't put me on the street."

She began to cry. I told her that I didn't know if I was going to buy the house.

"Please buy it. That way I'll know I won't have to leave. You're a good man. You wouldn't throw me away."

The idea was to restore the house. It was still stately and with care could be made into a palace again. The asking price was nearly nothing and I would knock that figure down to a giveaway. The fighters could all live very close to the Petronelli Gym. It'd be a lot less expensive than having to put them up at Herbertine Walker's or the local Holiday Inn.

I assumed that Mitch Green would love it. But as we drove back to Newton, he voiced strong opposition.

"Nah, nah, Charle. You don't want to buy a old place like that. That a big old spooky house. They *always* be ghosts in a house like that. You be goin' down the hall late at night, and one of them ghosts sneak up behind you. Or come into your room in the middle of the night while you asleep, put they icy fingers on you face. Man, you don't want to have nothing to do with that shit."

Blood had still more concerns. He patiently explained them.

"You buy a big place like that for fighters, you gotta hire a woman to do the cooking and cleaning. And I'm *tellin'* you, old houses like that attracts witches. And them old ladies, they fuck with you, dude. They spit in you food or they scratch they asses while they cooking or doin' laundry or you sheets. They put a spell on you by touchin' you things. And they put a curse on you if they don't like you. Even that old lady grabbin' at you coulda been a witch, puttin' her fingers on you clothes. Charle, find someplace else. Don't buy that evil house."

The Boxer Who Drove Me Around

In some ways, those were very dark days. It was a town where having money—almost any money—separated you from most of the citizens. Brockton had gone in recent years from being a white, working-class city to a black city, and from there to a Dominican and Cape Verdean city. Crack was everywhere. Every doorway concealed a five-dollar hooker who would offer you a blowjob in exchange for a ride down the block. Crack dealers and prostitutes killed each other over nickel-and-dime disagreements. Nobody gave a fuck.

The fighter was noticeably ambivalent about hookers. He loved the way a lot of them looked. He'd roll down the window if a particularly striking woman walked by, especially if she wore either a very short skirt or tight hot pants. He had a thing about women's asses. "Bam," he'd bellow in his booming voice. "Pow! That ass is bangin', sister. Goddamn."

But he'd also become angry and morally offended.

"Man, that ain't right. I don't like to be seein' no black women strutting around with their titties hanging out like that. You can see their pussies; they got those skirts up so high with no shit underneath or nothing. They ain't got no respect for themselves or for their kids. I gotta live in this fuckin' neighborhood. It gives niggers a bad name."

"They're mostly Cape Verdean."

He laughed. "Okay, baby. But there's a lot of 'em nigger bitches too. And they shouldn't be walkin' the streets like this in broad daylight. No wonder they get in trouble. I'm tellin' you, man. They bring the shit on themselves. How you think it feels for a black man to see his women walkin' around like this?"

"If it'll make you feel any better, there are some of the Dominican whores down at the end of Green Street."

"I ain't tellin' nobody who you can fuck. They put themselves out there, they ready to get themselves fucked."

I should have seen the problem. One afternoon I walked into the gym and found it uncharacteristically quiet. I went into the office. Pat was sitting with a middle-aged white man who wore an inexpensive suit, had a full head of gray hair, and looked like the detective he was. Fighters often get in trouble with the law, but it was unusual to have the police show up at the Petronelli Gym.

Pat introduced me to the detective, and we shook hands. The cop didn't look unfriendly exactly. It was more a question of it being clear that he'd seen a lot of things and questioned a lot of people—an absence of gullibility.

"Have you seen the fighter today?"

"No. He in some kind of trouble?"

"No, probably not. We just need to talk to him. It's routine questioning."

Pat interrupted.

"Charles, one of the prostitutes from the neighborhood got strangled. I was telling the detective here that nobody from this gym would hurt a fly. Wouldn't you agree with that?"

"Absolutely. Why are you interested in the guy, Detective?"

"We're really not. We just have to be thorough. There are a couple of things we need to go over. I'm sure he'll be able to clear up the few questions I've got."

Just then the fighter arrived at the gym. He was brought into the office, and Pat and I were asked to leave. The door was left open.

Gym business went on as usual, but there was a definite unease in the air. Everyone kept one eye on the open door. We could see the detective behind Pat's desk and the fighter sprawled on a folding metal chair. From the gym itself, it was impossible to hear their voices. They both spoke quietly. That was unusual for the fighter. He had a big voice and was often very loud. He looked calm talking to the detective. At one point I saw him hold up both his hands, palms forward, toward the cop.

I knew he was getting special consideration from the Brockton police because of the Petronellis' standing in the community. As the managers and trainers of Marvin Hagler, as close friends of the late heavyweight champion Rocky Marciano, and as longtime citizens of Brockton, Pat and Goody were highly respected. And over the years they'd been good to the local cops.

This might not have mattered if it had been someone else who'd been murdered. But hookers were killed all the time in Brockton. Deaths of gang members, prostitutes, and crackheads were routine business. The police would send a couple of men out so they could say the killings had been investigated.

The fighter talked with the detective for about ninety minutes. Neither raised their voice the entire time. The cop came out of the office, walked over to Pat, shook his hand, and left the gym.

The fighter went into the locker room. Everyone followed him.

"The detective wanted to know if I knew some lady who got killed. She got strangled. He thought I might have knew her."

The light heavyweight Steve Detar asked, "Did you know her?"

"No, I didn't know her. And that's what I told the gentleman."

"So why was they askin' you about her?"

"The detective told me they think a fighter might've did it. She had masking tape and hand wraps around her mouth and on her body, he said. Man said she been strangled. He axed to see my hands. Ain't that some freaky shit? I told him 'go ahead and look.' I ain't got nothin' to hide."

Still, the fighter changed. Before his questioning by the detective, he'd enjoyed trips to check out the street. He'd never actually go with any of the women, but he liked talking to them, flirting with them, making his rude comments. Now he was noticeably on edge.

"Ain't no women worth putting your dick into here. Shit, man, they axin' for thirty or forty dollars just for a quick blowjob? I don't think so."

A little later we were driving aimlessly on an unpleasant rainy night. People on the streets of the Combat Zone in downtown Boston seemed to be looking for trouble. The cops were everywhere. Even the neon signs reflected in the puddles on Essex Street looked garish and ugly.

The fighter again began to talk about the detective. It had become a regular subject. He'd circle around it, then swoop in.

"I don't know why that white gentleman picked me out. Why me? 'Cause I'm a nigger? You think it's because I'm a black man? Man, it feels like the dude was picking on me. Like some kinda discrimination."

"Most likely it's because you're a fighter, with those hand wraps and tape they found wound around her. But maybe it's the size of your hands. If you were a real suspect, you'd have heard back from them by now. You'd have been brought in for questioning. Just be cool. Lie low."

"Lie low for what? I ain't done nothin' to lie low for."

"You don't think things get pinned on the wrong guy sometimes?"

"Yeah, I hear you. If he's a nigger, no doubt."

He eased my BMW out of the narrow street at the entrance to Chinatown and got onto Route 93 headed south.

"Where you going?"

"I don't know. I just feel like driving around. That okay?"

"Sure."

It had started to rain harder. The fighter began to drive fast. That didn't worry me; he was a very good driver.

Time passed with neither of us talking. Then he said, "You really think they'd blame me for it if they didn't have no proof?"

"I don't think they care enough because of who she was. But yeah, I believe they would if you weren't connected to Pat. The Petronellis have a lot of local juice."

"Do they really plant evidence and shit? I mean, could they have took some of my hand wraps from the gym?"

"No way. That's not going to happen."

"Well that's good. 'Cause you never know what a cop might do if he's told to pin something on a brother."

He was driving too fast. We got to Exit 4 and turned onto Route 24 South heading to Brockton. That seemed like a bad idea, but I didn't say anything. The fighter thought of me as his friend. He regarded me in a certain way.

I had a sense of what he was doing. And, as bad as I felt for the poor woman, I felt bad for the fighter too. He'd played his cards so close to the vest. I had thought he was going to be able to pull it off.

Then I thought, *I wonder if I'm in any trouble here.*

We were getting close to the neighborhood.

"Man, this isn't a good place for you to be."

"No, it ain't. It's not a good place for me to be, brother Charles."

We drove down Green Street. He stopped the car outside the Petronelli Gym.

"I gotta take care of a little personal business. Hang on."

He walked to the side parking lot toward the back of the brick building. I thought about moving into the driver's seat and taking off. But I waited.

A minute later the fighter was back. He drove deliberately now. His driving was faster than it should have been, but not frantic, not out of control. He knew the area well. We first drove down streets I knew, and then streets I didn't know. We didn't travel far, but I had seldom strayed more than a few blocks from the gym. It was a bad neighborhood in a bad town.

"When you're a big dude, people *will* fuck with you. They will. You know me, man. I don't start no shit with nobody. I like being a professional boxer. I like what I do. I like driving you around. I like smoking my weed, but I ain't bothering nobody by doin' it. But nobody just lets me be."

He drove with a calm determination. We took small streets, twisting and turning into alleyways and through parking lots. Nobody was out on these streets.

"I always treat people with respect. But it pisses me off when someone tries to fuck with me. Just 'cause I don't talk good don't mean I'm stupid, man. I wasn't given any advantages growing up. I didn't have no father. My mother is dead. I got me a sister in prison. She's six foot six, man, and she's tougher than me. So, it's like, who's gonna watch my back, know what I'm sayin'?"

He slowed the car down. We were on a cramped street with parked cars on either side. There was barely room for the BMW to get through. At the end of the street was a small bridge. Off to the side there was an embankment with some water at the bottom. Just past this was an empty industrial area with an auto salvage company and a junkyard. That was it; that was all there was.

"You think I've been treated fair in the business? You're a normal size white man in a suit, who can talk good. So you get more respect than I do. You never threw a punch in your life. You seen what I had to go through to get where I'm at in boxing. But people treat you better than me. Don't that seem a little fucked up, sir?

I gotta look out for myself. Nobody else is going to do that for me. And if someone is disrespecting me after I've treated them nice, it's on me to take care of it."

He rolled down his window. He nodded toward the embankment by the little bridge.

"That's where they found her. That's where it got done."

He rolled up the window and we turned around and drove back over the bridge.

Nothing Good Comes from Kansas

I got a call from Pat Petronelli, who told me, "Chaales, I just got off the horn ("hawn") with Dick Meaks. Meak, I think. Dick Meaks, he's one of those scouts from out in the Midwest there—Kansas or Nebraska, somewhere like that—who give me an interesting piece of information. Might be something we want to look into."

Pat went on to explain that Meaks or Meak had tipped him off to a big white heavyweight from Kansas who'd made it to the Olympic finals and gotten to 4-0 as a pro, but whose career had stalled in the Heartland. He was looking for a manager with connections.

Pat had also gotten a scouting report on the fighter, who he referred to as Mac Foster—confusing him with the thunderous-punching black heavyweight from the '60s and '70s—that characterized him as very raw, big and strong, and "just a rough, tough kid."

A few days later I got a phone message from someone whose high-pitched, tremulous voice I initially mistook for that of a churchgoing spinster dialing a wrong number. It was Martin Foster.

"Sir, me and my family would like to come up to Boston whenever you're ready for us. I believe I gone as far as I can here in Kansas. I will be waiting for your call, sir."

I wasn't necessarily willing to sign on to support an entire family, but white American heavyweights with undefeated records and near-Olympic pedigrees were on the brink of extinction. With Pat's connection to Top Rank, it seemed advisable to see what Foster had to offer.

I brought Stanley Wright to Logan Airport to help with the Fosters' luggage and to give the stablemates a chance to get acquainted. Stanley went ahead to baggage claim while I parked the car. When I stepped inside the terminal, Wright was there, laughing.

"Did you find them? Did they get here alright?"

"Yeah, they're here."

He couldn't stop laughing.

"Okay, what's so funny about them."

"Charlsie baby, that's the goofiest looking white man I've ever seen."

"How do you mean?"

"He's just a big, fat white boy."

"He's fat?"

"Yeah, like *real* fat. He's this fat farmer-looking white motherfucker. His wife is cute, though."

"Does he look like a fighter?"

"No, he just looks like a farmer. Talks like one too. Come on, you'll see."

Seeing Martin Foster for the first time was deflating. I knew that it was unwise to judge by appearances, but Foster was going to be a tough sell. He had a terrible body even by civilian standards, and Wright had hit the nail on the head by calling him "goofy looking." Foster had a big, open face that looked like a pie plate, tiny eyes, a broken nose, and the polite bangs of an elementary school boy.

He *was* big, but his size was unimpressive somehow. Instinctively, I began grasping for usable descriptive terms that could mitigate his obvious liabilities: farm-strength, throwback, and Pat Petronelli's standby "just a rough, tough kid." I rejected "goober," "yokel," "hayseed," and "Klansman" as counterproductive. Likewise, I dismissed "turnip truck" and "East Podunk" as not being helpful to the cause.

To his credit, Foster wanted to go straight to the Petronelli Gym.

"Throw me in with whoever thinks he's the Big Dawg there."

Stanley said, "Josh Imadiyi. That man can hurt you."

Foster asked, "Is he a colored guy?"

"He's an African dude. He's not a nigger, like he ain't no brother."

"Well, then Josh is the guy I want."

No sane person would get in the ring with Josh Imadiyi. For "The Prince of Power" there was no such thing as sparring. You fought to get whatever you had, and every fight was a war. You didn't ask for favors, and you had no intention of giving any. Life had been hard in Lagos, Nigeria, and life turned out to be hard in Brockton, Massachusetts.

Josh was a Tribal Prince. It was a job that didn't pay much, so in addition to continuing his career as a professional boxer, The Prince of Power took up loan sharking, an occupation for which he was unusually well equipped.

I never understood how anyone, looking at Imadiyi, would even consider not making his payments. He wasn't a big heavyweight, but his density made him appear enormous. His head was as broad as an average man's shoulders, and his shoulders seemed as wide as a wall.

On the street Josh wore brightly colored native robes and an extravagance of totemic necklaces. He favored strong cologne. There were two sickle-shaped ceremonial scars under his eyes, gouges filled in with dark purple dye. His face was flat and impassive, his small eyes calmly observant. Fully clothed, his strength was evident; in boxing trunks, his musculature was outright unsettling.

One day on Green Street, I watched from ten feet away as a debtor stepped out of a banged-up clunker to intercept The Prince as he was about to enter the gym for his afternoon training. He'd come to let Imadiyi know that he hadn't brought his weekly payment, making an importunate gesture as he began to explain. Imadiyi serenely gripped the man's head, walked him over to his car, opened the back door, and, without haste, lined his left arm and shoulder up to the frame. He then slammed the door three times, breaking first the shoulder and then the arm. He turned to me. "Are you going upstairs? Do you know whether Stanley will be here today?"

This was the man that Martin Foster wanted us to measure him by. Martin was either going to shock me or he would have taken a long and pointless trip, albeit one that wouldn't wind up costing me more than the price of four roundtrip airline tickets and one night's stay in a nice hotel.

We checked Foster's wife Jackie and the two kids, Heather and Chris, into their room, and then called Pat at the gym to arrange for Josh Imadiyi to be there in an hour.

The sparring session was brutal. Four rounds of nonstop aggression by both guys, each trying to establish dominance. There was nothing about it that resembled sparring. Martin and Josh were each trying to take the other's head off.

Imadiyi was by far the heavier puncher, but Foster unflinchingly took every shot and immediately fired back, throwing looping punches that looked like someone banging the dinner gong.

I was impressed with Martin's ability to take a shot but didn't think he could fight. The four rounds were really entertaining if you had no business interest in them. Under the circumstances, I was very disappointed in what I was seeing; "rough, tough kid" might have been accurate, but those attributes wouldn't get Foster further than being a preferred opponent. I wanted to send him home.

Pat Petronelli surprised me. "Chaales, this kid is a little green, but he's gonna make a lot of noise in the heavyweight division. I think we got something here. He's a tough kid."

Admittedly, I was not a fan of tough kids, if being tough was all they had to recommend them. I'd always preferred stylish boxers—something Martin Foster was assuredly not.

It was here that I made my first error: I deferred to Pat's assessment over my own. It was a mistake I made repeatedly about Martin Foster. I finally figured out why veterans in the boxing business—men with sterling reputations as experts—didn't immediately spot Foster for the stiff he was. Older guys like Pat and Floyd Patterson—who trained Foster after I relocated him to New Paltz—had already made their millions and no longer had enough to occupy their time. They loved the fight game and missed their time in the spotlight. It was important to them to find things to do in the sport, so they would routinely overestimate fighters in order to say that they were grooming future champions.

Against my better judgment, I relocated Foster and his family from their farm in Kansas into one of my houses in Newton. It had been Mitch Green's home a couple of years earlier. I then set about getting Martin some local attention. It was an uphill task. The most influential boxing writer in the area was Ron Borges with the *Boston Globe*. Borges was an arrogant bully with a prognathic jaw that jutted from his enormous concrete block of a head. He was known more for attacking a disabled man and plagiarizing columns than for the quality of his writing.

When I first called Borges to see about getting Foster some space in the *Globe*, his immediate response was, "Never heard of him."

I scored some time on a few local call-in sports shows, and Foster, Tony Petronelli, and I tried to stir things up by issuing challenges to every undefeated New England heavyweight. All we succeeded in doing was getting the local managers angry at us.

Regional prospects were all perched in their positions very precariously. Only John Ruiz, backed by the loyal and often splenetic Norman Stone, seemed willing to take on all comers. Stoney was fueled by an anger that came from being slighted, coupled with a kind of enraged love that added up to all-in loyalty for those he considered to be on his side. He was virulently aggressive toward the Powers That Be, whoever the Powers

That Be were, real or imagined. The Powers That Be gave Norman Stone his own Power of the Enraged Outsider.

The Somerville Boxing Club was really his home. He would emerge from the locker-room showers, his lobster-red, ungainly body draped only in a small towel, women and children visiting the gym invited to gaze upon his outlandish figure. Stoney was a true innocent.

Most people couldn't stand Norman Stone, an outraged late-in-life homeowner upon whose lawn an atrocity had been committed by a neighborhood kid with a ball. Stone charged to the edge of his property line and delivered apoplectic outbursts with a Boston accent too thick to be comprehensible as English to anyone not from the area.

I was among the few who loved Stoney. He'd do anything for you. Of all of the local prospects, his fighter, John Ruiz, was given the least chance of success. At 195 pounds, there were serious doubts about whether he'd grow into a genuine heavyweight. He wasn't much of a puncher, and his *real* trainer, Gabe LaMarca, had given him a classic boxer's style that wasn't exciting to the average fight fan. To make matters worse, Ruiz never talked, never smiled. He was a good kid, but nothing about him would ever get him noticed.

I had gone to a few of Ruiz's fights and hadn't been impressed, although he was very sound. Aside from Fernely Feliz, the other New England prospects were equally pedestrian.

I got a clearer picture of Foster's ceiling over the course of his sparring sessions with John Ruiz.

Because Martin walked around fifty or more pounds heavier than John, I didn't anticipate his having a problem. LaMarca instructed Ruiz not to engage or get trapped on the ropes, which allowed him to effortlessly outbox Foster. Stoney's fighter couldn't miss with his jab; mine hit nothing but air. They sparred four rounds, realization dawning on me as it went that Ruiz was much better than I thought, Foster even worse.

When it was over, I tore into Foster. He was costing me a lot of money, and he had done nothing to suggest the expense was justifiable.

"What was wrong with you in there, Martin? You didn't lay a glove on him."

"He don't fight, Charles. He just runs the whole time. I tried to get him to stand and fight, but he just don't fight you."

"That's not his problem, Martin. It's your job to make him fight. If there'd been judges watching, you'd have lost every round. He was hitting you at will. He was using his legs, but he wasn't running."

"He don't have no power."

"Why should I care about that? If he'd had power, he would have knocked you out. Look, Martin, I'm not going to debate you. You're coming back here tomorrow and you better show me something. You're twice his size. Use your weight, use your strength. Get rough in there. Push him into a corner, lay your weight on him, dig to the body. Keep him trapped there. Shape up. I don't want excuses."

"Yessir."

Norman Stone came into the dressing room. He said, "Johnny was at the World Championships in Sydney. He was the runner-up. He's got a lot of amateur experience. Martin's a tough kid. He's a real diamond in the rough. He'll go a long way."

I called Tony Petronelli that night.

"You got to make him get rough in there, Tony. There's no way he should be letting that little guy dictate the terms. Stay on him tomorrow, okay?"

"He's just a little green. He's a tough kid."

Being a tough kid seemed to mean a lot to everyone else. To me, it just meant that you'd show heart when other guys were beating you.

The next day, Martin Foster fought differently. He was ungainly, but he bullied John Ruiz, roughing him up, keeping him trapped in the corner, and letting his hands go. He missed a lot of punches, but he controlled the action as thoroughly as Ruiz had the day before. He never hurt John, but he was the boss the whole time.

I let Foster know I was pleased with his performance. He had used his advantages in size and weight to keep a more talented, better-schooled fighter from doing what he wanted to do.

Two days later, they sparred again. Ruiz had already been schooled by Gabe LaMarca on how to deal with Foster's aggression. Inside, he would clinch, trap Foster's arms and spin himself off the ropes. He'd land combinations, move in and out, counter all of Martin's wide shots, land uppercuts when Foster moved in too wildly. Ruiz beat Foster up for five rounds.

The sparring session left Foster bleeding all over the locker-room floor, courtesy of a perfect uppercut.

"What happened, Martin?"

"I don't know, Charles. I just couldn't get off today. I didn't feel like myself in there."

"You don't think that maybe Ruiz had something to do with that?"

"Might have."

Foster couldn't say that Ruiz ran, he couldn't say that Ruiz wouldn't stand and fight with him. He couldn't say shit.

I knew that I was right about Foster and that the experts were wrong. The fat fuck couldn't fight.

And I knew that John Ruiz was much better than I'd thought. What I couldn't have known, despite Norman Stone's assertions, was that John Ruiz would put on forty pounds of muscle, reconfigure his entire style to become a mauling, grab-and-hold, roughhouse brawler, and twice win a version of the heavyweight championship of the world. Along the way, he made a lot more money than any of his New England classmates.

Getting a ringside illustration of how severely limited Martin Foster was didn't change anything. He was still undefeated. We could still challenge all the local prospects with impunity; none would take us up on the offer. He wouldn't ever have to fight Josh Imadiyi outside of the gym. And there were plenty of excuses to keep Foster from having to fight Ruiz for real.

Peter McNeeley was the heavyweight getting the most local attention, and he was probably the weakest prospect of the bunch while being the best risk-reward option, so we focused on him. To his credit, Martin Foster knew how to stir things up.

During radio interviews, he'd say, "He says he's the best heavyweight in New England. I say I'm the best. We're both undefeated. I don't understand why he won't meet me in the ring to settle things once and for all. Peter, why won't you fight me?"

Cliff Phippen, who helped Vin Vecchione train Peter McNeeley, was all for forming a vigilante group to come looking for me at this point. Vin Vecchione counseled that it would be smarter business if a more diplomatic introduction was made.

There was no real advantage to being the number-one heavyweight in New England if the up-and-comers were never going to get in the ring with each other. I could bypass building Foster as a Northeast fighter and go straight to moving him into world-title contention. He was now

8-0. Another year—six or seven more fights—was all it would take. I just needed to come up with the best possible marketing angle for an undefeated fighter who wasn't any good.

Floyd Patterson presented that angle. His imprimatur would confer instant credibility and likeability onto Martin Foster. Floyd would never train a heavyweight who couldn't be champion. And he'd never have anything to do with someone who wasn't of sterling character.

When You Come to the Booth in New Paltz, Stop. Pay the Toll

Although I can clearly recall the rationale for removing Martin Foster from the dead end of New England boxing, I'm at a loss for how I wound up relocating him with his whole family to New Paltz, New York. I remember thinking that having Floyd Patterson as his trainer would be a solid public-relations move. It could translate to an undeserved decision win or an overly generous ranking from time to time. Floyd had been the boxing commissioner for New York State, and that would sometimes come in handy.

I thought that Floyd would be a good trainer and that Martin Foster might be capable of learning something. I was wrong about both.

Floyd, a deeply complex man with simple tastes, had been made by time, fame, and the physical harm done him into a still more complex man, even as those things reduced him to involuntarily simplicity.

He was inordinately soft-spoken and genuinely introspective, yet he loved attention from the public and was voluble in expressing his opinions. Famous for most of his life, he was accustomed to receiving the kind of treatment reserved for celebrities. But he needed little and asked for less. Floyd knew he'd accomplished remarkable things but never thought of himself as better than anyone else.

Floyd was methodical to a degree seldom seen in anyone sane. Before our first meeting, he left a message on my answering machine.

"This is Floyd Patterson calling for Mr. Farrell. I believe we have an appointment for later today. I wanted to make sure you had directions to my house.

Once you're on Route 87 South, take Exit 18 in New Paltz. There's a toll booth after you've taken the exit. Stop at the booth. Pay the toll. If you miss the toll collecting receptacle, put your car in park, get out, and place the change in the bin. When the light turns green and the gate raises, go."

He then finished the rest of the directions to his house.

I liked him from the moment we met. There was all of the obvious stuff: his decency, his ironclad sense of fairness, his courage, his fundamental modesty, his discipline and resoluteness, and his kindness and generosity. Those were qualities that radiated from him; anyone could see them. He was all he'd been cracked up to be by hagiographers, but there was a lot that didn't translate easily to the page.

He was shockingly small for a heavyweight. He stayed fit and bore an uncanny resemblance to James Dean. There was a peaceful and nearly monastic solitude about him, a kind of nobility to his rituals.

Floyd's well-rehearsed set pieces never changed, and this kept outsiders from seeing what was really going on. He frequently forgot his wife Janet's name, and often couldn't tell her from her sister Connie, who lived with them. His surroundings were safe, his schedule firmly established in an easily replicable pattern. The people around him loved and cared for him, as did virtually the whole world. He didn't have the paranoia that many impaired former boxers finish their lives with.

Floyd was cranky. It was an oddly appealing trait—one that even further humanized him. He'd earned his crankiness.

Boxing had provided him with wealth and fame. His house was set on many acres of gently rolling hills. Deer grazed on his front lawn in the mornings. I felt at home in the refuge that Floyd had made for himself. There was space and no lack of comforts—the living room had a massive fireplace that blazed throughout the snowy New Paltz nights—but the Patterson's house projected an overall tone of pleasing rustic austerity.

Floyd was one of the few people I knew who shared my late-to-bed, early-to-rise hours, so we were well-suited to all-night conversations. For the most part we focused on boxing, but within that framework the talk ranged widely.

He talked often about his improbable post-boxing four-decade friendship with Ingemar Johansson, the man who first beat him for the heavyweight title and then lost it back to him.

Johansson was a freewheeling playboy of extravagant appetites. In recent years, the differences in the two men's weights had widened to more than a hundred pounds, yet they routinely ran marathons together,

Floyd deliberately holding back in order to finish the route with his friend, refusing to show him up.

Their families visited every couple of years, taking turns staying at each other's homes. Floyd found himself a national hero in Sweden, despite having taken back the crown from the only Swede to ever hold it. It was as if Ingo's countrymen were grateful to Floyd for letting him borrow the title for a little while.

Because Sonny Liston had always been my favorite heavyweight, I couldn't get enough of Floyd's stories about him. Curious to know about the kind of power Liston possessed, I once asked Floyd who the hardest puncher he'd ever faced was.

"Ingemar Johansson."

"Ingemar Johansson? How can that be? It's impossible. You fought Sonny Liston twice, Floyd."

Floyd returned a sheepish smile.

"Oh, yes. Well, let me explain. When I fought Ingemar, I thought I was going to *win*."

Floyd had publicly said a lot of negative things about Muhammad Ali, so I expected him to be reluctant to praise the man who'd referred to him as "an Uncle Tom Negro" and intimated that he was slow-witted. I was wrong about that. Floyd couldn't get over how great a fighter Ali was, and held him in a kind of awe.

"I never thought I'd meet anyone faster than myself," he explained. "Especially someone that big. His hands were very quick. But it's his feet that made him impossible to catch."

He elaborated, "The hardest thing to do in a boxing ring is to move backward at full speed for fifteen rounds. I know how hard I trained, and I couldn't have done it. But he just moved and moved on you, and you'd get so damned tired chasing him.

All the while, he'd be hitting you with jabs, getting you dizzy, and then moving out of range again. And he could keep you off balance with the jab. He had no power at all, but after six or seven rounds your head would be spinning."

"Was he the best you ever fought?"

"I don't know if he was better than Liston. They were both great. Archie Moore was too old when I fought him, so I can't say about him. I know there was talk of Marciano coming back to fight me. He would have been tough too. He was so determined. But I don't think he'd have been as hard as Liston or Clay."

Floyd's not calling Ali by his right name was a symptom of his crankiness, a minor way of getting a little dig in against Ali.

I had negative feelings toward Floyd's trainer/manager Cus D'Amato, stemming from stories I'd been hearing for years from people I knew were credible. I was told that D'Amato and some of his acolytes in Catskill and benefactors in New York City were chickenhawks. I believed it. In addition to the things I'd been told directly, the telltale signs were everywhere—the mentoring of young boys toward a heroic ideal of nobility by way of overcoming fear through courage, the priestly male comradery, the hubristic exclusivity, the total exclusion of women into the circle.

I felt that Floyd and I were good enough friends that I didn't have to hide my disdain for D'Amato. I also thought Cus had been a fraud as a trainer—one of those insecure and thoroughly uninteresting men who promoted themselves as mystics.

To my surprise, Floyd made no real attempt to defend D'Amato. While he never said outright that my suspicions about Cus and others were well-founded, he didn't deny them. And he kept saying that D'Amato was "a very strange guy."

He added, "Cus did things that prevented me from trusting him."

"Business things or personal things?"

"Both."

"Something was just not right about him."

"You could say that."

It was a brisk walk from Floyd Patterson's main house to a boxing gym that would have been state-of-the-art in the '40s or '50s—a perfect boxing gym for anyone who actually knew about boxing. You couldn't find a place to get into better condition.

Floyd knew everything about getting fighters into great condition. It turned out, however, that he couldn't train fighters at all.

I'd brought Martin Foster to live near Floyd in New Paltz because I had big plans for him. Those plans got derailed quickly when Top Rank's East Coast matchmaker Ron Katz pulled a bait and switch.

Katz told me, "I got a fight for Foster. It's on a Top Rank pay-per-view show in AC. You interested?"

"Very. But why the change of heart? You know that Pat has been trying to get Bob to sign Martin with Top Rank."

"Yeah, I know. But Foster can't fight. Look, I'm doing you a favor. He's gonna fight Terry Pitts, who's just a big light heavyweight. It's an easy win for your guy."

"If Foster can't fight, why do you want to get him an easy win?"

"It's the opener, so it probably won't make TV. You've got Floyd Patterson in his corner, and that ain't a bad thing. Also, it's only fifteen hundred bucks for an eight-rounder."

"I know Terry Pitts. We'll take the fight."

"I thought you would."

If Ruby and Betty had been in the car with my son Jesse and me, they would have said to turn around and drive home right after we were stopped for speeding just short of Atlantic City. I could always name-drop my way out of getting tickets, and the cop who pulled us over was properly impressed when I mentioned Floyd Patterson. He wished my fighter good luck as he handed me a $110 fine. I didn't see it for the bad sign Ruby and Betty would have known it to be.

A few blocks from the casinos, while we were stopped at a red light, a hooker strolled over. I rolled down the window.

"You boys looking to party?"

"No, thanks. This is my son."

"That's cool. I can give y'all a discount."

"That's okay. We're just looking for a safe place to stay."

"You in AC, baby. There ain't no safe place to stay."

The Boardwalk was cold on the day of the fight—not good for the fighters, especially those scheduled early and off TV. Martin Foster's parents, Ma and Pa Kettle, drove their camper all the way from the farm in East Podunk, Kansas, so Pa could try out his new video camera to capture their boy's first shot at the big time. Martin's hayseed wife and their two little hicks were there too.

Floyd had brought Janet along. That was okay with me. Janet was good company, watched out for her husband, and was nobody's fool.

I had the fun-loving factotum Chris Gingrow to run errands and keep everyone laughing.

We all adjourned to the coffee shop at the Trump Plaza near the Convention Center where the fights were held, with Floyd stopped every few seconds by rapturous fans.

I drew the short straw and wound up with Merle Foster seated next to me.

He lectured me about boxing, traveling cross-country in a camper, and, for all I know, the year's corn harvest, in his solemn incomprehensible bumpkin accent. I vacantly nodded my head. Then he said something that caught my ear.

"I'm sorry, Merle. Could you say that again."

"I said that Marty's got the best jab in the heavyweight division."

"He *does*?"

"Yessir. Don't nobody throw no jab nowhere near as good as Marty."

He looked at me with his hound's eyes. The farmer was serious.

"Including Larry Holmes?"

"I believe so. Oh, I ain't sayin' Holmes don't have a good jab. But I don't believe it's near as hard or as fast as Marty's."

How on earth do they make it to adulthood, I asked myself.

"Well, if his jab is that good, Merle, he should have no trouble tonight."

"I don't believe he will. With his natural talent and Floyd's guidance, there's not going to be no stopping him."

With these words of wisdom in my ear, I walked Martin and Floyd across the lobby, where we took the elevator to the Commission weigh-in. Foster introduced me to Larry Donald, the fighter who beat him in the finals to get the Olympic berth. I ran into Henry Grooms, the smooth-talking former NFL player who now peddled boxers around the Miami area. He had lucked into having his fighter Courtney Hooper in the ostensible main event against Charles "The Natural" Murray. A couple of months earlier Grooms had tried to pawn Hooper off on me, but tonight he wanted to keep him to himself. A few days later, he would call me to renew the Hooper pitch.

We got our licenses in order and were waiting for Foster to get on the scale when Ron Katz walked over.

"Terry Pitts is out. The Commission pulled him off the card."

"What are you talking about?"

"He's got a detached retina. They won't let him fight. He's been forced to retire."

"How long have you known this?"

"Just found out. But I found a substitute. Much easier than Pitts would have been. This guy fought Pitts and got dropped twice in four rounds. No problem."

"Pitts knocked this guy out?"

"No. It was a draw. But Pitts should have won."

He nodded toward a tall, gangly blond-headed kid surrounded by some small-town rubes.

"That's the guy over there."

"Is he even a heavyweight?"

"Barely. He weighed in at around two-hundred just now."

"What's his record?"

"I don't know. He's had a couple of fights. One was that draw."

"Give me two minutes."

I found Floyd Patterson talking with reporters. I pulled him aside to let him know about the new development.

Floyd had reached the point in his dementia where he could no longer remember anyone's name. In public, Janet would supply it, and Floyd would pick it up. Although he spent every day with Martin Foster, he didn't know his name.

"He's prepared very hard for this fight. I'm confident that he'll beat whoever they put him in with."

"If you have any doubts, we can pull Martin out, Floyd."

"He'll be very disappointed. His family came to see him. Believe me, Martin's ready."

"I'll tell Katz."

What happened next is my fault.

It took place before laptops, before you could send out a flurry of emails or go online to check out Boxrec.com. But I had my ear to the ground in those days; I knew what was going on in boxing. My opinion that Olympians were overrated clouded my judgment too. I didn't follow the amateurs, so hadn't heard of Foster's opponent. I also assumed that Ron Katz had no reason to lie to me, and that the best business decision for Top Rank was to put Martin Foster in a fight he could win. I believed in the marketing narrative of having Floyd Patterson in the corner. I okayed the fight.

That night, before moving to Foster's corner, I visited his family in the still nearly empty arena. They were seated together near ringside in order to get a good view of their Great White Hope. I was able to see a video of the fight not five minutes after it took place when I went to check on what I assumed would be a shell-shocked family.

Gingrow and I were squatting just under Foster's corner when he got hit by Tom "The Bomb" Glesby's first overhand right twenty seconds into the fight. I saw Martin's knees buckle and he went into a near-swoon. Gingrow said, "Shit. The fight's over." I was about to say something about Foster's having a good chin when another right put him down less than a foot away from us. The referee scooped him up as he was falling to the canvas, not bothering with the formality of counting him out.

In his peevish, schoolmarm voice, Foster protested. "I ain't hurt. He's got no power. I'm fine. Don't stop the fight."

Floyd led him back to the corner and sat him down.

"Floyd, tell him. I'm fine. I can fight. Tell him not to stop it, Floyd. I'm okay. I can beat him."

He kept trying to stand up. I was in the ring now, and I told Martin there was nothing more to do. The fight was over. I was going to let his wife and kids and the Kettles know he wasn't hurt.

I found five faces as blank as apple pies—open and honest and trusting and uncomprehending. Foster's wife and kids didn't seem to understand what had taken place. His mother had a bitter expression, seemingly directed at me.

Merle offered me his video camera. "I got the whole thing."

The fight began, and there was a lot of hooting and hollering from the clan. "Go, Marty." "Go, Daddy." Obviously, that didn't last very long. Jackie Foster's voice is soon heard saying, "What happened?"

Then Merle's. "Marty got knocked out."

The Postmortem

Floyd Patterson was telling a small group of us about losing for the first time. We were sitting in the coffee shop of the Trump Plaza, across from the AC Convention Center where Martin Foster had the night before been effortlessly removed from the opportunities afforded undefeated heavyweight prospects.

Earlier that night, Floyd had rejected an overture of friendship from Donald Trump himself, preferring to maintain a Zen-like solitude while gloving up his soon-to-be-knocked out fighter. It had been a night of missed business opportunities, some of them justifiable.

"I think I had about fifty pro fights," Floyd began.

"You had sixty-four, Floyd," I said.

"I did? Sixty-four?" Floyd gave a slight smile. "I didn't realize I'd had that many."

Floyd thought about it for a moment.

"Gee, that's a lot of fights. But what I meant to say is that I remember the first time I lost. I felt terrible about it—like I'd let everybody down. But I learned so much from that loss."

"Floyd, you were just a teenager at the time. And you lost a *decision* to Joey Maxim, who'd already had over a hundred pro fights and was a former world champion. Besides, Joey was a great fighter. Martin got knocked out in the first round by a guy with *seven* fights, and he hadn't even won all of them. It's not the same thing at all."

"I understand that. But . . ."

"Martin," Janet filled in.

"Martin can use this as a learning experience. And he can be more determined than ever to make it. I predict that he will still become the heavyweight champion of the world."

Even Merle Foster looked dubious. Martin kept his head down. It had been a long short night for him.

I didn't care that Foster and his wife and parents were sitting right there. I didn't like any of them and was relieved at no longer having to pretend he could fight.

"What can Martin learn from getting knocked stiff in thirty seconds, Floyd?"

"Maybe his defense will get better. Maybe he'll realize that anybody can be knocked out."

These potential improvements didn't fill me with optimism. Foster was just too slow and too dumb. And knowing he could be knocked out would take away the only thing he had going for him: the projected confidence of someone certain that he'd be the one standing after a firefight. Some opponents, seeing Patterson in his corner, and knowing that he was fighting out of New York, and that he had management willing to invest in him, and hearing about his—until last night—undefeated record, would infer that Foster was a much better fighter than he really was. Sometimes that would be enough to get Martin a win.

Patterson ascribed skills and qualities of character to Martin Foster that he didn't actually possess. These incorrect assignations caused him to see solutions where there were no solutions, to project instances where Foster, in some kind of fistic predicament, would summon up a hidden reserve that could turn a bad situation around. Floyd was picturing what Floyd Patterson would do—things Martin Foster would never have the talent or courage to do.

Foster, meanwhile, was still stuck on the one point he took away from his loss.

"That ref shouldn't have never stopped the fight," he opined. "I just got shook is all. I was fine. I wasn't hurt or nothin'."

"So, if you were to fight Glesby again, you'd do it the same way?"

"Yessir. Oh, I'd be a little more careful about his right—he got a little power there—but I know I'd catch him with something in a round or two."

His father, mother, and wife all nodded their heads in agreement, each chewing contentedly.

It was true that his loss had left Martin Foster a little bit hangdog, but that appeared to be the fight's only negative repercussion. Seeing him knocked silly hadn't shaken his family's confidence in him; it hadn't shaken his self-confidence. And Floyd saw it as a chance to go back to the drawing board. Of course, none of them was spending their own money. Floyd even praised me for "sticking with . . ." here he, as always, forgot Foster's name until it was whispered to him by Janet, "with Martin."

Apparently, none of them could see that I had already begun looking for the best way to cut him loose.

Sometime around 3:00 a.m. I was back in the coffee shop with my son Jesse. He didn't like the boxing business, so stayed outside it. Still, we were talking about what had taken place at the Convention Center. Ron Katz came in. He had been looking for me. He smiled when he saw me and plodded across the room.

"I told you that Foster couldn't fight."

"Jesus Christ, Katz. You think I didn't already know that? What the fuck does that have to do with anything?"

It was important to Ron Katz that he find me somewhere within the vast Trump Plaza to bring me his big news.

Nearly one year to the day after Martin Foster had his first loss in Atlantic City, I got a no-hard-feelings phone call from Ron Katz looking for a scouting report on Josh Imadiyi. Top Rank was considering him as an opponent for Tom "The Bomb" Glesby for an upcoming *Tuesday Night Fights* show. I told Ron that Imadiyi had never fought anybody of note and that he had a terrible chin.

Less than a week later, I watched with satisfaction as The Bomb, semiconscious and bewildered, was picked up on mic asking his cornermen "what happened?" as he was carefully placed on his stool after being stopped in the second round by The Prince of Power.

I hoped that somewhere nearby Ron Katz was asking himself the same question.

Lifting Slightly from the Ashes (or the Corn or Soybeans or Whatever the Fuck)

After Martin Foster got steamrolled in Atlantic City, I did what a manager is supposed to do. I bought him an easy knockout win less than two months later, sending him to Raleigh, North Carolina, for a fight against Eddy Curry that Foster didn't know was fixed. I didn't bother to go along. Everything had been set up properly.

Although you generally want your fighter to be victorious, a smart manager will understand that opportunity can come from nearly every result, and that winning and losing isn't always—or even usually—the best way to look at the big picture. The door that closes from a loss will result in the opening of a different door if you are alert to the signals.

This opening came through a phone call from Dennis Rappaport in New York, who took Foster's wipeout as an indication that he'd be easy pickings for his undefeated heavyweight Melvin Foster.

Rappaport held every card: He had the better fighter; he also had Billy Costello fighting the main event in his hometown; he was the card's promoter, so he probably had the judges; and he was a major player in the boxing business.

But I was fed up with Foster, worn down from doing all the heavy lifting myself. Supporting his family was costly. It was a nuisance to make the four-hour trip to New Paltz, but I didn't want to give him a chance to stop working hard. Martin Foster may have been a lot of things but when supervised he was not a slacker in the gym. Terrible physique notwithstanding, he was indefatigable. Because he looked terrible but was actually in great condition, there was always an outside chance that he could spring an upset on someone who took him too lightly and didn't bother training for him.

When Rappaport offered the insult purse of $1,500 for an eight-rounder, I decided it was time for Foster to sink or swim. I took the fight at some level hoping it would be sink.

In Kingston on fight night, Martin Foster was nearly knocked out again in the first round. I was sure the fight was over when I saw the telltale buckling of the knees and the semi-swoon. But he recovered, and although outboxed for the first half of the fight, came back to at least not be outfought for the second. I could see a generous judge giving him three of the eight rounds, so was shocked when all three judges turned in identical 76-76 cards. We had a draw.

The draw had the weight of victory. It led to Foster's biggest opportunity to date: a rematch with Melvin Foster on national television two months later as the co-feature of *Tuesday Night Fights*. Roy Jones Jr., the best fighter in the world at the time, would be main-eventing in his hometown of Pensacola, Florida.

The Chapter Where Floyd Patterson Calls Me a "Stupid Motherfucker"

It was a shock to hear Floyd Patterson, the mildest mannered of men, yell at me, stuttering as he did, "No, *you're* the st-stupid motherfucker!"

His assessment of me was based on the identical assessment I'd made of him a moment earlier. I'd called Floyd a stupid motherfucker because he had acted like a stupid motherfucker. He'd called me one because he had a very incomplete picture of what was going on.

It was two weeks before Martin Foster's scheduled rematch with Melvin Foster, their television debuts at the national level. I had taken the unusual step of booking Martin in another fight before the rematch in Vin Vecchione's bailiwick of Whitman, Massachusetts. Floyd and I had argued about my decision in Foster's hotel room, where the fighter was stretched out on the bed less than an hour before he was to be in the ring.

Floyd angrily told me, "I predict that if he . . . this fellow"—he couldn't remember Martin's name—"fights tonight, he will wind up exhausted. He will be knocked unconscious and carried out of the ring on a stretcher when he fights on television next week."

"Floyd, you will see that I know exactly what I'm doing. Tonight, Martin is going to send a message to Dennis Rappaport and Melvin Foster. This fight will bring Martin to the rematch tuned up and loaded with confidence. Now you've put it in his head that he's going to be carried out of the ring, you stupid motherfucker. I am his manager so I make the decisions about who and when he fights. You are way, way out of line."

I had already fixed the outcome of Martin's fight with Troy Sutherland—a guy who'd never been in the ring before—so that it would end in about a minute.

Of the eight fights on the card, Vin Vecchione had fixed four of them, Foster's included. The remaining four were gross mismatches.

"When this fight is over, I'll expect an apology."

Floyd was somewhat mollified by my speech, and more than taken aback by its vehemence.

"If I turn out to be wrong, I'll apologize. But you've scheduled the fights too close."

"You *are* wrong, and you'll see that. You've undermined me and you've damaged Martin's confidence."

The last part wasn't true: Martin Foster was immune to crises of confidence. He rested peacefully throughout the argument.

The Foster–Sutherland fight went as scripted. As promised, Floyd Patterson apologized from fomenting unwarranted tension. The night was a success all around, but it wasn't without its own strangeness.

Peter McNeeley, still a year away from his brief time in the spotlight with Mike Tyson, was on hand to finally meet Floyd Patterson, the man who had knocked out his dad Tom in defense of his heavyweight title thirty-two years earlier in Toronto. Tom would be along a little later in the evening to reminisce with his old rival.

Peter introduced himself to Floyd at ringside before the show began.

"Mr. Patterson, I've always wanted to meet you. You defended your title against my dad in Toronto many years ago. He always says it was the highlight of his career."

"Really? Who is your father?"

"Tom McNeeley."

"Tom McNeeley! I haven't seen Tom in years. Is he doing well?"

"Yes, he's great. He'll be here tonight."

"Tom will be here? I'd love to see him. It's been so many years. Will you bring him back?"

They arranged to have Peter bring Tom to the pressroom later in the evening, and Floyd got set to work Martin's corner.

There was a brief but touching reunion with Tom McNeeley and Wilbert McClure, who'd been two terms behind Floyd's class of '52 as an Olympian and was now chairman of the Massachusetts Boxing Commission.

The years since their encounter had been good to Tom McNeeley. Now in his sixties, he had become enormous, but impressively so. He looked the picture of radiant good health with his full head of snow-white hair and a twinkle in his blue eyes. His dry wit remained intact.

Tom was now about a hundred pounds heavier than Floyd, which made the fact that Floyd had bounced him onto the canvas eleven times in four rounds hard to picture if you hadn't seen a film of the fight.

The two former rivals spent some heartwarming minutes together, laughing and hugging as Peter looked on, spellbound. Then Tom left amid promises to not let so much time pass again between visits.

A moment later Peter returned alone.

"Mr. Patterson, I just wanted to tell you how much it meant to me to see you with my dad. I know it meant a lot to him too."

"That's wonderful. Who's your dad?"

"Tom. Tom McNeeley."

"Tom McNeeley? Your father is Tom McNeeley? I fought him! I haven't seen Tom McNeeley for thirty years."

There was something in the air when we got to Pensacola; I could tell that the consensus among boxing people was that Martin Foster would win the rematch with Melvin Foster. More than that, I could feel insiders jockeying to poach my fighter.

One member of the USA *Tuesday Night Fights* broadcast team was the former lightweight champion Sean O'Grady. A pro at fifteen, "The Bubblegum Kid's" gimmick was blowing pink bubbles while making his way to the ring. His 86-fight pro career was now a decade behind him, but he had retained the wide-eyed cornpone of an Oklahoma teenage bible-class valedictorian. But Sean was the son of Pat O'Grady, one of the wiliest fight hustlers in the history of Midwest boxing, and he had been taught the slippery ins and outs of the business.

Martin Foster let me know that during the standard question-and-answer period used as the televised introduction to the fighters just prior to their bout, O'Grady asked about the possibilities of managing him. He had boasted of his own connections in the business and suggested that Foster's career could move ahead much more quickly under his guidance.

More tellingly, the day before the fight Dennis Rappaport asked if we could get together at the hotel restaurant.

Dennis Rappaport was a reviled boxing figure to some. He had made ungodly amounts of money in the business, most of it through the promotion of Gerry Cooney, the Moby Dick of boxing. Boxing is a cynical and xenophobic business, instantly resentful of anyone seen as an outsider, especially a successful one. But Rappaport's success had not come through dumb luck. He understood business, he understood money, he understood the inherent racism that existed with a large segment of boxing's fans—although he was no racist—and he understood how to listen to people who knew what they were talking about.

I liked and admired Dennis. At the press conference earlier that morning, he had outplayed me before the newsmen and the locals. I had put on a jacket and tie, and made the standard short pitch for the area, the network and promoter, for the worthy opposing side, for Roy Jones, and for my fighter's chances of winning. I'd closed by saying that former two-time heavyweight champion and US Olympic gold-medalist Floyd Patterson was Martin Foster's trainer, and that he'd told me that Martin too would wind up a heavyweight champion. I'd ended with something stupid like, "When Floyd Patterson tells you something, you can count on its happening."

Rappaport had had a suit custom-made for the occasion. He began his spiel by talking about Pensacola—its white-sand beaches, its welcoming people, and its being the home of the world's greatest fighter, Roy Jones Jr. He talked about what an honor it was to be invited to such a glorious, sunny city, and how proud the local citizens must be to live in such a wonderful place. Years of being near the top of the game had given him impeccable mic technique.

Round one had already gone to Melvin Foster.

After we had seated ourselves in a booth at the back of the darkened restaurant and exchanged brief pleasantries, Rappaport got to the point.

"Does your kid beat my kid tomorrow?"

"I think so. You've got the better fighter. And he was robbed the first time around. But Martin is bigger and stronger, and he comes on as the fight progresses, so the extra two rounds favor him. Having Floyd Patterson along buys us the audience and that will help us with the judges. If Melvin doesn't catch Martin early, I think we probably win the fight."

"I follow. I've been thinking along those lines too. Do you think Melvin is a big puncher?"

"No, I don't. Maybe at cruiserweight, Dennis, but not at heavy."

"I've been building him up to be another Joe Frazier, but now I'm wondering."

"He's too small. He's only five-eight or so."

"Well, here's my point, Charles. Melvin needs to beat Martin to remain credible. He's going to be a hard sell otherwise. Would you consider letting me come in with you if Martin wins tomorrow night?"

"If he wins tomorrow night, I don't need anyone. If he loses, nobody will want him except as an opponent. I know that wouldn't interest you."

"No, you're right. Unless he wins, he does me no good."

"I wouldn't have taken the fight for this money if I didn't think Martin was going to win. Once he wins, there'll be plenty of options for him. Dennis, as much of a pleasure as it would be to do business with you, I'll take my chances alone. I'm sorry."

"That's what I thought you'd say. I don't blame you. I thought it was worth a conversation."

We stood up, shook hands, wished each other good luck in tomorrow's fight, and went our separate ways like the fine gentlemen we were.

The day before the fight also brought a visit from Ma and Pa Kettle in their prairie schooner, arriving just in time for me to pick up their tab at the restaurant where Martin, Floyd, and I were having dinner.

Their previous experience with seeing their son in action had taught them nothing. Merle Foster reiterated his strongly held opinion that Marty had the finest jab in the heavyweight division. Beating Melvin Foster tomorrow night was a foregone conclusion, after which Martin's career would be right back on track.

"I seen this feller Marty's gone be fighting. He's too small for Marty. And he's real fat. I don't think it'll go more'n three or four rounds with the shape Marty's in."

During dinner, several diners made their way respectfully over to the table to shake Floyd's hand or ask for an autograph. The owners came by with a surprise for Floyd. They had fixed him a staggeringly large mound of fried calamari, the specialty of the house. Floyd noticeably blanched at the sight of this truly stomach-turning pile of entwined tentacles.

"Oh," I said, "I can't believe you brought this. Calamari is Floyd's favorite dish. He'll want the whole order for himself."

I felt a sharp kick under the table.

"But the thing is, once a fighter, always a fighter. Floyd gets as nervous the day before a fight as the guy he's training. In the case of Martin, more nervous. Floyd's stomach is really delicate. Would you mind packing this for later?"

A doggy bag as big as a valise was brought to the table as we were getting ready to leave. I paid the check and started to put down the tip. I felt a restraining hand on my arm.

"I'll get this," said Merle Foster.

Merle Foster carefully placed a dollar bill on the table—his tip for a meal that had run about a hundred dollars. I had to sneak back into the restaurant to make things right.

The two generations of Fosters went their separate ways while Floyd—weighted down with his to-go order of calamari—and I walked back to the hotel. We passed a trash can on the corner, and I mentioned to Floyd that he could now unburden himself.

"Oh, no. I can't do that. Someone might see. They'll think I'm ungrateful."

"What are you going to do with it? You're not thinking of eating it, are you?"

"No, I'm not going to eat it. Let's look around for a dumpster some-where in the back of one of the buildings. But not too close by."

We wound up learning a lot about the back alleys of Pensacola, going blocks out of our way in search of a hidden dumpster.

"Floyd, I have an idea. Why don't you stage the Floyd Patterson Celebrity Calamari Auction, and you can donate the proceeds to some local charity."

"Should I autograph them?"

Before reaching the hotel, we found an art gallery that exhibited the paintings of local black artists. Patterson asked if we could go in. He looked carefully through all the artwork, then bought an expensive paint-ing to bring home to New Paltz. His doing that was quintessential Floyd Patterson.

I had told Martin how to fight, but made the mistake of not getting up into the ring to give him advice between rounds.

I allowed Floyd to make Foster's fight plan, figuring that, as his trainer, it should be his call. The plan was the exact opposite of one that might have worked.

It was so bad that after the seventh round Foster came back to the corner and forlornly said, "Floyd, tell me what to do."

Given his lack of talent, there was only one strategy that would have given Martin a chance.

To have won, Martin would have had to turn the fight into an unsightly brawl, draping himself over Melvin, fouling him constantly throughout the ten rounds, upping the ante as he went, digging his dinner-gong round-houses into Melvin's soft gut and lower, leaving him no punching room, and to forcing him to drag around the extra 240 pounds that would be placed on his shoulders and neck in addition to the fifty surplus ones of his own.

Melvin Foster was more gifted, more technically proficient, a better puncher, had a better chin, moved better, and had a higher ring IQ than Martin Foster.

Martin had only a few advantages: he was much bigger and he was in better condition. He benefited from whatever subliminal messages the judges would get from his having Floyd Patterson in his corner. And he was white.

Floyd's advice? "Use your jab and box him." Short of "let him punch you in the face," you couldn't invent a less effective approach. Martin was on the way to losing every round when, late in the eighth, he managed to cut Melvin over the eye. It was a fairly bad cut. I yelled up at him before the ninth, "Do whatever you have to do to open up that cut. Butt him if you have to. He's tired. You've got two rounds."

The cut had been opened by a punch. Even if a butt caused the fight to be stopped, Martin would probably get a TKO win. He might be disqualified or lose a technical decision; both would be better than a lopsided loss.

Martin Foster tried, and he may have actually won the last couple of rounds, but Melvin was too cagey, and he hung on without any serious further damage being done to his eye. All three judges scored it 98-92—eight rounds to two for Melvin Foster.

I cut Martin Foster loose. Sent him home to East Podunk. I cut Floyd Patterson loose too, although I was going to miss the long evenings of talk and pots of coffee. We'd become good friends.

Foster still owed me a lot of money. We agreed that if something came up in the future where he'd have a chance to square the debt while putting some cash in his pocket, we'd reunite just long enough for that.

My Heavyweight Gets a Title Eliminator and I Am Stuck in a Crowded Van All Afternoon with Naseem Hamed: The King's Hall, Belfast

Braverman asked, "Can your fat white kid fight at all?"

"No."

"I mean at all."

"No."

There was a short pause on the line.

"Well, that's okay. Don will give him the shot anyway. What's his record? We just need someone with a good record. It's short notice."

"He's 11-2-1."

"That's fine. Besides, this South African kid can't fight much either."

"Is it Botha?"

"Yeah, Botha."

"No way my kid beats him, but he'll probably go the distance."

"If he goes the distance, we've got things for him to do. If he goes *rounds*, we've got things for him to do."

"With Botha? He'll go rounds. That's the one thing I'll guarantee you."

"Good. I'll have Connie send out a contract. And I'll send you a check on the side. We can chop that one up however you think is right."

I had a good working relationship with Braverman. He would call to ask my advice about fighters who were under consideration by Don King Productions. In exchange, he would get my fighters spots on King cards.

I'd had the good sense to buy Foster a just-in-case win a month after his loss to Melvin Foster. No Floyd Patterson involvement, no publicity, just a no-frills trip to Raleigh with three other fighters to put wins on their records.

Foster's opponent, James Cowan, was an encouragingly too-muscular former football player in the Canadian League. He'd never fought before, and arrived at the Ritz with Bermuda shorts and low-topped sneakers as his boxing gear. Before the fight he called me into his dressing room with a last-minute plea that Foster not hit him in the face since he was wearing hard contact lenses that might shatter.

I assured him there'd be no head shots if he promised to fall down at my signal. The fight looked like exactly the sham it was, with a visibly petrified Cowan cowering and blinking wildly through his contacts. The crowd starting laughing the moment they got a load of Cowan in his sneakers and shorts, and were booing before the first minute had passed. In the corner I had to instruct Foster—who, as he'd been told, was not throwing any head shots—to shut down the sideshow.

A few seconds into the second round, as Cowan pitiably beseeched the referee with an outstretched arm to let him be excused, the fight was stopped.

Based on this kayo victory, we found ourselves in Belfast one month later, with Foster fighting Frans Botha of South Africa in a title eliminator for the right to take on Michael Moorer for his version of the crown.

I understood that Foster was a sacrificial lamb. He understood it too. But I drilled into him the idea that Frans Botha was no killer.

It was freezing cold in Belfast that March. The city was toxic, embroiled in the height of The Troubles, with checkpoints in every shopping center where armed policemen went through the handbags of old women doing their marketing and book bags of children on their way home from school. Armored tanks did slow routine sweeps of the center of town under heavy verbal bombardment from the overflow of drunken traffic staggering from the many bars. Belfast was on high alert; everyone held a grudge. It was an angry and aggrieved town with two or three partially bombed-out buildings on each block.

People drinking in the bars below us were belligerent, assuming that everyone staying at the hotel was a rich foreigner, and mostly being right. Fists were shaken at us; oaths mouthed. We were somehow seen as being collusive with the armed patrols circling the area.

One late night, a young woman stumbled from the bar directly across from us and caught me looking at her. She immediately executed an about-face, dropped her drawers and shook her ass at me. It was exactly the kind of thing that Betty would have done as a young woman: "Póg mo thóin."

I'd been booked into the hotel room next to commentator Al Albert's, forced to overhear his half of garbled conversations, spoken in an affected British accent, with room service: "I'd like a spot of tea brought up. Yes, yes, a spot of tea. No, tea. Te-ay. A spot of tay."

I wondered what besides tea might have been added to those pots after catering got a load of that British accent.

I was hanging out with Tony Petronelli in his room one night, going over Foster's fight strategy. The phone rang and I picked up. It was Pat Petronelli. He recognized my voice, but was already committed to what he'd expected to say.

"Chaales, it's . . . *Dad*!"

Because many of the fight people were decamped in the same hotel, it was inevitable that we'd run into each other in its restaurant, a glass-enclosed space that overlooked the town square.

Botha's guys hung out there, and I found myself growing to like them. The two members of his team were West Coast veteran trainer Jackie McCoy and former WBA heavyweight champion Gerrie Coetzee. They were keeping company with ace cut man Chuck Bodak, the goateed, shaven-headed octogenarian eccentric who made his own silver and turquoise jewelry and came to the ring with headbands festooned with slogans about whoever's corner he was working.

King hadn't set aside additional money for a third cornerman, and I was unwilling to spend any more of my own on Martin Foster. Tony Petronelli was the only one I'd brought to work his corner. Neither of us was really a cut man, so Bodak offered his services.

Ordinarily I'd have never considered letting someone who might be said to be working for "the other side" near my fighter's corner, but I knew a lot about Jackie McCoy, who was seen by everyone in boxing as the most stand-up of people. Although he knew every trick in the book, it would have been beneath him to set me up. It was also evident that McCoy, Coetzee, and Bodak saw this fight as a free win for Frans Botha. We were going to need a cut man for Martin Foster. Chuck Bodak, whose reputation had been cemented through his televised work with Oscar De La Hoya, was one of the best.

The day of the final press conference and weigh-in was gray and cold with a steady mist that managed to find its way through outer layers of clothing. Everybody was in a grim mood. A van came to the hotel to bring some of the fighters to the proceedings.

Martin Foster, Tony Petronelli, and I stepped from the chill into an overheated van already semi-crowded with fighters, including one tiny creature who, with his enormous ears and pointy little teeth, appeared to be a vampire bat. The tiny creature was talking. Although I recognized Prince Naseem Hamed immediately, my subconscious frantically tried everything at its disposal to disavow acknowledging his presence.

I knew he wasn't going to stop talking. And he didn't. Prince Naseem Hamed was a major fistic star in the UK, idolized as much for his flair and style as for his boxing unorthodoxy and big punch. But it's safe to say that I've seldom met a less charismatic or more tedious human being. He was a runt, a pipsqueak. He was a fucking popinjay. As tiny as he was, his energy took up every vestige of air in the crowded van. It was like being trapped in a wet chimney flue wearing a soggy woolen overcoat.

Hamed bragged and bragged, animatedly throwing demonstration punches that caused fighters who had actual fights scheduled on the card to duck.

"Nobody can do the shit I do," he opined. "Nobody has my kinda flair. And nobody gets up when I hit 'em."

There was some irony in all this. I was managing Freddie Norwood, who would have destroyed him had they fought. It would only have agitated the insecure Prince if I'd told him that, and the unpleasant atmosphere inside the van would have multiplied tenfold. I kept my mouth shut.

I got a close look at Frans Botha at the weigh-in. At 231¼ pounds, with short arms, "The White Buffalo" was a roly-poly little fatty with a crooked smirk and a whitish-blond patch of hair perched like an ill-fitting rug.

Botha's record of 29-0 was more impressive than he was. His best opponent to date had been the tricky Mike "The Bounty" Hunter. Hunter, despite being a light puncher, had managed to drop The White Buffalo on his way to losing a split decision that he'd deserved to win.

Despite his dubious credentials, I knew that Botha was better than my fighter and that business reasons favored him getting the nod were Foster to put in the performance of a lifetime.

I was past the point with Foster where I was willing to boost his naturally inflated, but now experientially deflated, ego. I no longer gave a fuck about him. I was there to collect a payday and to see if he could lose skillfully enough to allow for a few future paydays. He owed me money, and I was in Belfast to get a little of it back.

At a local gym, Tony and I had tried to give Foster a fight plan geared to provide maximum short-term utility: unless an extraordinary opportunity presents itself, lose the fight, but do it in a way that allows the door to stay open for purses of similar sizes.

As Tony worked the pads, I told Martin, "Use your legs and your jab. Botha's carrying too much weight, so make him chase you. You're in better shape than he is. Move all ten rounds. Once he gets tired, if you can dig to the body without putting yourself at risk, do it. But I want that jab in his face all night, and I don't want you standing still. He can't punch, so he's not going to knock you out. Just go the distance and King will bring you back. You got it?"

"Yes, sir."

Even though Martin Foster's jab was nowhere close to what Merle Foster thought it was, he had a decent jab. It was the only punch he threw correctly. And, enormous waistline notwithstanding, he could move a little bit.

So, Objective Number One was to not get knocked out. Objective Number Two was to try to win the fight if it didn't interfere with Objective Number One.

❖   ❖   ❖

Showtime PPV sends someone with a handheld camera bursting into your dressing room after you've had the fighter gloved up for an hour or more. The camera is on a dolly, and the crew thrust it within a foot or so of your face, then gesture for you to follow them as they back up into the arena. They move slowly, but purposefully. The dressing rooms in King's Hall are below arena level, so you're moving on a slight incline from a relatively darkened area into one that is suddenly brightly lit once you've crossed the threshold into the Hall itself.

Unlike in the United States, UK fans go to the fights to *see* the fights, not to *be* seen at them. They come early and stay until the end. The card's main event was a rematch between WBO super-middleweight champion Chris Eubank and Belfast's own Ray Close one year after their first fight had ended in a draw. The rematch was among the most significant fights in the city's history, guaranteeing a full and wildly partisan house.

The enthusiasm trickled down to the card's preliminaries. When the crowd caught sight of Martin Foster, with Tony Petronelli, Chuck Bodak, and me accompanying him, the din they created was enormous, going straight up to the what looked like a pressed-tin ceiling, amplifying the volume and reverberating through The King's Hall.

We entered the ring, where Frans Botha was already waiting in the opposite corner. The lopsided sneer was still in place, but he suddenly didn't look so comical. Or so fat. The motherfucker somehow looked *big*. The ring, on the other hand, looked very small, as it always does when heavyweights are fighting.

We moved to the center to get the referee's instructions. Not for the first time, I felt grateful knowing that I'd be ducking back outside the ropes in a few seconds. There was just enough time to remind Martin Foster, "Remember, use your jab and your legs. Jab and move."

At the bell, Foster came out as instructed; Botha, the smile never leaving his lips, circled in nearly slow motion. He began waving his right glove in an exaggerated bolo—a kind of mocking gesture. Then he threw a wild uppercut from too far back, a sucker punch that everyone in King's Hall except Martin Foster saw coming. The shot evaporated Foster's nose, sending a scenic waterfall of blood down his chest and stomach. Martin started to drop, but stayed upright by holding onto the ropes.

Botha, still doing everything in slow motion, laughed. He repeated the absurd glove-waving pantomime, threw another uppercut that everyone in King's Hall except Martin Foster again saw, landed it on what would have been his nose if he'd still had one, and the referee stepped in to stop the fight as Foster sank to the canvas. One minute had elapsed from the opening bell.

Foster almost made it down the ring steps before his legs went out from under him. Luckily, Tony, Chuck, and I caught the fighter and managed to hold him up, then more or less carried him back to the dressing room.

We got him seated, and Bodak put the spit bucket on the floor in front of him.

"Son, your nose is broken. I want you to breathe in hard, then spit into the bucket. Just keep doing it."

"My nose ain't broke."

"Alright. But just do it."

An appalling amount of blood was spat into the bucket. It didn't stop. Martin would breathe in as hard as he could through his nose, spit a mouthful of thick blood into the bucket, repeat it again and again. His eyes were already closing up. It was terrible.

The doctor came in, explained to Foster that, yes, he *did* have a broken nose, and a badly broken one at that.

I saw Martin Foster at the airport the next day. His whole face was swollen shut; his eyes, blackened as a result of his broken nose, were barely slits. It was the last time I ever saw him and the last time we ever spoke. I explained that I was taking all of the money from the fight. He owed me a lot more than that. I also told him that if he promised never to fight again, I wouldn't come after him for the rest. I stressed how important it was that he quit boxing immediately—that his health was at risk otherwise. He was no fighter.

Martin Foster promised me that the Botha fight would be his last. We shook hands, then took separate planes back to different parts of the U.S. I was glad to be rid of him. He'd only needed to do one simple thing, but he couldn't manage even that.

Four months later, Martin Foster was back in the ring, now self-managed. Gary Mason knocked him out in the third round. He'd fight twelve times over the next two years, never winning again. He would be knocked out nine times, lose one decision, lose one technical decision, and fight one no-contest with Obed Sullivan, who would knock him out in the rematch.

I sued him in Kansas, using the Long-Arm Statute so I wouldn't have to leave Massachusetts. I was awarded a $72,000 judgment. Martin Foster filed for bankruptcy and I was eventually issued a check for a little over $200. I used the windfall to take my lawyer Michael Zinni—technically in for a third—out to dinner.

In the last two years of his career, Martin Foster earned somewhere between $2,000 and $5,000 for each beating he took. The heavyweights who punched him repeatedly in the head while knocking him out had a combined record of 212-13-4. Being generous, his purses averaged out to $4,000 per fight. For $40,000—not taking into account what he had to pay his cornermen—he voluntarily traded away whatever chance he had to stay whole. And he probably believes that in taking those fights he outsmarted me.

2000s

Jesus Enters My Life and I Dedicate Myself to Spreading His Word

Twice in my life when all hope was lost and I was sure I'd used up the last of my chances, Jesus came calling.

And both times that sad-eyed motherfucker was able to provide a temporary influx of cash until I could come up with a better way to bring in some money.

You'd think it would be tough for a white piano player to break into the hermetically sealed circle surrounding black Gospel music, but I didn't find that so. As in most endeavors—at least on earth—being white gives you an unfair advantage over everyone else. Being white jump-started me to the head of a long line of worthy black musicians.

It wasn't my first time around Black Gospel. Twenty years earlier I had been musical director of the Charles Playhouse in Boston, handling a live performance every night and then overseeing the after-hours sessions where headliners doing stage shows in the Theater District dropped in to unwind and try out new material. It was a fast track; the audience expected a lot, and the pros were a competitive bunch who brought the best out in each other.

The late-night gig was tougher than the official one. You had to be on your toes. There was no way of knowing who'd be coming in or what they'd do once they were onstage. If Zero Mostel dropped by, the range of things he'd try was impossible to prepare for.

One night a very young woman showed up, confidently walked to the piano, put her hand lightly on my shoulder and said, "I heard you last night and I'm not about to insult you by asking if you can play it." She gave me a thousand-watt smile. "Ease on Down the Road. In G." Then she ripped the whole place apart.

Noelette Leader was twenty-two and had already established herself on the national Gospel circuit. She was considering branching out to cross over into pop. A tune like "Ease on Down the Road" would let her show off her panoply of skills. She commanded the entire theater, making it her own, walking into the audience, strutting back onstage, waving other performers up to join her, marching to a table to do an impromptu duet with a customer. Noelette already knew every trick in the book. She would let the tune build to Saturday-night-prayer-meeting proportions, pantomime a shushing gesture so that everyone but me dropped out and she was whispering, then gradually bring everything back to thunderous volume. Up and down she took this flimsy flag-waver that had recently topped the pop charts, using it as the palimpsest on which she could pile layer after layer of music history. Noelette didn't believe in leaving any prisoners.

A couple of years later, I remembered Noelette when I needed someone to sing on my recording date for Columbia Records. We had kept loosely in touch. One afternoon, I got a call from her.

"Charles, can you play black church music? I *know* you can play black church music."

"Yeah, I can play black church music. You've got some for me?"

"I'm about to go out on tour. I got my band, but I lost my piano player."

"Now you found your piano player."

I'm a good Gospel pianist—Black or White—but don't have a lifetime of playing it in churches. The music has ironclad traditions. To do it justice, you have to be completely conversant with its history. I could fool most people as to my authenticity, then put on fireworks displays that swayed the doubters.

I started my Gospel career at the top. Noelette's warm up for the tour began at three local churches. She briefed me on the characteristics of each. She had funny, critical things to say about them.

"First we'll have to do the Bethel AME. That's the white black church where everybody has got a stick up their rear end. Bach was hired to write his oratorios for them. Just stay inside the lines there and let them get a good look at your hands. We'll be in and out in twenty minutes.

In Cambridge we'll do thirty minutes at the Aletheia. You might even see some of your own people there. *Could* be a few white faces anyway. But it's just gonna be your standard Baptist 'Jesus Loves Me.' Easy.

But. . . . *Then.* Then you gonna have you the real black experience, Charles. You going to see you some holy rolling, some happy feet. Word of Life Tabernacle in Roxbury. Here's where we pull out all the stops. I want you to do all your crazy stuff on the piano. Don't hold back. You'll see—they'll run up and down the aisles, fall over, kick their legs, speak in tongues. Tears be streaming down they faces.

"And those negroes can sing! You'll have to follow me close. I don't even know for sure what I'm gonna do. Might only play one song, two songs, and it's still gonna take an hour. I'll break off, talk some, go back to singin'. Like we use to do back at the Charles. Keep following everything I do, but don't stop playing. They do a whole lot of testifying at Word of Life. You'll love it."

Noelette adopted an exaggerated black voice. "But don't you *dare* flirt back with them married choir ladies. If they holy rollin' in the aisle, I better not catch you rollin' with 'em."

The experience prepared me for the Eastern circuit through DC, wrapping up in Norfolk, Virginia. It taught me that the Conferences were essentially trade conventions where everyone peddled their products. They also used the opportunity to draw a bead on the competition and to see where the music's cutting-edge was heading. The Conferences were a fascinating amalgam of hayseeds and slicksters, although it wasn't always apparent who was who. There were a lot of savvy Southern preachers who came on like splay-footed, "well, looky he-ah" farmers.

The tour was an education and I was glad to have played it, but I could see it wasn't for me. Too much of the pitch focused on people's troubles, along with the one-size-fits-all message that accepting Jesus into your heart would be the answer to your prayers. There was too much discussion about who "had passed" recently, about how "the sugar" had caused someone's amputation, whose nephew was in prison—just too many personal tragedies monopolizing the conversations, even if folded into an ongoing narrative of uplift.

When I left church music that time, I assumed it would be the last I'd ever see of it firsthand. I liked the music; I liked most of the people. But it wasn't my life. Little did I realize that I had barely dipped my toe into the holy water. I was about to be baptized in the wonder-working power of the precious blood of the Lamb.

Near the end of the century I washed up on Tampa Bay. I was in my late forties, recently removed from one set of circumstances and now rudderless in new ones.

I was down on my luck, temporarily broke and homeless, reduced to sleeping on park benches a few times. I was the damnedest homeless person imaginable. I still owned six houses, but every penny from the rents went to mortgage companies.

In line at a grocery store, a woman and I got into a conversation where the talk drifted to what we did. I mentioned that I'd once played music for a living.

"My nephew Rog is in a church band that needs a musical director. Is that something you might be interested in?"

In fact, I wasn't very enthusiastic or optimistic, but my need for immediate cash required looking into whatever presented itself. I got Rog's number.

I was surprised by his voice. He sounded like a Midwestern farmer, peppering the conversation with "my goodness" and "oh Lord." Rog's aunt was black. I had assumed her nephew would be black too, but his voice was white. Would I be directing a white church group?

"Rog, where do you rehearse? I can drop by."

"We're at the 34th Street Church of God. It's right off Martin Luther King."

In any city in the United States, you can rely on Martin Luther King Boulevard not only being in a black part of town, but in the poorest and most dangerous part.

Thirty-fourth Street turned out be a dimly lit pulp-fiction place where barely discernable figures grilled barbeque over 55-gallon oil drums.

An old woman flagged me down on the corner for a ride. Her name was Hattie. She got into my car without looking at me, then admonished, "Lock up, honey. You in the ghetto."

I was unprepared for the band that greeted me at the 34th Street Church of God basement. The members of Emmanuel were sensationally good and disconcertingly young. They all looked like models. I couldn't imagine why the minister thought they needed anyone's help, least of all mine. Had they been white, they would have been superstars. Being black relegated them to the basement of a run-down church in the worst section of a poor area of a crime-infested backwater town.

I sat in on one tune with them and was hired on the spot. Their working assumption was that I would whip the band into shape, and that their only mission—other than their Mission to serve God and Jesus—was to learn from me.

I received two of their CDs to learn their material. The recordings were slick, featuring tight arrangements and precise instrumental execution. The vocalists were all first-rate.

The music Emmanuel played was overflowing with exuberance. They knew the tradition inside-out, but youth kept their ears to the ground. When I complimented seventeen-year-old Jeff Williams on his slap-bass technique—a style of playing that I assumed was state-of-the art—he hung his head bashfully and told me he'd learned "that old-school stuff" from his uncle.

Emmanuel was the brainchild of the church's minister Keith Jacobs, an ardent and loquacious hustler/Believer. I'd never met him before, but Jacobs was far from new to me. He was the self-involved narcissist with the messianic work ethic, asking everything of his congregation, justified by his understanding that he was not asking for himself. It was evident his flock found him charismatic.

It seemed obvious that he was tapped out, so before my first rehearsal as Emmanuel's musical director I tried to make it easy on him.

"Keith, Emmanuel is a fine band. But I'm not a Believer, so, please, no proselytizing. This is a job for me. I'll only charge $100 each rehearsal, but you'll have to pay promptly. Not one late payment. Understood?"

"Understood and agreed, Charles. I hope you won't mind if we all pray for you."

Keith shook my hand warmly, looking me directly in the eye.

"That would be very Christian of you."

I Step Inside the Circle, Then Step Back Out, and Take Others with Me

The rehearsals showed me a lot about ways to teach music. I had fallen into the habit of writing out music parts, but Emmanuel wasn't made up of good readers. To teach them new material, I needed to switch to the method the players themselves used. Luckily, they picked things up at warp speed.

Many black churches' directors teach their bands and choirs using a pattern of innovation followed by immediate imitation. It's an ongoing cycle that always keeps tradition in view while seeing to it that the language expands. Church spirit that encourages sharing knowledge makes for a risk-free learning environment. Even really young kids gain access to what's being shared; it's not unusual to find five- and six-year-olds flawlessly mirroring whatever they hear. The interconnectivity of this kind of learning encourages unusual flexibility among the musicians. Everyone can play anyone else's instrument at least reasonably well.

On a level playing field, only good would come from this learning arc. But music isn't made in a cultural vacuum, and while being great at what you do and receiving unconditional encouragement to do it is a source of happiness and sometimes even a life-saver, it has its downside.

When I first heard Emmanuel nearly twenty-five years ago, they were dazzlingly precocious youngsters. When I recently checked in on my old bandmates on YouTube—now heavyset middle-aged men with kids of their own—I heard them playing *exactly* as they did twenty years ago. They haven't improved at all. Music that seems stunning when played by a teenager sounds no more than competent when done by an adult. Maybe that's okay. Maybe being embraced within a loving closed circle is more than fair compensation for never stepping outside of it.

Working with Emmanuel was rewarding, but I had concerns about what I was doing nevertheless. Black Gospel was loaded beyond capacity with great groups that all played slight variations of the same thing. It was often exciting music—especially at first—but it was governed by a conformity and conservatism that I found increasingly grating. To keep from being bored, I introduced elements that made the music more radical. Thinking competitively instead of cooperatively, I wanted Emmanuel to stand out among its peers. This probably did the group more harm than good, but it wasn't like I was running into opposition from them. Church people may never admit it, but there *is* a vigorous strain of competitiveness that runs through Gospel music.

If I did the band no good, at least I corrected some individual problems. Randol Walton improved his keyboard fingering, which helped him play more fluidly. I upgraded guitarist Geoff Caputo's—the other white player in Emmanuel—harmonic theory.

Jeff Williams was one of the most naturally gifted musicians I'd ever met, but some of the material was very tricky to pick up by ear. He had the habit, when embarrassed by a passage that he wasn't able to decode, of facing away from the band to "make adjustments" to his amp.

Whenever I showed Jeff what the chords were, he would pick them up instantly and never forget them. If he later discovered a different piece of music with similar chords, he'd hear them with no problem.

As satisfying as the band could sometimes be, I found myself growing increasingly emotionally dragged down, exactly as when I'd worked with Noelette Leader. The theme of having fallen into a despair that could only be overcome through the acceptance of Jesus Christ as your Lord and Savior seemed imprisoning to me. There was a strong suggestion that this was the default status of people's lives.

I could be temporarily invigorated by the fire-and-brimstone essence of tunes like "It's Gonna Rain" when the O'Neal twins sang: "It's gonna rain. It's gonna rain. You better get ready and bear this in mind. God showed Noah the rainbow sign. He said, 'It won't be water, but fire next time.'" I loved the absolutism of that kind of judgment.

Or "Jesus Dropped the Charges." I could sink my teeth into that. You fucked up, had your trial, and through some procedural impropriety got a free ride that permanently expunged the matter. Or maybe someone had paid God off. I knew something about that.

Whenever we played a tune like "God of the Second Chance," it made me wonder how black churchgoers could bear it. "God of the second chance, He'll never give up on you." The implication was that everyone else would.

Emmanuel's music, like a lot of Gospel, had a subtext of underclass living yoked with only modest available success here on earth. If you had anything grander in mind, you had to wait until heaven to get it.

A Garbled Mission of Mercy

The weather had gone crazily dark and stormy, turning the night into the cause for concern it so often becomes in South Florida. We had formed a decrepit caravan of cars. This futile exodus confirmed for me that, whatever else he may have been, Keith Jacobs was insane.

Emmanuel—band and choir—was scheduled to play a concert at the Zephyrhills Correctional Institution. Keith had been sent detailed guidelines for when we were to arrive and begin playing. Lights out at the prison was 8:00 p.m. No exceptions. We'd given ourselves two hours to get there.

Keith had also gotten vague directions. The band, choir, and members of the congregation had no choice but to bump along Florida's highways in their clunkers, making frequent stops by the side of the road to reconnoiter while being pelted by a driving rain. Keith's eyes burned with the fervor of the Chosen, tears from heaven joining his own ecstatic weeping to cascade down his gleaming cheeks.

By 7:00, and no closer to the prison than when we'd started, it was apparent that we couldn't possibly get there before the deadline. It was unfortunate, but it was time to go home. During one of the soggy huddles, I pointed this out to Keith.

"No," he said. "We *must* complete our mission. Someone will be saved tonight! If there is just one soul I can reach, it will be worth whatever we have to endure!"

The "I" and "we" weren't lost on me.

"Keith, they're going to lock up the prison for the night in an hour. We can't make it in time. We'll be turned away at the gate. They won't let us in."

"Oh, yes. Oh, yes! They will. They must! We are doing His work. The Lord has sent us into—I momentarily thought I'd heard "unto"—this night. One of God's children is out there who needs us."

"I'm sorry, Keith. But I'm going home."

When I was the only one who turned back, I was certain that Keith Jacobs hadn't lost his followers, although tonight's mission would fail. Keith Jacobs was a fuckup. It wouldn't be long before he'd be unable to pay me.

Heading to the next rehearsal, I once again ran into Hattie. She was standing near the corner where I first saw her. I rolled down my window.

"Hattie, do you need a ride?"

She recognized me.

"You can just take me down a couple of streets. Just go 'round the corner. Can I get fi' dollar from you? I'll suck your dick."

I gave her five dollars.

"Just take the money. You don't have to do anything for it."

It was obvious that she was relieved to get a no-strings donation. On the other hand, it was hard to imagine anyone taking Hattie up on her offer.

As I'd feared, the general consensus among the members of Emmanuel was that Keith Jacobs had tried mightily to be God's foot soldier on the night he attempted to bring the group to the Zephyrhills Correctional Institution. No one took the position that he was an incompetent and delusional megalomaniac.

I played the rehearsal, but Keith didn't come up with my $100. We went to a small room in the back of the church basement and he ceremoniously emptied his pockets, and then walked back to the rehearsal space and started to take up a collection. I felt uncomfortable about this. Keith and I went back to the private room where I returned the added money.

"You can make up the difference this week. But this can never happen again. I need to be paid in full for every rehearsal, and it can't be the group's money."

Keith said he understood, but no money arrived during the week. I called to let him know that I was out.

In the short time since I'd begun with Emmanuel, my fortunes had again changed and I was living in a house on Davis Islands, an upscale enclave kept safe and apart from the rest of Tampa by a bridge. Being there felt like an escape from the undeserved but ongoing small losses that defined the lives of Keith and his flock.

I thought I'd dodged a bullet until an enormous manila envelope arrived in the mail containing dozens of handwritten letters from church members.

Reading became more and more painful with each letter. The congregation beseeched me not give up on them, to not abandon them. Almost every church member took direct blame for my leaving. They had failed me. They vowed to do better. They promised to continue to pray for me. I had no idea how to reply to them. In the end, I didn't.

Emmanuel Becomes Indio

Being done with Emmanuel didn't mean that I was done with its musicians. I'd been thinking about putting together a band that would blur the line between narrative and music, between composition and improvisation, between live and prerecorded music, and between performance space and audience space. What I had in mind was difficult because it drew from such a diversity of sources—both playing and thematic—yet had to emerge as coherent and organic.

For Indio, I enlisted five players from Emmanuel. By the time the band got around to doing its first—and only—concert, it had expanded to ten pieces, including one nonperforming member. It wound up with two guitarists, one electric bass player, two drummers—one who doubled on organ and keyboards—a saxophonist, two percussionists, one piano player, and a composer/sound organizer.

I didn't want Indio to be a music band, but the players couldn't shake being one. That the music was often interesting, occasionally demanding, sometimes well played, and always energetic wasn't the point. I was never able to get across to Indio that it wasn't just a music group.

Indio's playing generally fell into two categories: a funk-driven pulse with jazz solos riding on top, and music that I'd written that was too hard to play to allow falling back on cliches. Randol and I were the only ones in the group who could fluently negotiate the difficult stuff.

The task was to consolidate the variety of idioms so a unified voice emerged. This needed to be managed even while two or three threads were being explored simultaneously. I never got the band to understand that they were free to come and go as they pleased, to play or not play, to regard *anything* that served the larger narrative of the piece as usable.

After six months of rehearsals, things had yet to coalesce. Indio wasn't speaking a new language, yet the players were bragging to the local musicians about "what a trip" Indio was. When something was on the line, the players instinctively reverted to being "a great band." Great bands have always been a dime a dozen.

Indio played its one concert, was enthusiastically received, and I immediately broke it up.

A Happy but Closed System

*Although the band Indio no longer existed, my own life had
become inextricably connected with its members. In joining
Emmanuel, I'd walked into the middle of a preexisting family.
Living with Sam, Randol, Rogerick, and our friend Jamal on
and off for a couple of years, I was at times part of that family,
despite the vast differences in our ages.*

*Hair and grooming products aside, the three guys shared
everything. They worked out together, went to clubs to hear
music and sit in, joined bowling leagues with their friends, and
spent almost every Saturday from late morning until early evening gos-
siping on the balcony of the condo Randol and I shared while he picked
up spending cash by giving designer haircuts and shaves. Randol was a
custom tailor too; the whole crew always dressed sharp.*

*Most Sundays the guys managed to run into every other black church-
goer in Tampa at Golden Corral, a toxic communal trough that passed
itself off as a restaurant. The place was a brightly lit all-you-can-eat
emporium that herded diners like cattle onto wooden rampways; hundreds and hundreds of happy parishioners in their church best socializing
companionably as they inched forward up a series of slow, graded inclines
to the head of the $8.95 all-you-can-eat chow line, where they painstak-
ingly heaped mountains of fatty, sugary, battered, and fried "Oh, Lord,
he went too soon" early-heart-attack fare onto their plates, washing it
all down with endless pitchers of sweet tea, and later making their way
back to the line for seconds, thirds, and—if they'd only eaten a small
breakfast—fourths.*

*The rent was always behind, and the electric and cable companies were
consistently cutting off service. Repo men would show up outside the
apartment in the dead of night and quietly drive their cars away. There
was a steady supply of phone calls from collection agencies.*

*Family members from Miami or Orlando, from down in Alabama or
up in Detroit, were constantly falling ill and dying, victims of high blood
pressure, heart disease, or occasionally—if they were the black sheep
of the family—violent misunderstandings with the police, rival gangs,*

store owners, or other family members. There were stints of incarceration. Money was always being sent to bail out "Cousin Henry down in Tuscaloosa." A pilgrimage of friends and cousins took turns spending a week or two sleeping on the couch.

They were all enmeshed in a social structure that would dictate where they could—or even would choose to—go in their lives. There were constant qualifiers in play: you couldn't simply do something; you had to "strive for" or "reach to achieve" it. It was a kind of optimistic underclass restrictiveness.

Suckers for opportunists who should have had their best interests at heart, the guys were bombarded by local ministers and pastors who'd pawn off pamphlets and brochures with titles like "The Steps It Takes to Become a Man," with chapters headed "How Not to Be Ignorant (Ignant)."

Jeff Williams stole my BMW 535i. It's not that he meant to steal it. His intention had been to borrow it for the little while I was out of town, have a series of photos taken of himself and his girlfriend posing in front of it as if it was theirs, pocket the twenty or thirty dollars in change that I kept in the center console—under the "we're all family here" rule—and then get it back to me. But he'd managed to have it impounded and wasn't able to bail it out. It sat hijacked and rusting away in the sun, trapped in a forlorn used-car lot way down on Florida Avenue in North Tampa. Jeff didn't have the heart to tell me. He was hoping that the car would be quietly auctioned off, and that its disappearance would slip my mind.

He had good reason to hope that the car thing would just go away. Jeff was still a kid, and his kid's way of dealing with pressure was to hunker down as his faculties crashed to a binary on-off that turned him into a smiling automaton.

Once there, he'd wait for it to all be over. That was not going to happen. Things would never all be over. He and his sixteen-year-old girlfriend had only a few months left to get ready to be parents. They'd make it and they wouldn't make it. The baby would be born healthy, with family, friends, and the church community to see to its care and happiness. The child would mostly be raised by grandparents, older siblings, aunts and uncles, and family friends. Jeff and his girlfriend would stay in the picture, making *or not making ends meet; not bad kids at all, but deeply unequipped to be parents on their own.*

I was angry at Jeff for leaving me to search for my car, pay its ransom, then find that it had grown irreparable in exile. I felt sorry for him too. He was gifted in a way that wasn't going to be recognized and that would do him little good.

At seventeen, although of average height, he already weighed 265 pounds, with hands as big as steam shovels—his nickname with the guys was "Hands"—and size fourteen shoes. Jeff, without having ever been in a gym before, could bench-press more than 300 pounds. His family was from rural Alabama, and he had what people liked to call "farm strength." The male members of his family, from way back in the country, were divided evenly between preachers and jailbirds. Some were both. The preachers formed a peripatetic band called The Traveling All-Stars, crisscrossing the Deep South, playing at any tent revival their cars could make it to.

During rehearsals, having fun, Jeff Williams came up with the most brilliant, funny, and unclassifiable pieces of performance art imaginable. While playing the bass, he would sing and talk, mimicking a local minister who'd made the evening news after being criminally charged for confis-cating food stamps from his impoverished congregation.

"I didn't steal no food stamps! I'm gonna try an' he'p the people!" Jeff's voice would soar up into a beautiful falsetto. "Ohhh, yeahhh. Woo-ooh." He would simultaneously dance his enormous bulk in spinning circles, flipping his bass around in elaborate patterns while playing funk riffs.

In concert, where a rehearsal replication would have blasted the audi-ence out of their seats, Jeff froze, silently retreating out of range of the spotlight to the back of the theater. He couldn't be seen back there, but you could hear him mechanically playing ones and fives.

The guys in the band didn't read. I don't mean they didn't read music; they barely read anything. Their parents didn't read, nor had their par-ents. Nobody wanted them to. It was so much easier to take advantage of them if they couldn't. They were lured into confiscatory business deals where they'd wind up paying for things that would sooner rather than later be taken from them. At one point, Sam's wife Tanika's father Israel came to the apartment I shared with Randol to ask if I could help keep his home from being foreclosed. His mortgage contract was jaw-dropping in its predation. The homeowner would wind up drained after paying for four or five years, default on the loan, and the house would be taken. Almost any show of resistance would back the mortgage company down. The lender knew that their foreclosure practices couldn't withstand any genuine scrutiny. They targeted borrowers who wouldn't know that they had rights.

I was able to help Israel with his mortgage problem, but was again reminded how blatantly the deck was stacked again black people. Israel was harder working than I'd ever been, smarter, had gone a lot further in school, and had a more reliable source of income. It didn't matter.

Randol Walton could barely read or write, yet received a scholarship from USF. It looked like a beneficial arrangement for him, but wasn't. Randol got no education at college. He was recruited as a teenager who could already play circles around anyone in the jazz program, professors included. The department wound up using him as its de facto bandleader, paying him nothing and shortcutting him through classes that he neither understood nor cared about.

A few years later, Randol, now married, fell into the same predatory real estate scam as Israel. He and Layesha had their house stolen out from under them after owning it for five months. They didn't even fight to keep it.

I recently watched YouTube clips of my old roommates. One was one of Jeff Williams playing at Rogerick Green's brother's wedding. Now in his mid-thirties, Jeff had ballooned up to around 400 pounds. He sounded very good, but no different than he had at seventeen, certainly no better. He still seemed to be enjoying himself.

While on YouTube, I looked to see which of the young players living in Tampa twenty years ago were still around. Corey Christiansen, one of the guitarists from Indio, had moved on, becoming an internationally known music educator and author of instruction books. Nearly all of the other jazz players—black, white, and Latino—were still there, doing the same gigs, playing the same tunes with the same musicians, recording in the same studios. None of them sounded any different.

So, maybe it's the sunshine that keeps everyone from moving around much—the cheap and easy living, the lowered requirements and expectations. The musicians in Tampa don't lack talent; nowadays jazz musicians everywhere play at the world-class level. But none of the locals were experimenters; they all reached their potential early, and it was an easy transition to go from attending college in the area—usually USF, sometimes Eckerd or St. Pete—to teaching for subsistence wages at the same schools where they'd gotten their degrees.

There's part of me that really gets it. There are joys in living in the sun, hanging out together, doing nothing much. Sam and Randol and Jeff and Rogerick were happier than I was. They were gregarious, connected to their families, to the community, to the music scene, and to their church.

I don't entirely know how to process where their lives have gone. I know that the four guys in the band—Sam, Randol, Rogerick, and Jeff—have all made it to middle age, and that three of them have achieved successes of a sort. Maybe all four have; who am I to evaluate what success is?

Sam and Tanika opened up two schools in Tampa: the Walton Academy for the Performing Arts and the Body and Soul Dance Center. Randol is the Arts Director at the Academy; Layesha teaches dance at Body and Soul and writes inspirational Kindle books. On paper, it looks like they've done well. But the orbit is identical to what it was when I knew them. On Randol's LinkedIn page he's listed as the Arts "Ditector" at Walton Academy. It's just a little off.

The school teaches black children to sing, play musical instruments, and dance—all in the identical styles that were being taught by church members back when I was in Tampa. These styles were not new when I got there. The kids are beautiful and they look happy. There's a safety net of sorts for them. They'll be looked after in the community, in the churches, and at the Walton Academy for the Performing Arts and the Body and Soul Dance Center.

Are the decisions the guys made to stay with what they know, to teach what they were taught, a savvy way of protecting each other and themselves? Does it come from a deep understanding that, once removed from that sphere, they're fucked? Is it an acknowledgment that white America is not interested in sharing anything with them, and that the smart move is to not to waste time bothering trying to get it to?

Or is this all a terrible blindness—a failure to see the swindle that is still taking place? I've never forgotten reading the religious-training pamphlet that cautioned the guys not to be "ignant." I can't help but wonder if they get it that in the traditional corridors of US power that seeing names like Tanika or even Randol or Rogerick only prompts a knee-jerk response. That maybe presenting yourself as the Arts Ditector isn't going to be much help on LinkedIn.

If I went to a prestigious learning academy's website and saw that the photos showed only white kids, I'd get the message. When I went to the Walton Academy for the Performing Arts website, I got an equivalent message, even if the reasons for its exclusivity come from entirely different angles and guarantee a different set of real-life results.

Who am I to voice these misgivings? I can't present a case that I've made more of my life than the members of Emmanuel or Indio, my erstwhile family, have made of theirs. But I'm stuck wondering what advantages and rewards they'd have received if they'd been born in this country with their same gifts and white skin.

The Antoine Palmer Project

The longer I'd managed, the more certain I was that much of the advancing of a fighter came from what you could accomplish in the back room. My experiment with Fernely Feliz that long-ago Saturday afternoon at Gleason's helped bring the point home. Unquestionably, Feliz could really fight, but my prep work before he got into the ring set the stage so convincingly that a couple of well-thrown jabs followed by an authoritative right cross was nearly all it took to complete the picture of him as unbeatable.

I wondered if a fighter required Feliz's talent—or even much talent—to be successfully marketed. Maybe finding a prospect in the dismal current climate didn't mean combing the bushes for good fighters, but only required a casting call: you sought out guys who *looked and talked* like movie versions of fighters.

Tyrone Booze thought he might have found someone promising.

"He's big kid, Mr. Farrell. Not like a bodybuilder, but like one of those big-boned kids from down in Alabama. Big neck, big legs. He's not fat, but he's real thick, know what I'm sayin'? Maybe 280. I ain't seen him fight yet, but he looks like he can really punch. He's gonna be real green, though."

Antoine Palmer turned out to be as green as Booze had warned, which made the Antoine Palmer Project even more intriguing. Bringing him along would be a pure act of invention.

Antoine was a dark, sullen, and ponderous young man who came with extra baggage in the form of a standard crusty but lovable old trainer—yet another guy called Pops—looking for a meal ticket. Pops had the kid living with him in a rathole over a gym where he instilled old-guy boxing wisdom. It was all bullshit, but I'd take it. Pops could be worked into the Antoine Palmer Story.

The Tampa/St. Pete/Clearwater area had a lot of wealthy, sports-obsessed young day traders who dreamed of bankrolling projects in exchange for being visibly connected to them. Being in a fighter's dressing room, walking into the ring with him, having free ringside seats, being up on the dais during press conferences were lures that coaxed these suckers out of their money. I already had a few optimists lined up through Tyrone and Rogerick Green.

I'd arranged for my friend Eric Snider, the senior editor at *Creative Loafing*, to do a feature on Palmer's first public sparring session. Eric understood what I wanted written. Antoine Palmer had to be the new Sonny Liston—a scowling black menace barely held in check by his surrogate grandfather, the saintly Pops.

We had things scheduled for Jim McLaughlin's atmospheric 4th Street Gym in St. Pete, but Palmer's intended victim never showed up. Because Antoine was being brought in by a former world champion in Tyrone Booze, had a manager and a trainer, and an article was being written about him, none of fighters in the gym were willing to spar with him.

We made sure that Palmer scowled and raged through the gym, giving Eric "I just want to hurt people" quotes while taking swipes at the heavy bag.

Everything was going perfectly.

Then a smallish white man fucked up the whole deal. He was a very fit light-heavyweight kickboxer who offered to spar with Antoine Palmer.

"I'm not a pro or anything, and I might not be big enough for your guy, but I can maybe give him a little work for a few rounds. I'll move around in there with him. The thing is, if he's just too much for me, I'll stop, okay? I don't want to get hurt."

The kid was so nice that I hated the idea of his being a sacrificial lamb, but somebody had to be. I'd pay the guy. I went to talk with Palmer and Pops.

"Antoine, that guy standing over there is willing to spar with you. He's not a pro. You've got about eighty pounds on him, but don't hold back. Take his head off. Get him out of there as fast as you can."

Palmer nodded his head. I nodded my head at Pops. Pops nodded back at me. Tyrone and I nodded at each other. Eric and Tyrone and I all nodded at Pops. It looked like an episode of *Dragnet*.

Thirty seconds into the first round, I turned to Tyrone. "This kid can't fight."

"Not a lick."

Eric Snider whispered, "I can't write anything about him. He's terrible."

The point wasn't lost on Palmer's undersized sparring partner. He may have been a nice kid, but there was no way he was going to miss his opportunity to beat up a huge guy in front of an audience. He was gaining fans, who naturally rooted for the underdog.

Before the end of the first round, Antoine Palmer's nose was broken. We quickly discovered that old Pops was about as good a trainer as Palmer was a fighter.

"Don't you remember none of what I showed you, Antoine? Use your motherfuckin' jab! Don't be standin' there lettin' him hit you? What's *wrong* with you?"

"I'm tryin'."

"Tryin' ain't good enough. Now beat this boy's ass."

I wanted to tell Antoine not to listen to Pops. To lay his extra weight down on the little guy. Grip him in a bear-hug and hold tight. Don't worry about the jab. Don't worry about boxing at all.

Things got worse. Antoine wasn't in shape, so his punishment increased the longer it went. He was taking a real beating now, and lovable old Pops was screaming nonsense at him from the corner. Palmer was such a beginner that he kept looking over at where the screaming was coming from, desperate for help from anywhere.

I said to Tyrone, "We should stop it. No sense getting him hurt."

"Let's let him get through the round so he can hold his head up."

I didn't like seeing Palmer being pounded the way he was—he was now basically just cowering and flinching—but Tyrone was right. It was crazy to imagine that he'd ever fight again, so he should be allowed to retain as much of his dignity as he could.

Pops put an end to all that.

"You fat, lazy motherfucker," he yelled, "You're ruining it for both of us. You get your ass out there for another round, and don't let this boy beat you. Don't give me no excuses."

In the third round, even the kid who was destroying Palmer seemed to have misgivings about it. Still, for someone who wasn't a real fighter, he gave Antoine a good going-over.

Palmer seemed to be crying as he yelled back through his bloodied mouthpiece at Pops. They were engaged in an active argument even as Antoine was getting mugged. It was surreal and brutal, and I'd have to pay the sparring partner for it.

It ended after a thousand years, but Pops's tirade continued as Palmer, still in his trunks, attempted to escape to the parking lot. The trainer stayed glued to his side, a haranguing Chihuahua to the fighter's St. Bernard.

Finally, Palmer had had enough.

"Back off me, man."

"I ain't gonna back off you. You let a little white dude beat you in front of all them people. You're gonna have to do better or we'll lose our sponsorship. You think people gonna pay you if this the best you can do?"

"I'm tellin' you to back off."

"Or what, nigger?"

"I don't care if you are an old man. You leave me alone or I'm gonna knock you out."

Pops's face tightened. "If you raise your hands up to me, I'm'a blow your head off. You just try me."

It seemed like the right time to intervene. Tyrone blocked Pops's path while I moved Antoine away. There was a lot of yelling back and forth between them, but the two freeloading frauds were being moved in opposite directions, so it was okay.

The Antoine Palmer Project had come to its semi-dramatic end. Or near its end: I got a phone call the next day from Pops, who wanted me to know that Antoine could do much better, and then asked if I'd still be subsidizing the two of them. A few months after that, with Christmas approaching,

Antoine called to ask if I could send him some holiday cash. When I'd answered the phone, he'd identified himself as "Antoine Palmer, the fighter."

How Chase Bank Ended My Life as I Knew It

In 2009, my circumstances, which hadn't been good since I'd gone legitimate, went into a nosedive. Around the time I turned forty, I'd picked up some real estate with an eye to turning my assets legitimate. Now, nearly twenty years later, I had fallen into unrecoverable mortgage debt. Trying to pay it off using civilian methods drained all my resources. I cannibalized the cash that I'd taken out in refinancing, watching the pile steadily dwindle from a million dollars until it all ran out.

Chase Bank had started foreclosure on two of my properties—one the home I'd lived in on and off for over forty years.

I'd been a fool, taking cash out on two loans that were so predatory that they became illegal seven days after I'd closed on them. The broker was aware that the loans were about to be declared predatory. He told me, "These aren't going to be around much longer."

He just didn't bother to tell me why.

Chase scheduled an auction for the sale of my primary residence—the sign had been placed on my lawn in the dead of night—one day after an injunction temporarily suspended it.

I literally chased one of the vultures who hover over these auctions down the stairs from the vestibule of my house. He wouldn't step out of his convertible sports car so I punched a dent in it, hoping that would goad him into action. It didn't. He tore away from my house as fast as the car could accelerate.

The foreclosures led to my filing a lawsuit against Chase that lasted five years and left me, even after paying my lawyer about $100,000, $1.4 million in debt—a place where I will remain for the rest of my life.

Chase Bank became my life. They phoned ten times a day, demanding information. I'd hang up on them. Representatives were sent to my houses. I'd threaten to throw them off the porch.

That winter in Boston, I lived without heat or hot water in a first-floor apartment of one of my houses. I cut back to four meals a week. This involuntary austerity program forced me into making some decisions. One was to toughen myself up again.

I worked my way back into shape, dropping forty pounds to the 135 it had been more than thirty years earlier. I ran three to four miles on alternating days. I did at least 300 sit-ups six days a week. I brought my bench-press back to 260, just thirty pounds from what had once been my best. I did 350 pushups a day.

These weren't Guinness Record Book numbers, but they were acceptable for a sedentary guy pushing sixty. And the workouts made the lack of heat more tolerable. I still wasn't able to overcome my living conditions. They were too tough.

During that time Rudy Diamond was doing the maintenance of my houses. Rudy had been a pro wrestler in the old WWF—an enormously powerful man who was the perfect choice if you needed someone terrified, beaten up, or shot. His gig in the WWF was to protect his fellow wrestlers from altercations in bars and clubs and to cool out dressing-room squabbles. His backstage nickname was AK47 Diamond. Chief Jay Strongbow once had to warn Andre the Giant to stop making racist comments around Rudy or risk being mowed down.

Rudy Diamond was one of the toughest individuals I'd ever met, but he was a horrible handyman, as likely to do damage to things he was trying to fix as to bring them back to functionality. The results of his work were dangerous, and I often had to pay off outraged tenants in order to avoid lawsuits.

I still thought I might be able to hunker down and make it through the winter bumping along with Rudy, taking three steps forward, two steps back, and hoping that that the sum in the spring would total somewhere around zero.

But two disasters occurred within days of each other. Some basement pipes to the first floor burst from the cold, and the boiler for the second-floor apartment gave out. These weren't problems I could tough out. My tenants needed heat, and the house couldn't withstand frozen and burst pipes.

Rudy would fuck it up if he tried to fix these things. The house would wind up flooded. My tenants would all burn up in an electrical fire. There'd already been a terrifying incident the previous winter. Rudy had supposedly fixed the old boiler. In the middle of the night, I received a frantic phone call from one of my tenants. Smoke was coming into the apartment from somewhere below. When I arrived at the house, I found *a thick fog roiling through the entire basement, making it impossible to see even an inch ahead. Without thinking, relying on memory, I groped my way through the murk to the boiler and flipped the switch. Then I retraced my steps and made it back outside. I left the basement door open to the cold so that the smoke would clear. I sat on a snowbank, my hands black with soot, and tried to figure out what to do. I considered calling the fire department as a safety precaution, but knew that the Board of Health would file criminal charges and make me put my tenants up in a hotel, so I left it alone.*

This time, instead of rolling the dice with Rudy, I wound up calling a shady old Jamaican operator named Isaac. Isaac practiced a kind of zombie fix-it: he could get dead things to run at half speed for a short while. He pulled no permits, honored no departmental codes. As with Rudy Diamond's, the results of Isaac's work were usually dangerous; what he knew about heating, cooling, and electrical systems he'd taught himself back in spliced-and-duct-taped Kingston. But he was a shade more competent than Rudy, and his services came cheap. Isaac was always paid in cash, and he showed up whenever he felt like it, often in the dead of night. If I wasn't planning to be around when it was time for him to get paid, I'd leave cash in the basement, under a brick by the furnace. He'd send someone around to pick it up. Later he'd come out to do the work. I'd receive no receipt.

I didn't trust Isaac. And I don't think that Isaac trusted me. His posse of silent young Rasta jailbirds was afraid of him. Isaac carried a clunky old-fashioned pistol that had been a Saturday Night Special before falling on hard times. I was wary of leaving cash out for him, but he wouldn't do any work without being paid up front, despite having done dozens of pre-paid questionable fix-it jobs for me over the years. The modus operandi of these operations was to get things to work through the next week or two—and sometimes for just a night—until rents came in and there was money to do things semi-right.

Compromised living conditions kept me from thinking clearly. I'd forgotten that, in dealing with people, perception is nearly everything. The way you present yourself determines what you can get someone to do. You're never the only one in trouble, and people in trouble will take risks for anyone they think might be able to help them.

I was getting no leverage because I was telegraphing my circumstances. The effects of that kind of behavior are always cumulative: you make justifiable mistakes that eventually lead to beginner's mistakes. Instead of recognizing that Isaac was just scraping by—and his minions maybe not even doing that—and making him believe I was the answer to some of his problems, I let him flip the equation so that I was jumping through hoops to get him to do his haphazard work. I'd forgotten that, for poor people, the promise of money made by a person thought to have money works as well as actual money. It might even work better: actual money ends the transaction; the promise of money brings hope for the future.

Shell shock had set in. Each day brought multiple new crises, along with thirty or more emails calling them to my attention. A slate roof started falling apart in a number of places, bringing water through the ceilings in two of the three apartments. I couldn't afford to fix it. Even if I'd had the money, nobody would have been willing to go onto the roof in all the snow.

A family of aggressive raccoons had settled into an attic crawl space off the third-floor bathroom. Through a hole in the second-floor ceiling, the alpha male was starting to reach into the kitchen in an attempt to break out a panel. This scared all of my tenants, particularly bin Jhang, newly arrived from China as part of an exchange program with Harvard Medical School. He left a voice message on my answering machine: "Charles, the animal . . . it is here right now! I can see its craw! You must help me!"

Because of the house's decrepitude, the tenants, previously good about upkeep, relaxed and started treating the place like a homeless shelter. It was a strange, slow downward drift. Although their apartment was unsafe, often without heat or hot water for brief periods, menaced by raccoons and occasional squirrels, and subject to blown fuses, the tenants took an increasingly laissez-faire attitude about living conditions. This attitude began with the maintenance of their own rooms, spread by silent mutual agreement to the living and dining areas, and finally to the kitchen, which sprouted an outlandishly fecund wetlands around the sink.

This lack of cleanliness next extended to the tenants' wardrobes, grooming, and hygiene. The formerly stylish bin Jhang took to wearing the same black turtleneck sweater for days on end, then weeks, and eventually all the time. Paul Hobbs's boxer Haley stopped being housebroken, but none of his roommates seemed to care.

The conditions of the apartment freed the roommates from any remaining bonds of civility. They grew to accept each other as they were, *stubbly faces, gray teeth, and all. Those who had girlfriends lost them. Paul Hobbs, who had been attempting to reconcile with his wife, wound up divorced and barred from visiting his baby daughter. It didn't seem to matter. The television was on night and day, whether or not anyone was watching. The tenants spent all night in their rooms, listening to talk radio, the sound turned way down in the wee hours. Although all were in their twenties and early thirties, they began to act like old men. They complained like old men too, relieved as they were to no longer be held to accepted standards of dignity.*

Paul Cao's father called to ask if his son was still living at the house, and whether he was alright. Paul had stopped communicating with his parents. Then Paul Cao and bin Jhang got into some kind of code-of-honor war. During the middle of the worst blizzard of the year, Paul's parents showed up from DC with a rental truck to move him out. His father struggled up the long, snow-covered front stairway and knocked on my door. "Something is wrong with my son. We just found out he's left school. He didn't tell us. Does he seem normal to you?"

The City of Waltham issued a criminal complaint charging me with illegal use of a two-family dwelling. They started sending around building inspectors, health department inspectors, and the guys from the fire department. Citations would arrive listing code violations and threatening fines of up to $350 a day per violation.

These crises caused me to make a couple of unusual decisions.

"Good with Niggers"

"He's good with niggers." Or "good with *the* niggers." The loan sharks would say that. "Charles is good with niggers. He can handle them. They like him."

And so the phone used to ring, and Donnie Done or one of his crew would tell me, "We need help with some black guys. Maybe you can talk to them before it turns into a problem."

Meaning that it was still possible that if I reasoned with them there might not be a problem. Nobody wanted a problem. It cost money. And it was a problem.

I'd spent a lifetime around black people, in music, in boxing, and in my daily life. I'd often lived with black people. I got along with black people. My second wife, long departed, was black.

But I didn't try to act black around black people. I knew that it was tough being black. That was why I liked being white; it gave me an advantage in nearly every exchange. It wasn't fair, but I would have been insane not to use it.

When I went to collect money from black guys, I didn't pretend to be the muscle. I never threatened anyone. I didn't carry a gun. I'd been sent as the last lifeline they'd get before bad things happened to them. My real job was to explain the situation, and I was generally able to do that.

There were risks, which was why I was paid well for what almost invariably was simply a conversation or even a short monologue.

Back when I was a gangster, I had carried out this kind of job maybe ten times over a decade.

Then I got into some trouble with other gangsters, so I stopped being a gangster and became a citizen.

Many years passed. Over time I forgot most of my survival skills but picked up nothing to compensate for the loss. I got old and fat and soft.

One afternoon, amid a million calamities, the phone rang.

"A thousand bucks you don't know who this is off what I just said."

"If I'm talking to Donald Donatello, he owes me a thousand bucks."

"That'll teach me never to gamble. How are you, Charles? Long time."

"It has been a long time, Donnie. How are you doing?"

"Doin' good, Charles. Doin' real good. But you know me. I don't call nobody just to shoot the shit. I know you're outta this thing now, but I got something that's kinda in your line. And it's easy."

Any other time, I'd have brushed Donnie Done off, and he would have accepted it. But I was in bad shape and was ashamed of myself for being pushed around by people I owed money—lightweights I'd have once rolled right over. And I was broke.

"Tell me about it."

"Really? No shit? I didn't think you were gonna even listen to what I had to say. But, you know, fuck it, at least make the call. It's just a little situation. A couple of brothers out there in East Providence. Real brothers—same mom and, for all I fuckin' know, same dad. Young dudes, nothing heavy about them. They're into me for ten. I could send Richie S., but he'd want a fifty-fifty split. I ain't gonna do that 'cause this isn't hard money to get. I can give you a dime for the ride to Providence. You should be up and back in an hour. If it gets more complicated, we'll renegotiate. Believe me, Charles, these kids aren't gonna give you no back talk. You know what to say to these guys."

"Are they around to be found? Am I going to have to go searching for them?"

"Yeah, I got everything."

"What do they look like?"

"What do they look like? They look like two ghetto niggers tryin' to show they've hit the lottery. So they look exactly like all the other young niggers you might see. C'mon, Charles, you know me. I can't tell one black guy from another. They got the hoods, they got the fake gold bullshit around their necks, they got fake diamonds in their teeth, and you can see their fuckin' underwear."

"In other words, niggers."

"What can I say? No disrespect intended."

I had been a gangster for a long time. I'd mastered a self-deception bordering on hypnosis. I may have seemed impassive, but I was inwardly coiled; life lived in a state of perpetual readiness, geared up to hurt others and to protect myself and my own. The word "fear" was never allowed to enter my consciousness.

Now I understood that fear had been with me every moment; it was the condition that triggered each action I took, each decision I made. This realization left me with an enormous vacancy. If I wasn't the man who I thought I was, who was I?

I knew that I wasn't a tough guy although I had done the physical work required to convince most people that I was one. Those I couldn't fool, I left alone. I wasn't brave, something I'd managed to overlook.

I had blustered my way into owning millions of dollars' worth of real estate without actually knowing what a mortgage was. I had backed down professional heavyweight fighters by telling them that I was going to the trunk of my car to get my gun when I didn't have a gun. I had stormed the home of a city official who had tried to shake down a friend of mine. I had nearly torn a 400-pound man's eyes out with a gardening tool when he wouldn't take no for an answer. I'd gambled over $400,000 on one boxing match, lost, and shown no outward disappointment.

It was fake. All of it. I'd been a fraud masquerading as being fearless. After walking away from gangster life, it took me two full years to stop hyperventilating. I'd have to take huge surreptitious gulps of air when no one was looking. Going to retrieve Donnie Done's money, I no longer had the tool of self-deception to help me collect. I was just a scared and unprepared old man.

But less scared when I finally saw the James brothers.

There was a lot of dirty snow clogging the streets in East Providence, and the houses testified to years of neglect. The neighborhood seemed oddly divided between the working poor—mostly white and Portuguese—destitute black people, and newcomers whose drug and stolen-goods businesses were bringing them decent incomes. The brothers Demetrious and Skeebo James fell into the last category even though their house on Jenks Street was a dump.

I had arrived before sunrise that morning. I knew the guys might not be staying at their house overnight, but going to their place was the best place to start. They would be around sooner or later.

It had been a long time since I'd done a collection, but I still knew some things. Wear a good sports jacket, a white shirt, no tie, expensive slacks. If it's cold, wear a quality overcoat. But it's better not to. If the James brothers dressed to signify their status, so would I. It was important that they read the signals: 'This guy's a cop,' followed by 'No, he's not a cop, but somebody sent him.'

I was hoping for something easy, and I got it. At about 9:00 a.m., two young guys came out. I crossed the street decisively but not too fast, showing neither fear nor hostility. The first few seconds are the most critical ones.

I got to them, and said, "Demetrious James. Skeebo James. Donald Donatello sent me. You'll want to straighten things out with him."

They exchanged a look. They were nervous; they didn't know where to place me. And they were very young kids.

Skeebo said, "Man, are we in trouble?"

"You could be. We don't know yet. Is there anybody else in the house?"

"No."

"Okay, let's go back inside. Mr. Donatello wants this taken care of. He sent me to work things out, so don't do anything that'll make it worse. You know what I'm saying?"

"Yeah, you ain't been sent to do nothing to us, right? Donnie Done. . . . Mr. Dontelle send you to, like, work somethin' out, right?"

"That's all I'm here to do."

I knew they'd have guns in the house, but I wasn't overly worried about that. My being there meant they were on Donnie's radar: important enough to bother with, and that if he'd meant to hurt them, nobody would be talking to them. That knock on the door would have been the last thing they would have heard before the roof caved in on them. I had to assume they knew that, and there was a good chance we'd reach an agreement. If they were dumber than I thought, I could still be at some risk.

It turned out that the James brothers weren't dumb. They were afraid of what Donnie Done might have done to them and they understood that they owed him money. They also seemed a little petulant about how much interest Donnie was charging.

"It ain't right that he want ten thousand dollars back. We only borrowed sixty-five hunnit. That's a lotta interest, mister."

"Is that what you agreed to?"

"Yeah, it is. But a coupla things fell through. We knew Mr. Dontelle axing too much, we didn't think it wouldn't make no difference 'cause we was gonna have the money in a coupla days anyways. But we got caught short."

Demetrious chimed in.

"Yeah, got caught a little short. Ten is a lot."

"Can you give me half to bring back to Mr. Donatello?"

"Nah, we ain't got half. Lemme talk to my brother for a minute, okay? Figure out what we got."

Demetrious and Skeebo walked a few steps and conferred. Skeebo, who seemed to be the spokesman, said, "We got about thirty-four hunnit."

"Okay, let me make a call."

The Jameses eyed each other nervously,

"Really, man, that's what we got. If you need to take it with you now, we can't get no more. This all the money we got."

I fooled around with the cell phone that Donnie Done had lent me, holding up my hand for them to be quiet.

Here's what the James brothers heard: "Don, I'm with the two guys now . . . yeah, at their place . . . they don't have all of your money . . . thirty-four of it. Okay, let me ask . . . hang on. . . ."

"Mr. Donatello wants to know if you can get the rest in a week."

'We ain't bringin' in that kind of change. Could we, like, maybe get a month, ax him?"

I shook my head no at them, held up two fingers. Two weeks.

"They can't get it in a week, Don. I'm trying to see if they can do it in two."

"If Mr. Dontelle give us three weeks, I know we can get the money up."

"How about three weeks? I think they're good for it . . . they're not playing games with you, Don . . . they won't be able to manage it . . . yeah, that's what I'm saying . . . twenty-two a week for the next three weeks, then they're square . . . okay, hang on. . . ."

"You'll deliver the money each week for the next three weeks? Do that, and Mr. Donatello says he won't even charge you points. It's a good deal for you guys, better than I thought you'd get."

"Yes, sir."

"Okay, Don . . . yes, they'll drop the money at the store in Somerville . . . yeah, they understand that . . . I'll drop off what they give me today . . . okay, okay . . . very good . . . I'll see you in an hour."

"You guys did the right thing. You don't want Donald Donatello looking for you, and you don't want to owe him money. Just make sure you get the next three payments to him on time. Give me what you've got and I'll deliver it."

Donnie Done thought it was hilarious that he'd okayed the payment plan in a phone conversation I'd had with dead air.

"Jesus, I'm a more reasonable bastard than I ever thought I was."

I got a couple of calls from Donnie Done after that, letting me know that the James brothers had made their payments on time.

A month passed before I heard from Donnie Done again.

"I got another thing for you. Maybe even easier than the last one, and for a lot more money. You even get to go on a vacation. Interested?"

"Sure. But I can't promise this won't be the last one, okay?"

"Okay. We'll do it on a per-event basis. If you decide that's it, just say the word. Need you to talk to a dude named Elgin Bragg. That's B-R-A-G-G. He's been a steady account. So, you know, over time the numbers get bigger and bigger. No problem. We're talking twenty, maybe even thirty over a weekend. But three weeks ago, he wants to go a hundred on the Pats. Ordinarily I'd say no, but this Bragg was brought in by

FK, so that carries a lot of juice. Long story short, he's missed his first two payments. Looks like he's gone desperado. But I know where he is. He's out in Vegas, apparently hitting the sportsbooks pretty hard. So he can pay me. Maybe he figures I don't stretch to Vegas."

"You've got guys in Vegas."

"I do got guys in Vegas. But two things. Even if this is a simple diplomatic exchange, the best split I'm gonna get from a collector is I give up a third. The thing is, I don't really know what kind of guy this fucker is. I don't think you'll have a problem with him, but I have to be a little careful, and I have to tell you to be a little careful, because he was brought to me by FK. Which means don't let things get heavy. You don't like the vibe, walk away. I'll pay you something for the trip, and put somebody else on it."

FK. Franny the Killer. Things got serious the minute his name was mentioned. Everybody liked Franny. He was a charming guy, smart and funny. He was generous and helped his friends. But "the Killer" was a job description. And though he never strayed outside the reservation, no one who knew Franny wasn't—at least in some small part of their brain—a little afraid of him. It would be imprudent to cause harm to someone who might be a friend of Franny the Killer's. Donnie was right about Elgin Bragg having juice.

You may think that, because he'd vouched for him, Donnie Done could ask Franny for his help bringing Bragg into line. But that's not how things worked. Donnie was a professional, so it was up to him to decide how much credit to extend to a customer. And you didn't want to make something Franny the Killer's business that didn't need to be. Not even with $100,000 at stake.

Franny the Killer's involvement also went a long way toward explaining why Donnie Done asked me to talk to Elgin Bragg rather than sending a real collector. If it turned out that Franny and Bragg were close—which was unlikely—my being dispatched to try to retrieve the money would be seen as no more than a goodwill gesture, something for which there could be no residual hard feelings. It was a tactic of restraint.

It was no problem finding Bragg once I got to Las Vegas. Donnie's contact there pointed him out to me. He was staying at the MGM Grand. I even knew what floor he was on. It was just a question of being unobtrusive and getting on the same elevator.

He nodded at me when I joined him on the way to his floor.

Once the doors had closed, I said, "Donald Donatello intends to collect what you owe him."

Most white people don't know this, but the color can drain from a black person's face.

"I've always intended to pay him."

"Except that you haven't. And nothing you've done shows that you intend to. You've missed scheduled payments. You skipped town. And you're making bets at Caesars."

"Will you let me explain? Please."

"Go ahead."

"Okay, I had bets that would pay off, but I knew Donnie wasn't going to take them with what I owed. Nobody else in Boston would have either. Once I missed a payment, I was in trouble. I had money, but not enough. I came out here to get my bets down. And I've made back a lot of it."

He took a deep breath.

"Look, man, I'll be honest with you. I'm scared of Donnie Done. I don't want you to kill me. Can't you tell Donnie that I've got almost all of his money? I'll get the rest to him soon. I swear I didn't come here to skip out on Donnie Done."

"Now let *me* explain a few things. Donald sent me here to get his money. He didn't send me to kill you. He sent me to talk some sense into you. We may be able to handle things without you winding up with a bigger problem than the one you've got now. How much money can I bring to Don?"

"I have about $78,000."

"And when can you get up the rest?"

"Maybe six weeks? Something like that."

"Let's see if Mr. Donatello will accept that. It's not my call."

"Am I going to get hurt?"

"Not by me. I'm the goodwill ambassador. You won't want to deal with whoever's the next line of negotiation. Deal with me, assuming the option is there."

"I will. I'll deal with you. I just want to settle this, then forget it ever happened. Shit, I'm scared."

"If you don't fix this problem, you're going to get hurt."

"I don't know how I ever got into this. This isn't me. I just want it to be over."

"Right. You do. You have the cash with you in Vegas?"

"In my hotel room safe."

"Let me call Donald. I'm going to have you talk to him after I do."

"Can't you just straighten it out? I'll give you all the money, and you can bring it to him. What if I say the wrong thing?"

"I just want to establish with him that I've got most of the money and that your intentions are good. It's a way of normalizing the situation. Just don't argue with anything he says.

"Why? What's he going to say?"

"I don't know. Just agree with him."

I got Donnie Done on the phone, brought him current, put Elgin Bragg on the line, then checked out. I was suddenly exhausted. I'd come in poised to straighten out a bad, maybe dangerous, situation, but I'd wound up encountering a suburban high-school science teacher who happened to have black skin. He'd just gone briefly on tilt. But he was finished. He was so finished that he had wanted to hand a stranger $78,000 without even finding out for sure if he'd really been sent by Donnie Done.

I felt like a fighter who'd geared up for a twelve-rounder against an opponent who might be too tough for him, then wound up scoring a knockout in the first minute. There was a quick jolt of adrenaline, followed by psychic depletion.

My job was still not done, but I felt like telling the two guys to just work things out for themselves so I could go home. I needed to sleep.

It was all okay; they were going to work it out. I could pick up whatever money Bragg had to give and head back to Massachusetts.

As distanced from this event as I'd suddenly become, I continued to practice due diligence. Elgin Bragg would experience an emotional backlash and become angered and humiliated once he got over being terrified. It would be a lot easier to act out against me than it would to defy Donnie Done. I moved myself back to high alert. I'd seen people make costly errors after they'd let their guard down. They had thought the game was over when there were still a few seconds to go before the final buzzer. And, as Elgin Bragg himself now knew, anything could happen in those last few seconds.

The next day I flew back to Boston with Donnie Done's money. We settled up and I went home.

Being a gangster, you were either in or out. It made no sense to do it part time. It might have made sense if there'd been black guys I could talk to every minute of my life. Otherwise the risks were too great, the rewards too small. I had $10,000 in my pocket. That wouldn't make a dent in the million-plus I owed. I was always going to owe a million-plus.

There would now be heat for the winter—a good thing. But in the end even that wasn't going to matter. I'd decided it was time to move again.

The Semi-Long Goodbye

With the exception of the few times I took work because I needed the money, I stopped playing in public by the late 1970s. I continue to practice piano three hours a day because the discipline does me good.

It would take a lot of thought for it to become clear that music was part of my past but wouldn't be in my future. Before giving it up, I made a number of attempts to reclaim it, though.

Hope Springs Eternal

Around Christmastime of 2004, I flew to London to record one album and put the finishing touches on another with saxophonist Evan Parker. I had more or less abandoned playing pure music, but since we were going to be recording the hybrid "Hope Springs Eternal" anyway, I didn't want to pass up one last chance at it with the most advanced saxophonist since John Coltrane.

I hoped Evan would agree to take on a grueling dialogue that would require us to play nonstop at full speed and volume for forty-five minutes straight. Because Evan uses circular breathing, he'd be able to fulfill the music's physical requirements. He was up to the challenge.

The session was even harder than I'd feared. My fingers began to come apart a few minutes after we started playing—bleeding, nails breaking, and skin scraping off. For Evan's part, his tongue split down the middle early on, and he was forced to play while swallowing blood. I kept hoping that he'd have to stop so that *I'd* have an excuse to stop. I got very close to quitting a number of times, but I'd tell myself, "That's Evan Parker. He's the only saxophonist in the world you want to play with. And this is the last time you're going to do it." It was enough to goad me into continuing. But I couldn't stop thinking, "You mother*fucker*. Will you *please* stop playing so I can go home?"

The real reason I'd come to London to record with Evan wasn't to record a music album. It was so we could do the music component to *Hope Springs Eternal*—an album of answering-machine messages from people in the boxing game, painstakingly looped and sampled to form an extended narrative.

The Penguin Guide to Jazz Recordings (eighth edition) favorably reviewed both of the albums. *Hope Springs Eternal* is described as "one of the strangest records in this book" where "fragments of voice and speech do leave an indelible mark." Richard Cook writes about my playing on *Glossolalia*: "Farrell may be quite a technician, [but] one wonders at times if he is actually listening to his partner in these duets."

I was listening to Evan. I just wasn't necessarily *agreeing* with him.

(Not) Coming to Terms with Ornette Coleman

Ornette Coleman was the best-known musician I played with in the 2000s, but I hadn't sought to play with him. Ornette first heard me on a Jim Schapperoew recording. He called me in Florida, which led to several lengthy phone conversations, and we wound up getting together at his condo in New York City. We quickly became friends and wound up playing together regularly for a few years.

Although our music never really clicked, we liked getting together, and decided to form a quartet with Jim and bassist Henry Grimes. Grimes was my choice because he was an emotional touchstone of '60s avant-garde jazz, a voice of ironclad authenticity.

I had high hopes, but the quartet proved to be an unfortunate mishmash of sensibilities.

The $75,000/$750 Dollar Quartet

Even before we went into rehearsal, there was a problem. Ornette was now pulling in $75,000 a concert. I could expect to make not much more than 1/100 of that. In a co-led group, I wasn't willing to be paid less than anyone else. We agreed to rehearse the quartet anyway. We'd worry about how to handle money later.

Henry Grimes had resurfaced after disappearing—assumed dead—for thirty years. On his return, his playing was identical to what it had been in his prime. I looked forward to playing with him.

My goodwill toward Henry held until the moment at Ornette's when I was introduced to his wife, Margaret Davis, who single-handedly made me wish I'd never laid eyes on Henry Grimes.

As I shook Henry's hand, Margaret told me, "Henry is a legend too, you know."

Less than a minute later, she added, "Henry is a genius too, you know."

Because I'd suspected that the quartet might not work out, I'd asked a friend to videotape the afternoon's session. I seldom keep souvenirs, but this seemed worth making an exception for.

Margaret said, "What do you plan to do with this video?"

"Nothing. Keep is as something to remind me of this afternoon."

At that point, I already knew the group was going nowhere.

"You're not going to sell it on the black market, are you? A lot of people try to sell Henry's concerts on the black market."

"No, Margaret. I'm not going to sell it on the black market."

"Because people do, you know. People make a fortune selling Henry's concerts on the black market, and Henry doesn't see any of that money. I'm not sure I should let you take it."

I held my tongue. I didn't say that, as great a bassist as Henry was, his value on this video was that it was the only time he'd recorded with Ornette Coleman. YouTube was already overloaded with videos of Henry Grimes since his return to public playing.

"I'm not going to sell it. I'm not even going to let anyone see it. Why would I? We sound terrible. I'd be embarrassed if people heard it."

"Henry didn't. Henry didn't sound terrible."

"I didn't say Henry sounded terrible. I said *we*—the band—sounded terrible."

Meanwhile, Henry, Jim, and Ornette were standing around, listening to a conversation I should have known not to have.

Ornette, who really did always put music first, said, "We just need to play together a lot more. If we rehearse, it will sound good after a while."

I knew it wouldn't. More important, I knew that Margaret Davis would show up for every rehearsal. I did something ungracious then. I told the players, "This is a waste of time. I'm going home."

Ornette, clearly shaken, asked, "Are you mad at me?"

"No, man. I'm not mad at anyone in the group. But I know when something isn't working."

"Can we try one more tune?"

"You and Jim and Henry can. I'm done."

"Okay. You're sure you're not angry?"

"I'm sure."

By the time I was out the door, the trio was already artlessly slogging their way through a blues in C. It just wasn't a well-matched trio, and it had been an even worse-matched quartet.

From Ornette to the Copa

Despite the travesty of our attempt at putting together a quartet, Ornette Coleman and I remained friends and continued to spend afternoons playing duets together. I valued my time with him.

On a warm, cloudy June afternoon, Ornette and I walked from 9th Avenue to his condo on West 36th Street. I was in New York so we could play. Later in the evening I'd pick up a bullshit award from the Boxing Writers Association of America at the Copacabana.

Recent years had brought Ornette a Pulitzer, a MacArthur, and a Grammy, along with the wealth that went with them. After having been famous for a long time, he was finally getting his financial due. He'd bought an entire floor of a prewar building that had a private elevator that took him to his penthouse. Its doors opened onto nearly three thousand square feet of open living space, branched out in one direction onto a small rehearsal room and in another toward the darkened recesses of three bedrooms. A high-tech kitchen was incorporated into the open area. Fourteen-foot floor-to-ceiling windows overlooked 36th Street.

It didn't look like the home of any jazz musician I'd ever met. But I'd never met Miles Davis.

In Ornette's practice room, there was a wall-sized blowup of the controversial Vietnam-era photo of Nguyen Ngoc Loan's point-blank pistol execution of a Viet Cong prisoner. I never found the blowup conducive to creative improvising. Maybe Ornette did.

Ornette hated his condo. He was certain his neighbors in the building didn't like black people. He told me that someone was sneaking into the place and stealing things, breaking things.

I met some of his neighbors while waiting for the elevators in the lobby. Far from not liking Ornette, they all seemed flattered to share his address. And given the security in the building, the coded elevator, and the various locks to Ornette's door, it was clear that no one was breaking into his apartment. Whenever I came to see him, everything was in exactly the same place as the time before.

Still, I sort of got it. This sudden elevation of his standard of living had been thrust upon him through channels he didn't understand by sources he didn't know.

Ornette talked about a youngish Japanese vocalist with whom he'd recorded and whose career he asked me to supervise. She wasn't good, and could go only as far as her association with Ornette allowed.

"You know, I slept in the same bed with her once," Ornette said. He was small, frail man with a quiet voice that had a slight lisp and the hint of a Texas accent. "I don't remember if we had sex." He pronounced it "thex."

"That means you're either getting fucked a lot or you almost never get fucked."

He laughed.

"Yeah. I suppose I ought to remember whether I fucked her or not. But I worry about whether I'll get some woman pregnant. I think there are women who want me to get them pregnant. That's why I almost never have sex. I don't remember the last time I had sex."

"So if you fucked her, you'd probably remember it."

He pondered that one. "I *think* I remember. Yeah, yeah, I'm pretty sure I've seen her naked." That came out "*nek*-kid."

"I hope for your sake that you have. Because she can't sing at all."

Ornette had obsessive, circular theories about music. Certain numbers and relationships buzzed around insistently in his head. They vexed him.

These theories got saddled with the reductive term "harmolodic." Intended to promulgate a complex system of logic, this combination of conventional music rules, substitution of visual relationships for intervallic ones, and misapplied and inaccurate information is at best naïve and at worst gibberish—a kind of theoretical double-talk.

"Okay," Ornette would whisper in his papery voice, "you play the piano. That's in C, ain't it? So, I play my A on alto and that's the same C. The trumpet player play his D, but that sound the same too. Then the bass player—he in the bass clef, ain't that right? —he play his E-flat, and that come out C too. So all these notes got different names, but they all the same sound. How is that possible? Or like they all got the same name, like if we all play C, but we got four different notes. So why we using these names? That's fucked up. See, a note don't care what you call it. It's just a note."

He was stuck. His language, both innovative and expressive, was a relatively closed system. He'd become a famous and important jazz musician, but was still in some respects a primitive player. Both his fame and his primitivism restricted him. Anyone famous who radically changes his voice risks losing their audience. Ornette was never going to change his playing. I'd played with him quite a bit, and I knew. He always ultimately played exactly the same way.

Ornette worried about dying before he'd had a chance to express what he needed to through his music. He couldn't explain what that music would sound like. He told me that his new music must be "spiritual," but didn't attach a compositional or improvisational blueprint to it.

People still ask me, "What was it like to play with Ornette?"

I tell them that he could play the fuck out of Ornette Coleman music.

Ornette Coleman was the only musician in the world who could play as he did. His playing had unearthly beauty. Hearing him while he stood a foot away—knowing that what you were playing was connected in the air with what he was playing—was a unique privilege.

Most of our duet playing was not successful. I was not interested in being Ornette's accompanist—which is why I walked out of our rehearsal with Henry Grimes and Jim Schapperoew—or playing the obvious or redundant. I struggled to find a compatible voice that compromised neither of us.

We would stumble for half an hour before some sonic lever might get tripped.

The first time that happened was when I realized that I was playing with someone who was like a blues musician. It was more productive to filter what Ornette played through things that he'd heard during his early life—things that defined him as a person—rather than thinking in terms of form or structure.

Replacing music with biography worked. For the next forty-five minutes, we played music that was eerie, full of screams and wails, moving back obliquely to packed Texas juke joints from the 1940s but then rocketing into the future. It was more Ornette's music than mine, since we were using his story as its emotional fulcrum, but it was honest dialogue.

Ornette asked to hear the CD I recorded in London with Evan Parker. He listened for a couple of minutes. He didn't approve of Evan's approach.

"He's playing notes. He's just following you, playing with his hand close to the keys of the saxophone. He's a good saxophone player, but he's thinking about the *saxophone*. What you playing is an *idea*. It ain't notes."

He insisted that we try to play what he'd heard on the CD, with an eye to recording it together. I disagreed with him about Evan Parker's playing. He was more reactive than instigative, but that worked because Evan's response time was so quick, his technique so extraordinary, and his ear is so uncanny.

Ornette didn't negotiate the music well. Once we'd begun to play, the alto veered off quickly toward familiar territory. Some of the music was good, but good only on Ornette Coleman terms, which wasn't the point.

After twenty minutes, we stopped.

I said, "It's different than what Evan was doing, just a different approach."

"Let's try again. I think I can get it."

I had to be at the award dinner soon and started to beg off but Ornette was intent on attempting to play what he'd heard on the CD.

"Charles, let's play for just one more hour."

It popped into my head that I was trying to talk my way *out of playing* with Ornette Coleman. That was insanity.

We did another forty minutes. The music had some value—and was even good in spots—but it didn't represent a truly different approach for Ornette. He was just adding his playing to mine, the way that I often just added my playing to his.

And I inadvertently broke his piano, busting the D-natural next to middle C by hitting it too hard. Ornette was actually more impressed than upset by that.

We finished up, hugged goodbye, and I got ready to go.

"I'll get it," Ornette said. "We just got to play a lot more."

He never did get it, and I never found a reliable way to play well with him. Our voices were not naturally complimentary. Still, the music had its moments.

No one else had ever played like Ornette, yet somehow—largely on his own terms—he found a way to bring much of the world to his music. His desire to communicate produced something undeniable. That was what, despite our miscues and long stretches of mutual grasping at straws, kept drawing me back.

I caught a cab from Ornette's to the Copa and arrived too early. All the doors were locked, so I had to search around until someone from the kitchen staff stepped out for a smoke and let me in. Sneaking in through the kitchen felt appropriate. I almost slipped the guy a ten.

The Copa was a sprawling and disheveled dinosaur that now existed in some drab half-life. There was nothing remaining of its glory days when Latin bands played to packed houses of crazed mambo dancers. Trying to picture the two Tito's—Puente and Rodriguez—fronting their stylish *orquestas* here, I came up empty. I didn't think there were any ghosts in the building.

It turned out that I was wrong. The club eventually opened. An hour later, it was packed elbow to elbow with hard-drinking, red-faced, conspicuously nonfit boxing writers brushing up in their hearty frat-boy way against the pro fighters, all of whom were instantly recognizable by their impeccable posture and Zen-like personal containment. It seemed important to the writers that they establish tough-guy bona fides with the boxers, a pose that was tolerated with respectful equanimity. I found my way to my table, pried out a spot, and was immediately approached by event organizer Steve Farhood.

"Charles, I can't find a place for Jake. Can I put him next to you?"

I looked up, and there was Jake LaMotta—ancient and tiny, emanating icy hostility. Next to him was a woman forty years his junior, but by no means a young woman. She wore a low-cut evening gown, had dyed her hair jet black, and—ever the trooper—was beaming back and forth between Jake and me.

"I'm sorry, "she said, "I didn't get your name."

I introduced myself.

"Hi, Charles. I'm Denise. I'm sure you already know the champ. Hon, this is Charles."

LaMotta eyed me coldly. I partially stood up to shake. He gingerly extended two fingers, barely touching my hand. His grip was nonexistent—a combination of a fighter's traditionally delicate handshake and a form of dismissal. His eyes never left my face; the opaque eyes of a shark. It was hard to know whether the blankness came from cognitive decrepitude or the vestiges of a notoriously merciless fighter's refusal to cede any signals.

I thought about the current generation of fighters working hard to project menace and how childish it made them look. Jake, nearing ninety, was the genuine article. Whoever the fuck you were, Jake LaMotta was not afraid of you.

Over dinner, Denise chirpily carried on as interlocutor between Jake and me, conveying information to him and getting either a grunt in return or nothing at all. When the food came, she noticed that my meal was different from everyone else's.

"Oh, you must be a vegetarian! Jake, Charles doesn't eat meat!"

For the first time, LaMotta looked at me with some animation.

"You don't eat no meat?"

"Not since I was twelve."

"You don't eat no meat since you was twelve? You don't want no steak?"

Denise said, "No, Jake. He doesn't want steak." She had to raise her voice so that LaMotta could hear her over the din. She spoke very deliberately, one slow word at a time. "He's a vegetarian, Jake."

"He's a *what*?"

"A vegetarian. He doesn't eat meat."

"He don't eat no meat?"

LaMotta then settled down to eat his dinner, tearing into his steak with a single-mindedness of purpose that recalled the way he'd attack an opponent's ribs and midsection. The process seemed grim. It was hard to imagine Jake enjoying anything.

The Retirement Tour

I had hoped that the enthusiasm I'd felt as a kid for public performance—the excitement of all-or-nothing based entirely on what you had at your disposal that night—would return after I began meditating.

That didn't happen. My interests as a player had changed, requiring a new, extended language that I had yet to learn. Additionally, I found myself uninterested in the kind of communal vocabulary that improvisors, even at the most advanced levels, use.

Evan Parker had flown to Boston with Caroline Forbes to visit for a week, recording two albums and playing three two-set concerts during his stay. He chided me for my refusal to go easily along with this code of bandstand etiquette.

"Charles, it's called 'in concert' after all."

"That's one option."

There's no question that playing harmoniously together requires skill and cooperation, especially if you're using no formal guidelines. But traditions and conventions still emerge, as well as modes of behavior and propriety that severely restrict your choices about what to play.

The upshot of the visit was that, playing with the players I most admired, I was bored twenty minutes into the first set. I knew what the other sets would sound like. We'd play serious music that was going to take hard work—my fingers were going to be bleeding by the end of the first set; Evan might again split his tongue as he had during our duet recording session—with no room for slacking off or losing focus. That would no longer hold my interest.

The three nights of concerts went well, but when people asked when the group was going to play again, I had to tell them that it probably never would. Why should it? We'd said everything we were going to say. We could only say it again a little bit better or a little bit worse.

Who cares about a job well done? It may be fine as far as it goes, but it opens up nothing new, it is not a breathing thing. A conversation—playing "in concert"—seldom bears repetition. And bandstand etiquette provides almost no room for argument; it militates against difference of opinion even when disagreement would bring dynamism to the music. Bandstand etiquette doesn't value someone playing in the moment if that playing isn't congruent with what everyone else is playing.

I'm not saying that musicians should get up on the stand and fight all the time. But broadening the range of emotional interaction, no matter how you do it, adds possibilities for what might emerge.

I Don't Play Piano Anymore

I still practice the piano three hours a day, six days a week. It's always the same: two hours early in the morning of sight-reading Classical music or doing technical exercises, a short break, and then one more hour of sight-reading. I've been practicing the same way for over thirty years.

Back when I was gigging every night and doing TV, radio, and recording sessions, I practiced five or six hours a day. That was too much. After plateauing, my playing stagnated. With the three-hour routine, my playing will continue to improve incrementally for the rest of my life.

Until I realized that I couldn't stand music—something that came as a big surprise—I'd usually play another two or three hours a day for pleasure. I no longer do that. Aside from practicing, I seldom play at all.

How Your "Favorite" Music Slips Away

When you're young, it's important to listen to certain pieces of music over and over again to completely internalize them. Doing it helps you define your personal experience, allows you to better find out who you are and where you belong. The transfer of music from being in the air to being inside your head—with every nuance of a record committed to a depth of memory that finally might as well be the notes themselves flowing through your bloodstream—is a vital stage of self-recognition. Even if you're just looking for tribal affiliation, intimate understanding of a piece of music will start you in the right direction.

But those touchstones become less meaningful over time, whether or not you're able to recognize that they do. The external part—the "music" part—of the process nearly disappears. Hearing the tune winds up being no more than the trigger that brings you inside your own head, where you dutifully dredge up meaning that consists mostly of sentiment. The sentiment itself, over time, is entirely manufactured.

I was a sucker for this process until I caught myself hating all of my favorite music. I know the exact moment it happened. I was at a party where Miles Davis's "Kind of Blue"—a major signpost in my young life—was playing, and I involuntarily thought, "Oh, no, not this fucking thing again."

Hollywood Comes Knocking, and I Duck Out the Back Door

I'm not a writer and never meant to be one. But in 2011 a friend wrangled me a gig at Trinity College in Dublin as a keynote speaker for a "Cultures of Boxing" conference. This was way out of my line. I didn't really know what a keynote speaker did.

The conference went well, gave me the chance to become acquainted with Dublin—a town I connected with instantly—and to meet old friends and make new ones.

My keynote address was soon repurposed as an essay called "Why I Fixed Fights." Through the writer Brian Tuohy, it came to the attention of the editors at Deadspin.

Within days of its running, I had a dozen radio interviews lined up (three on NPR, one on CBC), had signed on for numerous online and podcast conversations, was referenced in more articles than I could count, became the recipient of multiple death threats, acquired two film agents, signed a TV development deal, and was bombarded with book offers and movie pitches.

On balance, this all sounds promising. It wasn't. But for a while, through my agents, I chased after what I should have intuited would lead nowhere.

Eventually a very small dollar sign wrapped itself around an offer from a struggling production company called Phoenix Pictures: $10,000 for a one-year option on the Deadspin article. It was rejected through my agent.

This led to a series of missteps by all parties—except my steadfast lawyer Michael Zinni—in negotiating an acceptable figure for the rights to the piece.

With neither side willing to get the ball rolling, weeks of silence passed. I fired my agent. And I stopped trying to deal with production companies.

My Hollywood writing career was over, but I wound up appearing in five movies. I played "Himself" in each one. I thought I had reasons to do them.

Mike Martinez's documentary *Reviled and Maligned*, about the maverick mortuary that accepted Boston Marathon bomber Tamerlan Tsarnaev's body, is a gem. And Mat Whitecross's documentary *The Kings*, about Roberto Duran, Ray Leonard, Marvin Hagler, and Thomas Hearns is a fine film.

There was also a putative documentary about Sonny Liston that somehow wound up on Showtime. My segment was shot in an empty warehouse in Paterson, New Jersey, presumably to establish some sort of underworld verisimilitude—whether the movie's or my own, I'm not sure.

But it looks as if I'm not going to have a lucrative future playing "Himself" in movies. Now I hear that there's a possibility that someone else may play "Himself" in an upcoming film. He's welcome to give it a try.

What happens now? I'm out of the boxing business. I'm through with being a gangster—even a small-time one. I don't like music anymore, so playing piano professionally isn't an option. Writing is an unreliable way to make a living.

So maybe the trick is to not *be* anything, to not *do* anything. The universe is benignly indifferent to whatever decision you make. Maybe the idea is to watch *it* instead of assuming that it's watching you.

Nico Is Nineteen

We settle into our sleeping positions—Nico either tucked into my chest with my left arm draped over him or at the bottom of the bed pressed against my feet—and don't budge until 4:15. Nico never wakes during the night. I seldom do. Although we both sleep soundly, there's a reassuring awareness of the other's presence. I used to set the alarm, but Nico internalized the time, wakes up automatically at 4:15 and moves, so I no longer need it. I start my coffee, take Nico for his first walk, and check email. I feed him, and then sit on the couch, reading and drinking coffee while he naps in my lap.

Depending on how you measure time, I'm either fifty years older than Nico or almost forty years younger. If I were able to reconfigure my own sense of time to verticality—as I often try to do—I would no longer think about that.

Once you know that you're going to die, you always know that you're going to die. I've got a lot of karmic debt to work off, and that will go better if I don't look back at my life as a road that stretches from point A to a point to be determined.

Nico is nineteen now—very old for a dog, even a Chihuahua. He's blind and deaf, but in good overall health. Doctor Rabaut tells me that he's "a really tough little guy." His appetite is good. He takes his medicine without coaxing and remains enthusiastic about getting treats that he uses The Big Voice to demand. Nico lives in a world almost entirely olfactory and tactile. He crawls into my lap to join me in meditating each morning at 5:30.

ACKNOWLEDGMENTS

To
Betsy,
Jesse,
Margo,
and
Paula,
with love and gratitude

THANKS TO (among the living)

Robert Anasi
Phil Anselmo
Debby Applegate
Tyrone Booze
Jay Bulger
John Carlo
Tommy Craggs
Michael Ezra
Caroline Forbes
Charley Gallay
Ryan Gattis
Eddie Goldman
Mitch "Blood" Green
Adam Hashian
Mary Istre
Amanda Kelley
Andy Komack

Bill Littlefield
Russ Lossing
Frank Lotierzo
Jeff MacGregor
Tim Marchman
Gordon Marino
Susan McKain
Peter McNeeley
Brian Moore
Gary Moser
Hamilton Nolan
Freddie Norwood
Richard O'Brien
Rob Osborn
Evan Parker
James Parker
Barry Petchesky

Tony Petronelli
Martha Plotkin
David Reich
Sharon Rivers
Carlo Rotella
Kyle Sarofeen
Bill Savage
Jim Schapperoew
"Iceman" John Scully
Glen Sharp
Sam Sheridan
Robbie Sims
Bonnie Snider
Eric Snider
Ken Steiner
Brian Tuohy
Mat Whitecross

(Low)life is set in 10-point Sabon, which was designed by the German born typographer and designer Jan Tschichold (1902–1974) in the period 1964–1967. It was released jointly by the Linotype, Monotype, and Stempel type foundries in 1967. Copyeditor for this project was Shannon LeMay-Finn. The book was designed by Brad Norr Design, Minneapolis, Minnesota, and typeset by New Best-set Typesetters Ltd.